THE TEACHING OF WRITING

THE TEACHING OF WRITING

Eighty-fifth Yearbook of the
National Society for the Study of Education

PART II

By

THE YEARBOOK COMMITTEE
and
ASSOCIATED CONTRIBUTORS

Edited by

ANTHONY R. PETROSKY AND DAVID BARTHOLOMAE

Editor for the Society

KENNETH J. REHAGE

19 NSSE 86

Distributed by THE UNIVERSITY OF CHICAGO PRESS ● CHICAGO, ILLINOIS

The National Society for the Study of Education

Founded in 1901 as successor to the National Herbart Society, the National Society for the Study of Education has provided a means by which the results of serious study of educational issues could become a basis for informed discussion of those issues. The Society's two-volume yearbooks, now in their eighty-fifth year of publication, reflect the thoughtful attention given to a wide range of educational problems during those years. In 1971 the Society inaugurated a series of substantial publications on Contemporary Educational Issues to supplement the yearbooks. Each year the Society's publications contain contributions to the literature of education from more than a hundred scholars and practitioners who are doing significant work in their respective fields.

An elected Board of Directors selects the subjects with which volumes in the yearbook series are to deal and appoints committees to oversee the preparation of manuscripts. A special committee created by the Board performs similar functions for the series on Contemporary Educational Issues.

The Society's publications are distributed each year without charge to members in the United States, Canada, and elsewhere throughout the world. The Society welcomes as members all individuals who desire to receive its publications. Information about current dues may be found in the back pages of this volume.

This volume, *The Teaching of Writing*, is Part 2 of the Eighty-fifth Yearbook of the Society. Part 1, which is published at the same time, is entitled *Microcomputers and Education*.

A listing of the Society's publications still available for purchase may be found in the back pages of this volume.

Library of Congress Catalog Number: 85-062666
ISSN: 0077-5762

Published 1986 by
THE NATIONAL SOCIETY FOR THE STUDY OF EDUCATION
5835 Kimbark Avenue, Chicago, Illinois 60637
© 1986 by the National Society for the Study of Education

First Printing, 7,500 Copies

Printed in the United States of America

Officers of the
National Society for the Study of Education, 1985-1986
(Term of office expires March 1 of the year indicated.)

The Society's Committee on the Teaching of Writing

Associated Contributors to the Yearbook

Acknowledgments

We are grateful to the Board of Directors of the National Society for the Study of Education for its support and encouragement in this project. We owe a particular debt to Margaret Early, a member of that Board, for her advice when we began to think of this collection of essays. We would also like to thank Robert Glaser, Director of the Learning and Research Development Center at the University of Pittsburgh, who gave us time and space for our work and whose good sense and good humor make the Center a model for academic collaboration. And, finally, we wish to thank the authors. They made our job a pleasant one.

DAVID BARTHOLOMAE
ANTHONY R. PETROSKY

The National Society for the Study of Education is deeply appreciative of the work that Professors Petrosky and Bartholomae have put into the planning of this volume and to their most competent assistance at every stage in the process of bringing it to completion. We are grateful also to each of the authors whose contributions illuminate the concerns of those who are close to current developments in the teaching of writing and especially to ways of viewing the processes of composition.

The Board of Directors of the Society initially considered the possibility of a yearbook on the teaching of writing in 1982. Persuaded that a book on this subject would be a useful contribution to the literature of education, the Board invited Professors Petrosky and Bartholomae to submit a proposal for such a volume. After the proposal was approved early in 1984, the editors and the invited contributors worked diligently to have manuscripts ready by deadlines that had to be met in order to permit publication in the spring of 1986. We are pleased that we can include this important volume in our Eighty-fifth Yearbook.

KENNETH J. REHAGE
Editor for the Society

Table of Contents

PAGE

THE NATIONAL SOCIETY FOR THE STUDY OF EDUCATION iv

OFFICERS OF THE SOCIETY, 1985-86; THE SOCIETY'S COMMITTEE ON THE
TEACHING OF WRITING; ASSOCIATED CONTRIBUTORS TO THE YEARBOOK v

ACKNOWLEDGMENTS vii

Part One
Introduction

CHAPTER
I. WORDS FROM AFAR, *David Bartholomae* 1

Part Two
The Teaching of Writing: Research and Practice

II. WHY WRITE?, *John T. Gage* 8

III. TEACHING WRITING: THE MAJOR THEORIES, *Anne Ruggles Gere* 30

IV. COMPOSING PROCESSES: AN OVERVIEW, *Patricia Bizzell* 49

V. THE WRITER'S KNOWLEDGE: THEORY, RESEARCH, AND IMPLICA-
TIONS FOR PRACTICE, *George Hillocks, Jr.* 71

VI. PROBLEMS IN PROCESS APPROACHES: TOWARD A RECONCEPTUAL-
IZATION OF PROCESS INSTRUCTION, *Arthur N. Applebee* . . . 95

VII. EVALUATION AND LEARNING, *Rexford Brown* 114

Part Three
A Look at the Schools

VIII. LEARNING TO WRITE AND WRITING TO LEARN IN THE ELEMENTARY
SCHOOL, *Mary Ellen Giacobbe* 131

IX. TEACHING WRITING IN SECONDARY SCHOOLS, *Miles Myers* . . 148

X. COMING OF AGE IN COLLEGE COMPOSITION, *Paul Kameen* . . . 170

PAGE

Part Four

Postscript

CHAPTER

XI. ON THE ROAD TO SHANGHAI: A THREE-YEAR PROJECT WITH THE
PUBLIC SCHOOLS, *Anthony R. Petrosky* 188

NAME INDEX 197

SUBJECT INDEX 200

INFORMATION ABOUT MEMBERSHIP IN THE SOCIETY 203

PUBLICATIONS OF THE SOCIETY 205

Part One
INTRODUCTION

CHAPTER I

Words from Afar

DAVID BARTHOLOMAE

The claim to attention of an ethnographic account does not rest on its author's ability to capture primitive facts in faraway places and carry them home like a mask or a carving, but on the degree to which he is able to clarify what goes on in such places, to reduce the puzzlement—what manner of men are these?—to which unfamiliar acts emerging out of unknown backgrounds naturally give rise.

CLIFFORD GEERTZ
The Interpretation of Cultures (1973)

The writers of the following chapters are not anthropologists, nor are they writing about faraway places. Composition instruction of some form or another surely goes on in every school in the country, and every reader of this book will have had some experience in a course that presumed to improve his or her writing skills.

There is, on the other hand, an unusual way of talking about writing, about thinking, about knowledge, and about teaching that could be said to belong to writing teachers—a way of speaking and thinking, a shared set of key terms and concepts, of examples and interpretations—that defines the order of things in this particular pocket of the academic community. I would like to force a sense of its unfamiliarity, to heighten its foreignness.

Writing teachers, or teachers who care about writing, *are* strange. There are not many of them. They tend to teach differently from other teachers, even in their own content areas. In my department, an English department at a large university, I can quickly make fundamental pedagogical distinctions among my colleagues by the kind and amount of writing that goes on in their classes. The teacher who, in a course on William Blake, requires regular short papers from

1

his students, who uses those papers for in-class discussions on ways of reading Blake, and who has students revise those papers, makes literature and the reading of literature something substantially different from the teacher who runs discussions, gives regular short-answer exams, and asks students to keep a journal of "impressions," or the teacher who gives lectures on Blake, gives two essay exams, and assigns a research paper due at the end of the term.

There are differences here of timing and genre. A big paper due at the end of the terms serves more as a test than as an exercise. A research paper asks students to summarize and arrange the opinions of experts; the short papers ask students to examine and experiment with their own structures of interpretation. The skills required for journal writing are not the same as the skills required for an essay exam. But my point is not just that the writing skills called upon in each course are different, but that Blake is different, as are the fundamental activities of reading and interpretation, since in each case writing holds students in a different relationship with their subject (Blake) and with professional expectations about what it means to be a reader of Blake. You "know" Blake differently if you have recorded your impressions in a journal, summarized articles from the library, or written short papers on specific textual problems. It is a matter of orientation. Some forms of writing give priority to commonplace, generally recognized, and generally acceptable interpretations of Blake's work. Others make those taboo, and value, rather, problems or paradoxes that break the pattern of set interpretation or received knowledge. It is not just what you know but the way that you know what you know that is shaped by the writing that goes on in these courses.

And this, of course, is what makes it so difficult to be a writing teacher, since you not only have to have developed that muscular habit of mind that allows you to look at a student's reading of Blake and see not only that reading but also the kind of reading it represents. And you not only have to know that, but you have to know how to talk to a writer, how to say something other than "good job" or "interesting" or "awkward" or "wordy."

When there is no writing, then the shaping of knowledge is of another sort altogether. One way of knowing the work of William Blake is to know (that is, to have a memory for) names, dates, places, titles, works, and a series of standard interpretations of major poems. All of this fits conveniently within the structure of a short-answer or multiple-choice exam. There are good reasons why our curricula should represent a variety of ways of knowing and understanding the subjects of academic inquiry. It seems, however, there has been little room in our schools for writing.

You can get an interesting view on this if you go back to the last NSSE Yearbook on writing, published in 1923.[1] The author, Earl

Hudelson, conducted a survey of writing in high schools. There is more than a half century between our classrooms and his, and yet the most surprising thing about his book is that its account of methods and aims does not sound at all primitive or old-fashioned.

Hudelson found that regardless of size and location most of the high schools in the country split instruction evenly between literature and composition over the course of a school year. Teachers generally assigned one or two themes a week.

Composition topics arise from the teacher more often than from any other source, though pupil interests, experiences, and observations are frequently the basis of written work, and assignments are sometimes related to literary readings. Practically all teachers designate their pupils' mechanical errors but do not correct them if the pupils themselves are able to do so. Emphasis in the teaching of composition is decidedly upon rhetoric, with considerable attention, however, paid to originality and with some stress laid upon thought, interest, style, and neatness. Models, class discussions, and conferences are the main devices used in attaining the desired accomplishments.[2]

The largest portion of Hudelson's book, however, is concerned with measurement, not with aims or methods. In the course of his study, Hudelson sent out selected student essays for teachers to comment on and rank and, to his horror, he found that there was little agreement. "When three teachers of English composition rank ten anonymous themes in order of merit," and when they not only fail to agree but when a single essay receives both the highest and the lowest ranking, then, Hudelson concluded, "obviously something is wrong."[3]

Hudelson's response was to construct a scale that could be used to synchronize national grading standards. He constructed two sets of writing assignments: one that would reliably elicit themes "typical" of student writing at a particular grade level and one that would reveal students' "maximal" abilities in composition. With these he constructed a scale (from 0-9) represented by sample student essays at each level from the standard topics. By studying the sample, he argued, teachers could give a national standard to essays written by local students. The typical scale would be used to place students at the beginning of a term; the maximal scale to evaluate their progress at the end of the term.

For Hudelson, the fact that teachers had trouble agreeing about what was good writing (and, most likely, about what writing is good for) was a sign that something was wrong and that teaching had to be shored up, or stabilized, by a general scale. It would have been possible to assume, however, that if something was wrong, it was not with the teachers' various judgments but with the assumption that writing should be read the same way by different people in different contexts. I am not interested in a discussion of testing here (for that, see chapter 6 in this volume on evaluation by Rex Brown). I do, however, want to take Hudelson's decision as symptomatic of a problem that has continually threatened the teaching of writing. When teachers or administrators or supervisors suddenly get a view of writing, when the drapes are pulled away and writing stands there for what it is, they are troubled by what they see, and their first response is to make writing go away and to put something else in its place, something that is not writing but appears to be able to stand for writing.[4] When they see, for example, that a writing class calls basic assumptions about knowledge or value into question (when a writing class raises the issue of whose job it is to interpret Blake, or whose job it is to judge the various interpretations students give of Blake, and to judge them as interpretations and not as spelling tests or tests of sentence construction), then they decide that it is all too messy and problematic, and they look for some alternative.

Hudelson's system of measurement carried with it a set of aims and methods for the teaching of composition. The point is nicely made in the 1923 yearbook by one of the teachers asked to write a response to Hudelson's study. M. H. Willing, in an abstract of the discussion of Hudelson's study that took place at the annual meeting of the Society, argued that not only do teachers have difficulty knowing how to read students' themes (knowing what to see and what to value), they are also overburdened with too many of the things anyway, and if the themes serve only as practice for the sake of practice, then maybe they are counterproductive. Maybe they are encouraging bad habits, and maybe success in composition may not be identical with success in theme writing. "The first and most important effect of scientific measurement upon writing composition," he said, "will be to encourage the revival of drill on the composition fundamentals in high school. High school teachers will be required to learn how to teach such humble things as spelling, punctuation, functioning grammar, and sentence sense, in ways that really establish habits instead of through red ink suggestions from which only the conscientious profit."[5] The question then, as now, was not whether students *should* study spelling, punctuation, functioning grammar, and sentence sense, but what happens when such instruction is allowed to displace writing. Willing said, "Theme writing cannot be abandoned, but its usefulness as a check on progress or a device for emphasizing general merit must, I think, become its chief justification rather than its relatively small value as a method for fixing the many elemental habits essential to a satisfactory general performance.[6]

The chapters in this volume all argue, in one way or another, that writing (and writing itself, not some substitute or stand-in) should be at the center of the curriculum because of the ways it can develop the many elemental habits essential to a satisfactory general performance. These habits, of course, are habits of mind, not behaviors, and like all well-developed habits of mind they tend not to be "fixed." A writing teacher, then, is also a teacher who knows how to look at writing, not turn away, and who takes pleasure in looking into matters that are not fixed.

Writing teachers, it should be clear, do not always come with writing courses, and they are not always found in English departments. In some circles, you would get a good bit of argument about whether all of the three teachers cited above (the teachers teaching a course on William Blake) should properly be considered writing teachers. Some would say that the research paper is a "canned" exercise and serves no real purpose until a student is prepared to do some actual research (as opposed to conducting a raid on the library). Others would say that the journal assignment is a way of avoiding all the responsibilities to audience or to the conventional structures of knowledge that real writers face. You would probably find the greatest agreement over the teacher who assigned short papers and revisions, but still there would be questions over what those short assignments asked for, what was taken as a suitable occasion for revision (do you revise the lousy papers or the good ones?), over how one assignment would lead to another, and over whether it is appropriate to spend so much class time on writing when the course, after all, is a course on William Blake. The chapters that follow will represent the variety of responses to these specific issues in the teaching of writing.

I said that you do not always find writing teachers in writing courses and that they are sometimes housed in departments other than the English department. What characterizes writing teachers, I think, is not that they have a set of "methods" for the teaching of writing, but that they have a commitment to writing as an intellectual activity and to what that activity can produce in the classroom. They would, in other words, have made conscious choices about the variety of assignments listed above, choosing one or rejecting the other on the basis of how they wanted students to read William Blake, how they wanted students to see the activities of reading and interpretation, and not because they had a term paper lesson or a revision lesson or a journal lesson that they could plug into the semester in the third week.

I am trying, then, to force the recognition that writing teachers are strange, unlike other teachers in the schools. I do this not to reserve any special status or privilege (or forgiveness) for them but as a way of preparing readers who look in on them from the outside. This book is immediately addressed to those involved with issues in education but who are not located within the community of writing teachers and researchers: legislators, supervisors, principals, researchers from other disciplines, parents (we would hope), concerned citizens generally. The authors were given the task of taking an issue or area of instruction that they knew well, something of immediate concern to the profession, and of representing it to those on the outside. I hope those readers will come to this book, look (at least first) at the big puzzling picture, and ask, "What manner of men and women are these?" The biggest barriers to curriculum development have been failures of cooperation and failures of understanding. We have certainly not lacked proposals, research reports, or new and innovative methods. While this book is meant as an overview of work in composition, it has its share of specific recommendations. I would hope that these readers would not carry them away, like a mask or a carving, without a sense of the culture that produced them and of the roles they play within that culture. A good writing program is a local expression of a generally agreed upon attitude toward writing—what it is, what it is good for. There are no set guidelines here, partly because writing is like that, too messy for guidelines, and partly because, as Hudelson discovered, it all depends on who is looking at it. This is not to say that every opinion is as good as the next. If you look here, in this book, you will see the way professional writing teachers think and talk about writing—what they notice, what they value, what they take as a problem or a solution. In other words, those on the outside need to get a sense of the people to understand best the use of their tools and artifacts.

The book is also, however, addressed to those who are within the community of composition specialists—those who teach writing, who read the journals, go to meetings or conferences, attend in-service training, conduct and publish research, and who establish their professional identity through these activities. I would like these readers, too, to read the essays as though they were visitors to foreign territory. It has become easy to take our branch of the discipline for granted—with its established projects, major figures, standard examples, and theories—as a natural part of the academic landscape. This book offers a scholarly overview of a moment, in 1985, in the history of the study and teaching of composition. I can think of no other book that does this quite as well. It would be a useful exercise, I think, for those on the inside to foster an ethnographer's naive point of view as they read it, looking for the systems that govern our behavior and our thinking, looking for the secrets we keep and the truths we take as self-evident. The authors of the following chapters were certainly not able to free themselves completely from the push and shove of our discursive practices, but with a remarkable consistency they were able to take a critical step beyond the standard arguments of the profession, pushing hard, for example, at some of the complacencies of the "process approach," putting "writing across the curriculum" in a historical context, bringing basic questions (like "Why Write?") into specialized discussion, and looking at the political implications of presumably "neutral" uses of writing.

FOOTNOTES

1. Earl Hudelson, *English Composition: Its Aims, Methods, and Measurement*, Twenty-second Yearbook of the National Society for the Study of Education, Part 1 (Bloomington, Ill.: Public School Publishing Co., 1923).

2. Ibid., p. 7.

3. Ibid., p. 32.

4. For discussions of this phenomenon, see William E. Coles, Jr., "Freshman Composition: The Circle of Unbelief," *College English* 31 (November 1969): 134-42; Patrick Hartwell, "Grammar, Grammars, and the Teaching of Grammar," *College English* 47 (February 1985): 105-28; and Mike Rose, "The Language of Exclusion: Writing Instruction at the University," *College English* 47 (April 1985): 341-60.

5. M. H. Willing, "Methods of Teaching English Composition," in Hudelson, *English Composition: Its Aims, Methods, and Measurement*, p. 167.

6. Ibid., p. 168.

Part Two
THE TEACHING OF WRITING:
THEORY AND PRACTICE

CHAPTER II

Why Write?

JOHN T. GAGE

There is no question that students *should* write. Without exception, it seems, reports and studies dealing with educational quality in recent years have advocated more writing, at every phase of learning.[1] This renewed interest in writing results from the belief that writing is not simply a "skill" to be mastered and then applied neutrally to knowledge, but the ongoing reflection of students' developing understanding of ideas. The slogan "writing to learn" seems to have replaced "learning to write" for many teachers, because they believe that there is a direct relationship between students' development as thinkers and the discovery of meaning in the struggle to compose discourse. It seems inconceivable that any suggestion to have students write *less* would be taken seriously, so powerful is the current belief that composing lies at the center of learning. In the face of nearly universal agreement that students should write, it might seem unnecessary to discuss the reasons. After all, if we agree that students should write, the relevant question changes from *why* writing should be emphasized to *how* to do it. With all this agreement, however, I think the need to address the question *why* is even greater, because if we assume the answer we are in danger of forgetting that different justifications for writing depend on different assumptions about what education is for, and these will yield different pedagogies.

The question of why students should write needs attention, then, lest we adopt methods that do not fulfill genuine educational objectives. In response to the recent call for "writing to learn," we might inquire "Writing to learn what?" It happens, I think, that the answer to this question, in relation to some ways of teaching writing, is not consistent with certain values of a liberal education. Other ways, however, support those values. Behind every methodology is an ideology. The neglect of ideological discussion in favor of exclusive attention to method, then, is risky indeed.

The ideological, or philosophical, assumptions behind composition will concern me in this essay. It is necessary that I write somewhat abstractly, although I do not wish to ignore some practical implications that follow from such a concern. I trust that the essays in the rest of this volume will adequately survey available techniques of teaching composition. In discussing the justifications that might support such techniques, however, I would like to begin with a reminder that these justifications are not of recent origin. They are not responses to any recent "literary crisis," but echo the earliest attempts to reason about human knowledge and its relation to the written word. I want to begin, therefore, with a sketch of some ancient responses to the question "Why write?" These responses raise issues that are never resolved once and for all but require rethinking by every generation. The ideas discussed by Greek philosophers about the value of writing continue to be relevant to current pedagogy, and a brief look at them can help to clarify major issues facing those who would defend the teaching of writing today.

Some Old Wine: Eloquence versus Wisdom

In Plato's *Phaedrus*, the philosopher Socrates attacked writing as a false art, which, if taught to youth, would lead them away from the honest pursuit of the truth. Socrates practiced an oral art of discussion which he called "dialectic" and which consisted of questions and answers between people who sought to discover transcendent truths. In order for dialectic to proceed *toward* new discoveries, it required that people be able to question each other, a process that is not possible, Socrates maintained, when the written word separates a speaker from the living presence of an audience. More importantly, however, Socrates questioned the motives of the would-be writer: a writer was someone who wished to persuade an audience of a predetermined conclusion, entering into the process of communication only in order to prevail. Socrates saw writing as manipulative and therefore dishonest. In such a one-way communication, a writer's own mind could not be changed, since the object of persuasion was to win one's argument, not to discover truth in dialectic fashion. Socrates maintained that he engaged in the oral art of dialectic, not to persuade, but to arrive at self-knowledge. He thought of this as the genuine end of education, and he thought of writing as an obstacle to this process.

Socrates' critique of writing takes place in the context of his attack on a group of philosophers called the sophists, who were the first teachers of composition. They were professional speech-writers who used their knowledge of "rhetoric" to compose speeches on any subject, with no regard—as Socrates complained—for the truth. They also wrote and sold handbooks containing techniques of speech writing. Socrates' most critical discussion of these handbooks, and of the sophists' advice to writers, is found in Plato's *Gorgias*, where he charged that the sophists are skilled liars, people who make a living by making "the worse case appear the better." Their handbooks of persuasive devices were morally indefensible, for Socrates, since the better the sophists were at manipulating language—the more skilled technically—the worse they were as spokesmen for the truth. Knowing and practicing the art of writing persuasively, for Socrates, were dangerous to the soul, because they did not depend on knowing the truth. This art depended instead on knowing how to write well on any idea indiscriminantly, whether true or not. Socrates condemned the art of rhetoric, then, as a false version of dialectic, because even though it seemed to use the same techniques of argumentation, it disregarded the thing that mattered most: a desire to "know oneself." It substituted "belief," gained through persuasion, for genuine self-knowledge. It was because of the tremendous power of the rhetoricians' techniques for gaining belief that Socrates feared writing would have a bad effect on those who practiced it. Socrates advised his student Phaedrus to avoid the rhetoricians, lest he be seduced by their skills into giving up his search for wisdom.

Aristotle, as a student of Plato, was familiar with such ethical objections to the art of rhetoric: that it substituted eloquence for wisdom. Aristotle, however, sought to provide a different kind of defense of this art, one which did not defend writing as a means of gaining power, as the sophists had done, nor which condemned writing as an obstacle to the truth, as Socrates had. Aristotle instead attempted to relate the art of persuasion to the discovery of knowledge. In the first place, Aristotle did not believe that the way to protect students from the harmful effects of the skilled rhetoricians was to avoid teaching the skills. He believed that the answer to the problem of people being led to believe lies by means of the rhetoricians' tricks was to teach them what the tricks are. Aristotle thought that if people understood where the persuasive power of language came from, what "the available means of persuasion" are, they would be less likely to be easily persuaded by them. His antidote to the power of sophistical rhetoric was to advocate teaching people how it works, unlike Socrates' solution, which was to keep this knowledge from corrupting his students. Artistotle believed that if people understood how skilled writers attempt to manipulate them, they would be less manipulable, and the effect would be a greater ability to detect false arguments. He thought, in other words, that the best defense against powerful writers was to educate the audience in the art of persuasive writing, so that "the worse case" could not appear the better. He wrote a treatise on rhetoric, then, which taught people how persuasion works. His was not a handbook on how to persuade, but a critical anatomy of persuasive techniques.[2] In that treatise, Artistotle emphasized the importance of honest persuasion, but acknowledged that dishonest persuasion also uses the same techniques. He said it was not the art that made the sophist, but the motive. The ability to write well could be used as a means of promoting the truth as well as promoting falsehood, as Socrates had said, but Aristotle added that only if people understood good writing could they be alert to the difference between honest uses of rhetoric and dishonest ones.

Aristotle believed that the process of honest persuasion was a means by which people could discover what they should believe. Socrates had distinguished truth from mere belief. Aristotle was not so quick to make this distinction. For Aristotle, there are many questions which people must decide for which knowledge of the truth is simply not available. The process of attempting to persuade other people of answers to such questions should involve a search for the best reasons one could discover. Thus, when Aristotle discussed the art of rhetoric, he did so in an entirely different way from the way in which the sophists had done in their handbooks. The sophists taught writing as a "bag of tricks," a set of persuasive techniques that one could use to prevail on any side of a question. They advocated the use of many techniques for making ideas sound better than they really were, techniques for hiding weaknesses in one's own argument, and for giving one's writing eloquent stylistic flourishes for the sake of diminishing the audience's capacity for judgment. Aristotle, on the other hand, taught rhetoric as an intellectual, rather than as a technical skill. For him, it was an art of searching for the best available reasons for believing something, and of arranging those reasons in logical order and in a clear style. The sophists believed that any reason was good if it worked. Aristotle taught that a writer's skill actually amounted to an ability to reason well. It required that the writer be willing to argue only for positions for which good reasons could be found. Thus, Aristotle believed that the honest practice of rhetoric, as a search for good reasons, could result in one's changing one's own mind.

Two premises underlie Aristotle's defense of writing, at least for the purposes of this discussion. The first is that there is such a thing as "contingent, probable truth,"[3] a category of knowledge that Socrates had rejected as false and self-deceptive. Socrates sought a pure method of dialectic which would provide only pure truths, truths untainted by human motives and conditions. Rhetoric, for Socrates, was the opposite of dialectic. For Aristotle, rhetoric and dialectic were parallel arts. Both were means of discovering knowledge in the realm of ideas where absolute truth is beyond reach.

Thus, as a second underlying premise, Aristotle did not think that there could be anything like a "systematic" set of "rules" that could lead to knowledge. Argumentation, or rhetorical inquiry, led to knowledge by means of circumstantial reasoning which was not logically pure, even though it tried to be reasonable. Aristotle admitted, in other words, that people believe for reasons that are not always strictly logical, and thus writing could not be reduced to any set of systematic and logical procedures. Aristotle thought of rhetoric as unsystematic, but no less valid for that reason.

In this controversy in antiquity, essentially three ideologies of composition are represented, three very different answers to the question "Why write?" The first is that of the sophists, for whom writing was a source of power. Writing well enabled one to manipulate the beliefs of others, and it was one of the skills one needed, therefore, to get ahead in the world of politics and commerce. The second is that of Socrates, who thought of writing as an obstacle to knowledge of the truth. In reaction to the sophists, he saw the *mere* skill of writing well as a means of self-deception. The third is that of Aristotle, who, in reaction to both the sophists and to Socrates, viewed writing itself as a means of discovering knowledge. The practice of persuasion, when it involved the search for the best available means of reaching a conclusion, led the writer through a process that enabled the discovery of adequate, sharable grounds for belief. Technical skill was necessary, of course, but for Aristotle writing was essentially a thinking skill.

These three ideologies relied, furthermore, on three essentially different theories of what knowledge is. The sophists justified their approach to teaching writing skills because they did not believe that there was such a thing as knowledge. They thought that all ideas were equally unknowable and sought to substitute the ability to win one's case for the unattainable goal of wisdom. Socrates, on the other hand, believed in the human capacity to know transcendent truths, and he valued reason as the only means by which such absolute knowledge could be attained. It was knowable, then, but not necessarily sharable in human discourse. Aristotle, as I have already suggested, admitted another kind of knowledge and a way of knowing it. Aristotle thought that contingent, changing truths, unlike certainties, could be known through reason, but not without taking human motives, passions, egos into account. Thus, knowledge about such matters was the same as agreement, and it was attained by the rational use of persuasion. In similar ways, theories about what knowledge is and how one gets it continue to provide tacit support for ways of teaching writing.

You will be happy to know that I do not intend to trace these three ideologies "throughout history," as my students like to say. These issues never go away, and different times have produced different ways of viewing them. I intend to leap forward to the present day, instead, and to say how I think these ideologies look to us. The forms in which we encounter these controversies have changed, but the basic issues nevertheless persist. The relation between writing and knowledge, the ethical question of writing as a technical skill, the question of whether writing and thinking rely on "rules"—these issues continue to be debated, and positions on them continue to give rise to teaching methods.

Some New Bottles: Competency versus Independent Thought

The difference between writing as a technical skill and writing as an intellectual process continues to divide writing pedagogies. While there are few modern-day sophists claiming that ideas do not matter, numerous approaches to teaching writing are carried out *as if* ideas do not matter. Such approaches simply ignore content in the interest of form. If the teacher's mission is to drill students in the basic rules of correctness, then chances are that the ideas contained in the students' sentences will not be subject to the teacher's assessment. No one is telling these students that their ideas are unimportant; but the students are not being asked to write ideas at all—they are being asked to write sentences. Such approaches are usually defended on the ground that writing is a *competency*, that is, an ability to construct written artifacts that have certain definable, formal attributes, such as subject-verb agreement or, at a higher level of sophistication, topic sentences for every paragraph. In effect, this technical approach to composition assumes that writing can be mastered by learning *what* the attributes are and by practicing them in exercises, apart from real writing situations. When competency in writing is attained, students are assumed to be able to perform in situations where writing is called for. But this competency is thought to be developed in the English classroom, where approaches to composition may stress drill and error-avoidance, define forms of sentences and compositions, or prescribe the use of different strategies of organization or diction. Whenever the prescribed form is independent of the specific intellectual content of the student's composition—when assignments prescribe that a theme be five paragraphs long, for instance, or that each paragraph contain three supporting details, whether they are required by the writer's purpose or not—it is apparent that ideas serve only as a convenient means to the end of learning such patterns, rather than the very substance of the writing. To facilitate the practice of such skills, students are usually provided with topics to write about, as if students can be expected to write as well about other people's ideas as about their own. Composition textbooks are full of such topics: "Write a narrative essay about the first time you . . ." "Write a 500-word essay that compares and contrasts . . ." Such topics at times attempt to imitate real writing situations, but the need to master a given form usually makes easily controlled, and therefore inherently uninteresting, topics preferable to the adventurous and sloppy kind that emerge from the students' own thinking.

The method I have just described—the prescribed form to be filled in with arbitrarily selected content—has come under attack by those who would exchange its "product" emphasis for teaching students the "process" of writing instead. The recent popularity of teaching the "writing process" has not, however, guaranteed that the quality of the student's thinking will be relevant to the processes the student is guided through. The "process-approach" to teaching writing emphasizes the stages of composing by offering students procedures that will help them in choosing topics, gathering information, organizing their thoughts, composing, and revising. While the approach is a clear alternative to the drudgery of filling in empty rhetorical forms, following prescribed procedures for each "stage" of the writing process does not necessarily invite students to do their best thinking. Any of these procedures, such as the use of different "heuristic" strategies for inventing things to say about a topic, can be reduced to a repetitive exercise and taught as a skill to be mastered in a thoughtless way, as if competency in the prescribed heuristic procedure were more important than the quality of the ideas it may (or may not) help the student to discover. The new demand for "process over product" answers only part of the objection to technical mastery as the aim of writing instruction.

The exclusive teaching of technique will always be accompanied by the claim that writing is, of course, *more* than drill, and error-avoidance, and practicing organizational and heuristic strategies, and all of the other separate tasks of the classroom. No one denies that writing also requires independent thinking. But such approaches, at least in their extreme forms, give only lip-service to the aim of independent thinking and do not address it directly through teaching. This is the case, presumably, because some of a writer's activities are assumed to be teachable while others are assumed to be unteachable. Sentence structure, grammar, mechanics, organizational forms, heuristic procedures—these are teachable. Having ideas, being sensitive to issues, caring about whether one is right, taking responsibility for finding good reasons—these are not teachable. So, even while it may be admitted that the latter activities, or attitudes, are essential for writers, these are not among the "skills" that technical methods teach. Students are assumed to be able to gain them on their own, at some point after the skills are mastered.

Based on a standard like that of Socrates, we might say that a strictly technical approach to composition, or a "competency in writing" model, assumes that "good writing" is defined by the same characteristics whether it is applied to a good or bad idea. Sentences can be manipulated according to different grammatical or syntactical principles, heuristic or editing procedures can be followed, and essays can be written that adhere to the required form or length—all without the quality of the ideas contained in that writing coming under any scrutiny at all, by the student writer or by the teacher. If the terms of a writing assignment are strictly formal, as in the traditional "five-paragraph theme" or the equally traditional term paper which must have citations from x number of sources, then it is clear that such an assignment can be fulfilled with good or bad ideas indiscriminately. And, if students have been taught to view success on such assignments as fulfillment of the technical requirements, however these may be defined, then it will no doubt occur to them that the best way to ensure success is to keep the ideas as simple and meaningless as possible. If successful writing is defined as technical skills only, then students may be learning an unspoken lesson that is unintended by the pedagogy, namely, that ideas do not matter. Socrates would say, I think, that they are learning that the truth does not matter, or that the way to succeed in writing is to *seem* to be saying something without really troubling to ask whether it is true.

If writing pedagogies stress the technical at the expense of the intellectual (even while claiming that the intellectual is important), then we may indeed question their effects in terms similar to Socrates' complaints about the handbooks of the sophists. Are we, by our ways of teaching writing, encouraging students to think that it is more important to be correct than to be right? Indeed, since "being right" is likely to be seen as the province of instruction in content areas alone, where the textbook presents the information and the teacher tests whether students have learned it, technical methods of teaching writing may be reinforcing the already prevalent notion that good ideas are judged more on the basis of authority than on the basis of the adequate presentation of reasons in writing. Such methods may well encourage an uncritical acceptance of ideas independent of the quality of the writing in which they are argued. From Socrates' point of view, what appears to be good writing as defined by the handbooks of composition may in fact be the worst sort, if the assessment of writing is entirely independent of whether one ought to believe what it says. The better the writing is in a technical sense, the worse it may be in an ethical sense, if "good writing" brings with it no responsibility to

examine ideas for their truth. A stupid idea is no less stupid for having
been written correctly, or eloquently. In his *Philosophy of Composition*,
E. D. Hirsch, Jr., has written, similarly, that "An A-plus success in
achieving a trivial or harmful intention is a trivial or harmful success,
and ought to be so judged."[4] For Socrates, the more eloquently such
an idea might be written, the worse it is for the author and for the
audience, since eloquence has the power to compel belief.

Some Superstitions about Writing in School

We do not need Socrates to guide us in speculating about the
potential effects of strictly technical writing pedagogies, however. We
can ask, simply: What habits of mind, or attitudes, do they encourage?
It seems to me that strictly technical approaches to composition risk
some specific effects that need our consideration. I would like to
consider for a moment the possibility that some of the superstitions
that students frequently have about writing in school may be the
result of how they have been taught to write. These are superstitions
which students often have to be painfully untaught when they reach
college—that is, of course, unless the college classes they encounter
continue to reinforce them.

"My only writing problem is grammar." This is a comment I
frequently hear from students in writing classes. I have decided that
students believe it because they have been taught grammar and little
else. They have probably been subjected to prescriptions and
proscriptions deriving from principles they do not understand and in
jargon they do not comprehend. They believe that grammar is a
mystery, known only to English teachers, and that their own failure
to learn every nuance of grammar is going to get them into trouble as
writers—because it always has in the past. When these students write,
they think about having to follow the rules, and in consequence their
attention is diverted from what they are trying to say. Writing
becomes, as I mentioned above, error-avoidance. For such students,
grammar is a gigantic, invisible mine field through which they must
navigate or be destroyed—when they least expect it—by red ink.
They have often suffered this sort of injury; their teachers paid
attention to the correctness of their writing and never noticed whether
they had an interesting idea or not. Shell-shocked, they stopped trying
to have interesting ideas, because these only made errors more likely.
Such students express the hope that someone will finally provide them
with the easy explanation of those complicated rules that will
demystify writing for them. But, of course, they will be forever
disappointed in this hope and will eventually give up, deciding that
they cannot be writers, simply because they have never been able to

learn "how to write," by which they usually mean spell or punctuate or distinguish "who" and "whom."

A corollary of this superstition is another: "Some people are writers and some are not." If students believe this, it is also because they have not mastered some technical competency that has been the focus of their writing instruction, some competency that has been taught as the *sine qua non* of all good writing. But, more importantly, they have seen other students succeed as writers and have finally decided that such students differ from them in an undefinable but essential way. Writers, they assume, are different. Writers know how to do something that other people cannot learn. This belief is mixed up with another general superstition, perpetuated by the culture, that writers are special people, an idea that has its origin in the romantic adulation of writers as a class. "Writers are born, not made." "Writers are sensitive people, gifted with imagination." Writers, of course, are simply people who engage in the activity of writing, and everyone is a writer sometimes and no one is a writer all the time. This should not need saying, but it does. The romantic belief is a strong one, and it helps to kill the motivation of students who have struggled with mastery of technique.

I encounter the mirror image of this superstition in students who think writing classes are beneath their dignity. "I already know how to write," they argue, as if writing competency were a matter of doing one thing—writing as analogous to tying one's shoes—over and over. The technical definition of competency suggests that a skill is something that one either acquires or one does not and that it is acquired once and for all. It is as if there were a "writing" switch inside each student's mind, with an *on* and *off* position. The metaphor is odious. No one knows how to write in that sense. Writing is not a competency in that sense. It is an activity, always undergone in new situations which change the nature of the task, with greater and lesser degrees of challenge and uncertainty. There are learnable techniques and attitudes that can help one to approach a writing problem, but there are no techniques that will make it go away. The student who believes, "I already know how to write," is self-deceived. He or she has no doubt had teachers who rewarded technical competency as if the constantly challenging and imperfectable problem of thinking had nothing to do with it. No student who had always been pushed in writing assignments to think better, simply because better thinking is *always* possible, could come away with such an easy and deceptive confidence.

Both the confident and the unconfident writers I have just described might share the further superstition that "there is a right and a wrong way to write." In other words, many students have learned to view the technical principles of good writing as good because these principles have been taught as absolutes, on the basis of the authority of the teacher or the textbook. "Why follow this rule? Because it is a rule, that's why." Writing becomes, if not a quasi-religion, then a quasi-science, in which the essentials are taken on faith. It is something that students are told to do in certain ways, theirs not to reason why. And, not surprisingly, students find this comforting. None of the responsibility of thinking about writing is really theirs; all they need do is follow the "rules."

Finally, students sometimes reveal the unexpressed attitude that writing is not important to them because they can do without it. And what they do when they do without it has been more important to them in their education than what they accomplish when they compose. "I get good grades in other courses," students sometimes tell me, or "My other teachers don't care whether I write well." I recently read a student evaluation of a literature class in which the student attempted to argue that the teacher had been unfair because he had included writing skills as a basis for grading. Writing for such students is separated in their minds from learning. They think of it as something that can be done *in addition to* learning, but not as directly related to what they know or how well they think. This attitude does not develop solely as a result of what they have accomplished, as students, without writing. It can also result from their success as writers, in a technical sense. Students who develop mastery of formal principles, but who are nevertheless left unchallenged intellectually by writing tasks, can readily come to view writing as unrelated to the rest of their education. Furthermore, they can be reinforced in this attitude when they know that they have written on mindless subjects (by their own account) but have been rewarded for their technical skill—as well as when they have written thoughtfully but have been wholly excused for technical lapses in their writing. In either case, they will view writing itself as an intellectually inferior "subject" for the same reasons many teachers do, because it is not somehow the real stuff of learning. Writing teachers are often assumed by their colleagues in other fields to be no more than grammar cops, people who police "good writing" but who have no real function in the intellectual development of students. Composition programs, likewise, can be viewed by colleagues and administrators as providing "service courses"—those necessary but unfortunate auxiliaries to real education.[5]

Utility versus Responsibility

If technical approaches to writing are justified by the goal of competency, what justifies the idea of competency as an end of education? The answer most frequently heard is a utilitarian argument, which amounts to an ultimate superstition about writing and education in general. Students are said to need to write in order to carry on the business of their lives, whether to get better grades while in school or to get better jobs later on. The payoff, they often believe, will be a tangible one. Good writers, they believe, are wanted by business. Students who do not learn to write will find themselves behind in their advancement toward economic prosperity. For similar reasons, good writers are said to be needed to benefit the society. While these aims are not easily disregarded, we might recall Socrates' complaint against the teaching of the sophists, to the effect that their art was dangerous because it gave one power while it led one away from the pursuit of wisdom. The sophists were vocational education specialists *par excellence.* They promised to provide one with a marketable skill, a capacity to stay on top of situations and to advance one's own cause successfully. But, as Socrates observed, the skill did not distinguish between good causes and bad ones, it did not make one more able to perceive goodness or justice, and it provided one only with standardized tricks that work in standard situations. It did not teach independent thought or the ability to reason.

The difference between teaching writing as a strictly technical skill and teaching writing as the exercise of independent thought and the ability to reason can be found in the answer to a simple question: Is it possible to succeed fully in this writing task (whether from a textbook's or the teacher's directives) without having a good idea of one's own? If the answer is yes, then what is learned by performing the writing task can be said to exercise the student's competency at the expense of failing to exercise the student's judgment. Such tasks may teach a limited procedure, or process, but they may also misrepresent what the procedure is good for. If writing is good for the writer in any other than a utilitarian sense—if it serves to clarify or improve the writer's understanding—then it must provide the occasion for genuine inquiry and the exercise of responsible judgment. These are what writing teaches students, if it requires them to have ideas of their own and to accept the responsibilities that come with having them. All of the technical aspects of writing can be taught in this context, because those aspects—such as correctness, efficient sentence structure, or a coherent organization—are among the responsibilities that writers accept when they are engaged in the communication of ideas that matter to them. But when taught as isolated skills, apart from the writer's commitment to an idea, these matters can reduce a student's sense of commitment to thought rather than increase it.

This "test" is not so simple as it sounds, however, since by asking the question we are faced with the inherent difficulty of saying what a "good idea" is. What makes an idea "good"? Certainly we cannot expect to agree on the answer, especially if we were to set out to say whether this or that idea measures up. A few generalizations might help us remain aware of the need to keep asking the question, however, as we assess the kinds of writing we ask students to perform.

In the first place, a good idea need only mean one that a student comes up with through independent thought and decides is significant enough to require communicating. While it is unlikely that such ideas can be invented by teachers and assigned to students, this does not mean that teachers will encourage students to look for them by allowing them to write about anything at all. Such ideas do not occur to people spontaneously, apart from their confrontation with issues of some kind. In other words, thinking is situational, in the sense that we respond with ideas of our own when we find ourselves in situations that demand ideas from us. Robert Frost once remarked that students cannot be taught to think by rapping them on the knuckles and shouting "Think!" They can, however, be put into situations that require thinking from them. Such situations are created for us by our presence in an audience—it is when confronted by the ideas of others that we look for our own. The desire to inquire after an idea presupposes the need to find one: thinking, like writing, is at its best when it is a search for an answer to a problem of some kind.

In the context of learning to write, a good idea need not be profound, nor does it need to represent the writer's final judgment on the subject. These qualities alone are needed: A good idea is one that a student comes up with in response to being confronted by a genuine conflict of thought. ("Genuine," like "good," is continually subject to our best judgment.) Such an idea, then, must emerge from exposure to the thinking of others, nor for the purpose of accepting it as true, but for the purpose of measuring it against one's own convictions. A good idea for writing, by these standards, cannot be one that a student feels solves no problem or one that solves a problem that is of no significance. It is an idea that the writer's audience does not already understand or accept—and it is this condition that makes it necessary for the writer to use all of the writing skills at his or her command to earn the reader's assent. Earning a reader's assent is not the same as persuading a reader to believe anything. When we have an idea that we feel ought to be of genuine interest to someone else, our first responsibility is to be sure that we have sufficiently good reasons for believing it ourselves.

Although I have criticized the utilitarian-competency justification for teaching writing by appealing to principles derived from Socrates, it should now be clear that I am speaking of "good" ideas for writing from the point of view of Aristotle. Writing about such ideas becomes a search for good reasons, motivated by the writer's response to an issue that demands attention. It is motivated neither by the sophist's desire to win the argument at the expense of truth, nor by the philosopher's desire to know truth in an ultimate sense. It is rather an encounter with ideas that demand attention but do not necessarily lend themselves to permanent answers or to ultimate conviction. These are the kinds of ideas that face us every day, as we confront issues of ethics and politics, of interpretation and evaluation, and they demand our best thinking because they urge themselves on us insistently as we listen to others take positions. If they are urgent enough, we attempt to find grounds for agreement; and if this really matters, then we attempt such persuasions by honest means. It is by this process that we teach ourselves to reason better, because in any genuine exchange of ideas our reasons will encounter resistance, calling for equivocation, qualification, and improvement. This is the responsible exercise of rhetoric as Aristotle conceived it: inquiry and honest argumentation practiced for the purpose of achieving cooperation among members of an audience who must continually struggle to come up with adequate, though not final, answers.

It is no wonder that these Aristotelian premises for defining ideas in student writing are less in evidence in classrooms and textbooks than the sophistical forms and strategies that seem most popular. The Aristotelian concept of a good idea for writing puts responsibility for thinking on each person who undertakes to write and on each person who undertakes to assess what is written. Teachers, in other words, are made responsible for exercising reasoning and judgment when they invite their students to do so. This responsibility hardly recommends itself to teachers who must show evidence in quantifiable terms—to students, parents, and administrators—that they are teaching students "skills." The problem of learning to write responsibly and well is only magnified in an educational setting where the measured result must be objective, and where human judgments are distrusted as an adequate basis for assessment.

Teaching students to write in order to solve genuine problems of thought is inevitably constrained by the way students learn to confront such problems in other educational contexts. Just as students are led to believe that there are technical approaches to writing situations, they are encouraged to think of learning as memorizing easy, reliable formulas for solving problems. Confronted by problems of thought, in whatever arena of knowledge, students are confident that there is a simple, dependable "key" that will unlock the answer. This key is not one that they have to forge for themselves, they think, but one that can be found somewhere, perhaps written as a rule or as a missing piece of information. And it is one which, when found, will guarantee a single unambiguous answer. Thus, students learn, I believe, to take no responsibility for finding their own answers by means of critical and rational thought, since they are confident that there will be a formula which, when applied, will make such thought unnecessary. Those who struggle to learn are those who have not yet learned some necessary technique or bit of information, they think, that will make the solution easy. Those who do not struggle may relax into the easy confidence that the techniques and bits of information they do possess will see them through. This habit of mind, encouraged perhaps by adopting the model of scientific education for all other fields,[6] is one reason that some students give up on learning—whether they are poor students or good ones—either because the mysterious element eludes them or because they have found success so easy they do not wish to risk going beyond it.

What has been missed in the education of such people is the difficult but significant habit of "critical judgment." In an essay that argues for critical judgment as the principle aim of education, Wayne C. Booth offers this definition: "To be genuinely critical—to judge on the basis of thought—is to have no easily predictable relationship with belief or doubt, with yes or no, with joining or splitting. The critical mind does not know in advance which side it will come out on."[7] What is hard for many to accept about this definition is that it really means that the critical habit of thought requires two very difficult attitudes: it requires the willingness to take responsibility for thinking for oneself, and it requires the ability to live with the perpetual condition of uncertainty.

These two attitudes are ones that writing can teach, perhaps better than any other academic process. But it cannot do so, as I have indicated, if technical mastery is viewed as an end in itself. How does writing instruction as something more than technique lead to the justification of writing as a way of learning? Aristotle thought that the honest practice of persuasion was a means by which people could come to know contingent and probable truths that could not be known in any other way. What does this mean in today's terms?

Better Writing and Better Thinking

Writing pedagogies do not have to place technique above content. It is possible for writing pedagogies to place students' responsibility for thinking and for judging their own ideas at the very center of the enterprise. The question of how writing might fulfill these ends depends on understanding that "thinking" and "judging," as such, can be taught only by indirect means. These are available to be assessed only through some kind of performance, such as writing. And good thought, good judgment, the kind we wish to teach students to practice, is in fact undefined, except in hopeful generalities like

Booth's. Such definitions are themselves acts of human judgment, and our judgments of how well our students make judgments are obviously limited by our own capacities to reason—without finally being able to ground that reasoning on the solid foundation of quantifiable knowledge.

This is where Aristotle's defense of writing becomes a defense of education in humanistic terms: Since we cannot know many truths with absolute certainty, and since we nevertheless need to act on the basis of thought, we must learn somehow to seek and accept the best available grounds for assent, however limited "best" may be. Rhetorical assent, the kind we daily forge out of genuine situations of disagreement, is not the same as truth. But it does the same job, in the absence of the possibility of truth in all situations. The practice of looking for good reasons, which for Aristotle is what a writer does, is justified, then, because good reasons provide the only basis for rational behavior. Without knowing exactly what it is, we wish to give our students the ability to exercise judgment, because without this ability their technical skills cannot serve them as rational participants in a world that is ever ambiguous but always calls for acts of judgment in new situations.

Judgment is not something that students should be assumed to lack when they enter any given stage of their education, or to possess fully when they leave that stage. It is a human activity that everyone exercises all of the time. But everyone exercises it better or worse at different times, and no one exercises it well all the time. This is why the growth of students' ability to exercise good judgment is harder to measure than the growth of their store of knowledge. It may even be impossible to measure. Students may not feel that they are thinking better when in fact they are, since, after all, as they become better thinkers the kinds of problems that they think about will naturally become more complex and they will continue to feel a familiar uneasiness about their ability to solve them. This uneasiness should not be something that students are conditioned to worry about. It is something that they need to recognize as the fate of thinking people, and to learn to live with, and to enjoy.

Students improve as thinkers in small, undetectable increments of change, brought about by the level of challenges they face. It is only when they are put into situations where better thinking is called for that they will be challenged to produce it. Such situations, of one kind or another, at whatever degree of difficulty, should be the aim of each course that students take. But lacking such consistency, students should at least know that they can create such situations for themselves, by looking for questions or problems within the material they encounter. This is a practice that is encouraged by writing, if writing is understood to be a means of clarifying problems and of inquiring into potential solutions.

Learning to become a better writer happens in the same way that learning to become a better thinker does. Students are not expected to take writing classes because they do not yet know how to write, nor should they be expected to have become perfect writers when those classes are over. Students always enter a writing class knowing something about how to write that that class will not teach. Some write well and others write poorly, but none would be in class if they were starting from zero or if they had nothing to learn. No writing class can complete the job of teaching students to write at their best. All writers, even if they seem to write effortlessly, are always learning to write better each time they take on and complete a new writing challenge—and each new writing task should be a challenge to them in some sense. The rate at which they will become better writers will be just as imperceptible as the rate at which they can be expected to become better thinkers; it will happen slowly, in small increments of change, in intuitive stages of progress that they may not even notice.

Just as they may not realize it when they are thinking better, students may not know that their writing is improving when in fact it is. The reason for this is the same one I mentioned before: As they improve as writers, they will naturally take on slightly more challenging writing tasks and find themselves in somewhat more difficult writing situations, and they will naturally attempt more sophisticated effects. As they do these, they may continue to feel inadequate to each new writing task, simply because it will involve using what they already know how to do to go beyond it. Again, this feeling of inadequacy is nothing to worry about. It is the way students should feel if they are learning. It is only when they give up in despair, because they have been promised too much, or when they feel too satisfied with their writing, that we should worry, because at that point they will have stopped trying to write better.

One difference, of course, between writing and thinking is that writing is tangible—it results in a finite product—while thinking is intangible and just goes on and on (or, sometimes, around and around). But this difference is also a reason why learning to become a better writer results in better thinking. Writing is thinking-made-tangible, thinking that can be examined because it is "on the page" and not all "in the head," invisibly floating around. Writing is thinking that can be stopped and tinkered with. It is a way of making thought hold still long enough to examine its structures, its possibilities, its flaws. The road to a clearer understanding of one's own thoughts is travelled on paper. It is through the attempt to find words for ourselves, and to find patterns for ourselves in which to express related ideas, that we often come to discover exactly what we think.

But notice that I said "attempt to find for ourselves." The idea that students must create the patterns of discourse that they use, when movitated to say something in the best way possible, is contrary to what I have been calling "technical" approaches to composition throughout this chapter. The forms cannot be *given* to students, whose task is then to fill them up with ideas, since in such cases the ideas will not have a purpose in themselves other than to satisfy the demands of the form. It is ideas which come first, in writing, and forms which satisfy the demands that face a writer who has them.

Thus, there is yet another important benefit to thinking that comes from the process of learning to write better, even if this benefit, too, is an intangible one. Writing is a process of finding and structuring ideas. Having ideas is what creates the responsibility for searching for a way to express them. Writing is an occasion for making ideas matter, and without ideas to compel it, it is empty exercise. Writing is the search, not only for the right words in the right order, but also for the right *reasons*. It is in this way that the serious attempt to compose one's thoughts in writing is what can lead one to the very important discovery not only of *what* to think, but *why*.

This is the most significant sense in which writing is a way of learning. Any student, in any class, can listen, read, collect information, pass multiple-choice tests, and even think deliberately about the problems or implications of the information learned about a given subject. But writing about that information has an effect that none of these activities alone can produce: It causes one to *need* to clarify that information, those problems, and those implications for oneself, to put them into relationships, and to explore reasons for saying what one has decided to say about them. Writing does this because it is sustained discourse, as opposed to the temporary and fragmented nature of thinking. Writing does this, furthermore, because it externalizes, for an implied if not a real audience, what is otherwise private and inaccessible. Thus, the possibility of being *read* creates responsibilities that thinking alone can neglect. Writing, because it is undertaken as a decision to be clear, forces clarity. But if it is also undertaken as a decision to be *believed*, it forces more than clarity. Any act of writing that does not stop with the mere assertion of random bits of information will force a writer to look for good reasons, and in the process of looking for good reasons the writer's judgment is being exercised along with the writer's composing skills.

William Irmscher has discussed all of the advantages I have ascribed to writing in a way that demonstrates that these are not separate advantages, but take place simultaneously. "Writing," he says,

is a way of counteracting our distractedness. It requires concentration, focus, and discipline, usually in a silent and solitary setting. Because writing is so much more deliberative than talking, it helps us determine what we know and what we don't know. In our minds, we can fool ourselves. Not on paper. . . .

Writing is often thinking about our own thoughts; that is, it permits us to distance ourselves from our thoughts, to separate the thought from the thinker—a kind of analyzing and assessing, a resolving of differences, and a final structuring. Perhaps most important of all, writing permits us not just to say what we have to say, but to *see* what we have to say. Thus we have a new concern for the *how* as well as the *what*, the manner as well as the substance.[8]

This justification for writing as a way of exercising and improving critical judgment implies a very different kind of pedagogy from the promulgation of technical knowledge and practice. This pedagogy will not be one in which the technical aspects of writing are ignored, however. Technical advice about composition can be taught as an end in itself, or it can be taught as a consequence of the responsibilities that follow from having ideas and wanting to express them.

The Writing Classroom Where Ideas Matter

It is the responsibility of teachers, and of those who administer curriculum, to attempt to make the writing class a place where ideas matter more than technique, so that technique can be taught as a means to a significant end rather than as an end in itself. The difficulty we all face is how to encourage students to want to be right, first, and correct only as a consequence of wanting to be believed. While many different pedagogies will satisfy this condition, certain features must be shared by them, it seems, if the writing class is to create problematic situations that call for the student's best thinking—situations that the students must write their way out of. What are these features?

First of all, a writing class must be a place where students encounter ideas and where they are free to respond to them honestly and critically. This means that reading the thoughts of others is necessary, not only to provide students with "models" of decorous writing, but to stimulate them to assert their own agreements and disagreements so that they can explore their own reasons along with the available arguments of others. The reading students do in a writing class must be critical reading, in the sense that students are not required to accept and memorize information on the basis of the writer's authority but encouraged to question the writer's conclusions on the basis of the quality of the writer's reasons. Critical reading is a process of measuring one's agreement with a conclusion against the quality of the case made in its defense. Writing students who are encouraged to undertake this process will not need to learn complicated or arbitrary "heuristic strategies" in order to come up with ideas for writing. Their ideas will result from their having adopted "stances" in relation to problematic ideas.[9]

Second, students must know that they do not write exclusively for the teacher. Instead, they write for an audience of other inquiring minds, who share their concern for finding answers. This definition of audience places the teacher-critic in the role of eavesdropper on a communication that is intended for others. The teacher helps the student achieve that communication, but it is the members of the class, with whom the student has engaged in critical dialogue about issues, that comprise the student writer's audience. (Or, if not the class, then some other real audience outside the class.) This implies that students also ought to be reading each other's writing and offering their responses. Too often, students write without any sense of a real audience who reads in order to hear what they have to say. Students know that teachers read in order to mark their mistakes. Teachers, as members of the student's audience and yet as authorities on writing, should not think of themselves as "correcting" student compositions so much as explaining aspects of the student's writing which inhibit or enhance its communication. This means that they ought to comment on technical matters as well as respond to ideas. They should respond as people who share an interest in the student's ideas and who are capable of judging those ideas based on the clarity of the writing and the adequacy of the support offered.

Third, thoughtful revision should be taught as a writer's responsibility, given the reasons for writing we have discussed. Revision is ordinarily perceived by students as a perfunctory exercise in cosmetic editing: correcting only the surface faults that the teacher has marked. When students revise in this way, they are responding to revision as a kind of punishment for their errors, rather than as a further opportunity to rethink what they have to say and their reasons for saying it. Revision cannot be a penalty for crimes against grammar; it must be an occasion for reassessing every aspect of the writing after having had the opportunity to see how others respond to it. Students must be encouraged to revise in order to satisfy themselves that they have presented their best thinking and that they have presented this thinking in such a way that the reader's potential understanding and objections are taken into account. Revision, in other words, is essential not because it is forced on students by writing teachers but because it serves the end that writing students should be aiming for: the earned assent of readers who are capable of deciding on the basis of the quality of the writer's reasons.

These are but three considerations that follow from the attempt to make writing serve the ends of a liberal education. Obstacles to bringing these pedagogical considerations to bear on teaching are plentiful, but teachers and administrators must ask themselves

occasionally whether the reasons that make change difficult are
becoming excuses for not trying. One reason, and potential excuse,
that I see as especially important is that teachers who feel inadequate
to judge the quality of students' ideas fall back on grading for
mechanics and grammar because they can have confidence in their
ability to recognize faults in these areas. Recognizing faults in
thinking is not only much harder, it is much more unreliable. It puts
the teacher at risk, because of course, when it comes to judging ideas
we are all equally dependent on our own ability to reason. No
handbook of grammar, no computer editing program, no sentence-
combining exercise, can tell us how to recognize a good idea. This is
not a rule-governed activity, and consequently it is imperfect. To
chance being wrong threatens the teacher's authority in the classroom,
and consequently, for the writing teacher, it is always easier to get
through the day if all ideas are allowed to stay safely equal.

Teachers *can* judge thought because they do it every day, when
they read critically writing that is addressed to them as thinking
persons. They must be as free to exercise their critical judgments in
their writing classes as they are elsewhere. For students to develop
their own critical capacities, they need to be in active, honest dialogue
about their ideas with a writing teacher. If this puts the teacher at risk,
it is only because thinking always puts a person at risk: It always
creates the possibility of being wrong, and if it did not, we would
never learn to think better. The risk of honestly facing real human
issues, as Aristotle taught, requires abandoning systematic means of
testing knowledge and engaging in the messy and unpredictable
business of argumentation, not knowing where you might come out,
but knowing that by entering the dialogue you are demonstrating an
ability to live with uncertainty.

Conclusion

Why write, then? My answer is because writing, more than any
other task, brings one face to face with important human
responsibilities. These include the responsibility to clarify and
structure one's ideas. More importantly, they include the responsibility to continue to inquire and argue, *toward* the truth as we are able to
discover it through the shared means of discourse, even while
knowing that the whole truth will always be beyond our means.
These responsibilities are as necessary for students as they learn to
respond as thinking members of the audience for others' writing, as
much as they are for them as they learn to compose their thoughts.
Thus, while writing as a competency is justified by claims to offer
students power, writing as the responsible exercise of judgment is
justified by a plea for tolerance.

FOOTNOTES

1. A summary of such reports is contained in *Education Week* 4 (September 5, 1984): L-51. The entire issue of this journal is devoted to literacy, with thorough discussion, from many viewpoints, of the relationships between writing and learning. For a review of eight recent reports on education that illustrates the technical/ intellectual distinction I discuss in this chapter, see Walter Karp, "Why Johnny Can't Think: The Politics of Bad Schooling," *Harper's Magazine* 270 (June 1985): 69-73. For discussions of teaching writing as a thinking skill in the lower grades, see *Perspectives on Writing in Grades 1-8*, ed. Shirley Haley-James (Urbana, Ill.: National Council of Teachers of English, 1981).

2. Aristotle wrote, for instance, that the function of rhetoric "is not so much to persuade, as to find out in each case the existing means of persuasion." See *The "Art" of Rhetoric*, trans. John Henry Freese (Cambridge, Mass.: Harvard University Press, 1926), p. 13.

3. For my extended discussion of this concept and its relation to methods of teaching composition, see "An Adequate Epistemology for Composition: Classical and Modern Perspectives," in *Essays on Classical Rhetoric and Modern Discourse*, ed. Robert Connors, Andrea Lunsford, and Lisa Ede (Carbondale, Ill.: Southern Illinois University Press, 1984), pp. 152-69.

4. E. D. Hirsch, Jr., *The Philosophy of Composition* (Chicago: University of Chicago Press, 1977), pp. 182-83.

5. For further discussion, see my "Freshman English: In Whose Service?" *College English* 44 (September 1982): 15-20.

6. See Wayne C. Booth, *Modern Dogma and the Rhetoric of Assent* (Chicago: University of Chicago Press, 1974), esp. pp. 3-40.

7. Wayne C. Booth, "The Uncritical American: or, Nobody's from Missouri Any More," in Wayne C. Booth, *Now Don't Try to Reason with Me: Essays and Ironies for a Credulous Age* (Chicago: University of Chicago Press, 1970), p. 66.

8. William Irmscher, *Teaching Expository Writing* (New York: Holt, Rinehart and Winston, 1979), p. 20.

9. See Wayne C. Booth, "The Rhetorical Stance," in Booth, *Now Don't Try to Reason with Me*, pp. 25-33.

CHAPTER III

Teaching Writing: The Major Theories

ANNE RUGGLES GERE

When the editors of this Yearbook asked me to write a chapter on current models of composition pedagogy, an image came immediately to mind. I would portray the dominant model as King Kong standing on the Empire State Building. Like the beast who swats biplanes away as if they were flies, this model remains impervious to the challenges of other approaches, dispatching them with the brutish power born of preeminence. Or so I thought before I began looking more closely at discussions of what goes on in the majority of composition classes today. First there was the problem of what to call this dominant model. In discussions of research, classes employing experimental procedures are usually contrasted with the "traditional" class, and names for these traditional classes include "formalist," "discipline-centered," and "current-traditional."

Each of these names has a slightly different origin and meaning. The formalist approach was described by Richard Fulkerson, who, moved by Charles Silberman's description of mindlessness in education,[1] considered how to address composition instructors who "either fail to have a consistent value theory or fail to let that philosophy shape pedagogy [and who are] in Silberman's terms . . . guilty of mindlessness."[2] As might be expected of one trained in English studies, Fulkerson turned to literary theory for a model and settled upon M. H. Abrams's four theories of literature,[3] claiming that "since the elements in an artistic transaction are the same as those in any communication, it seemed that Abrams's four theories might also be relevant to composition."[4] Fulkerson shifts Abrams's "objective" criticism to a "formalist" approach. According to Fulkerson's definition, this approach emphasizes certain internal forms, the most commonly valued form being grammar. For the formalist,

good writing is "correct" writing at the sentence level. In the classroom, one studies errors of form—in order to avoid them. But forms other than grammatical can also be the teacher's key values. I have heard of metaphorical formalists, sentence-length formalists, and topic-sentence formalists, to name a few.[5]

30

Fulkerson names two major figures in composition (Francis Christensen and E. D. Hirsch) who exemplify the formalist position. Fulkerson offers no evaluation of formalists' effectiveness, but I argue that they take an extremely narrow view of writing. While correctness or at least adherence to conventions makes writing accessible to readers, a model that looks only at this dimension cannot help students see language as a means of communicating with others or as a source of delight.

William Woods takes a slightly broader view as he places composition pedagogy within the context of educational theory. As Woods sees it, two general pedagogical theories—one student-centered and one discipline-centered—have dominated American education since the nineteenth century. Woods claims that discipline-centered teaching accounts for more of the composition curriculum, and he divides this discipline-centered approach into three subcategories emphasizing rhetoric, logic, and language. This leads to a description of three discipline-centered composition pedagogies, one of which is the "discipline-centered/language-based" approach. As Woods describes it, the "discipline-centered/language-based" model

gives rise to style books, manuals, handbooks and workbooks concerned with grammar, syntax, diction, usage, and style. Two extensions of this theory are the "educational technology" approach, which tends to produce auto-instructional texts, and the approach to teaching writing through various uses of exemplary prose passages.[6]

Woods arrives at this and his other descriptions of discipline-centered and student-centered teaching as a way of describing composition textbooks. According to Woods, each text represents a certain approach to the teaching of writing, and one of the instructor's tasks is to decide which one appeals and choose a text that fits the approach.

The term "current-traditional paradigm" was coined by Richard Young to describe what he saw as a tacit theory dominating composition pedagogy for most of the twentieth century. Borrowing his term from what Daniel Fogarty calls "current-traditional rhetoric,"[7] Young described the features of the current-traditional paradigm as

emphasis on the composed product rather than the composing process; the analysis of discourse into words, sentences, and paragraphs; the classification of discourse into description, narration, exposition, and argument; the strong concern with usage (syntax, spelling, punctuation) and with style (economy, clarity, emphasis); and preoccupation with the informal essay and the research paper.[8]

Although he draws on Thomas Kuhn for the "paradigm" concept, the name for and substance of Young's description derive from the features Daniel Fogarty ascribes to current-traditional rhetoric. Fogarty distinguishes between "a teaching rhetoric and the philosophy of rhetoric" in Aristotle's work.[9] The philosophy includes thought-thing-word relationships, abstraction, definition, logic, and dialectic, while the teaching rhetoric is exemplified in Aristotle's *Rhetoric*. In Fogarty's view, current-traditional rhetoric is essentially Aristotelian, but "time and expediency" have added elements of grammar, syntax, spelling, punctuation, and mechanics; modes of discourse; qualities of style; communication; divisions of words, sentences, and paragraphs; and specialized forms.[10] Fogarty goes on to note that students of Aristotle's day could have easily integrated philosophical concerns with their study of rhetoric, yet "today it is not only quite possible, but quite likely, that the average college student may never make the connection between his philosophy and his composition."[11]

Young does not address the disjunction between philosophical and teaching rhetorics, but he identifies as a problem the lack of attention to invention in the teaching rhetoric. For Young, both the delineation of the problem and its solution lie in paradigmatic terms, and he devotes considerable energy to demonstrating the applicability of the paradigm concept to composition or, as Fogarty calls it, the teaching rhetoric.

James Berlin appends the term "positivist" to "current-traditional," arguing that the epistemological basis for the current-traditional model is positivistic because it assumes that writing should assume an uncomplicated correspondence of the faculties and the world in order to "provide the language which corresponds either to the objects in the external world or to the ideas in his or her own mind—both are essentially the same—in such a way that it reproduces the objects and the experience of them in the minds of the hearers."[12] According to Berlin, the current-traditional model "demands that the audience be as 'objective' as the writer; both shed personal and social concerns in the interests of the unobstructed perception of empirical reality."[13] Further, he states that "in current-traditional rhetoric the writer must focus on experience in a way that makes possible the discovery of certain kinds of information—the empirical and rational—and the neglect of others—psychological and social concerns."[14]

These different origins—literary theory versus rhetorical history/philosophy of science versus educational theory versus intellectual history—for describing "formalist," "discipline-centered/language-based," and "current-traditional" demonstrate the difficulty of seeing the currently dominant model as a monolith. Satisfyingly dramatic as it is, the King Kong image does not work because the current model is more complex than this colossus suggests.

Closer examination of the definitions offered by Fulkerson, Woods, Young, and Berlin illustrates some of the complexities inherent in the current approach. Fulkerson can be commended for insisting that composition avoid the "value-mode confusion"[15] that results for both instruction and evaluation when instructors fail to think carefully about what they value in composition. And we can thank Fulkerson for recognizing the need to articulate values that have remained inchoate, but his method for solving the problem creates further value conflicts. Rather than looking directly at composition instruction to determine its nature and values, Fulkerson imports literary theory to describe four postures. The awkwardness of this borrowing is evident in the extent to which Fulkerson redefines and renames Abrams's terminology. Abrams's "mimetic" does not mean that "a clear connection exists between good writing and good thinking,"[16] and the translation of Abrams's "pragmatic" and "objective" to Fulkerson's "rhetorical" and "formalist" obscures more than it reveals.

Part of the problem with Fulkerson's terminology resides in its sources because terms borrowed from literary criticism fail to capture the essence of composition instruction. The limited definition Fulkerson assigns to formalism bespeaks, however, a greater problem. By concentrating exclusively on issues of form, Fulkerson omits concern with what produces the forms, thereby removing any possibility of connecting this model of instruction with a philosophy of rhetoric.

William Woods has a much less ambitious goal than Young or Fulkerson in that he considers only text selection rather than larger instructional questions. His attempt to connect composition instruction with educational trends such as "life adjustment theory," "academic reform," and the counterrevolution of the Dartmouth Conference suggests the importance of looking at composition instruction in larger terms, but Wood's analysis does not extend far enough into history. He claims, for example, that "college teaching of writing in America had its official baptism in 1949, when the NCTE founded the Conference on College Composition and Communication."[17] Nor does he explore the educational movements fully enough to demonstrate their philosophical roots.

To the extent that he draws on Fogarty's discussion of rhetorical history, Young offers a useful perspective on current-traditional composition pedagogy, but his attempt to place composition instruction within the scientific tradition is problematical. As Robert Connors has explained so well,[18] there is serious question about the applicability of the paradigm concept to composition, and Young, like others in composition, may have been unduly attracted to the glitter of science. The more serious problem with Young's approach is that it ignores the division between philosophy and composition. Even though he borrows Fogarty's "current-traditional" term, Young fails to develop the philosophy-composition division that Fogarty delineates. In turning to the philosophy of science, Young compounds this neglect.

James Berlin comes closest to making a connection between philosophy and composition pedagogy because he searches for the rhetorical theory underlying the model. In beginning this search Berlin notes that conceptions of writers, reality, audience, and language all contribute to the definition of a model: "To teach writing is to argue for a version of reality, and the best way of knowing and communicating it."[19] As he continues, however, Berlin moves to an advocacy position, claiming superiority for what he calls new rhetoricians, and his argument veers in the direction of intellectual history.

What Fulkerson, Woods, Young, and Berlin share, then, is a failure to connect what Fogarty terms the teaching rhetoric with a philosophy. This is not a problem unique to these four theorists; it has been the continuing problem of composition pedagogy. Because the teaching rhetoric has remained separate from a philosophy of rhetoric, it has been vulnerable to the ravages of "time and expediency."[20] The dominance of mechanical features (syntax, spelling, modes, style, and punctuation) in today's instruction derives from the lack of a coherent philosophy guiding composition pedagogy. When a discipline lacks a coherent philosophy, it can be shaped by the most anti-intellectual forces, and this is precisely what has happened to composition pedagogy over the years.

At the college level, composition instruction began with the introduction of a prescribed full-year freshman course and a half-year sophomore course at Harvard in 1874. These courses, like their predecessors, were stimulated by President Charles Eliot, who at his inaugural in 1869 lamented "the prevailing neglect of the systematic study of the English language"[21] and sought every opportunity to redress this neglect. Francis James Child, Harvard's Boylston Professor of Rhetoric and Oratory when composition courses were first introduced, could have played a major role in articulating the philosophy of these courses, but he did not. Rather, Child resented the composition courses he was asked to teach and devoted his energies to finding a way to escape them. Child's real interest was English literature, and he became this nation's first professor of English in 1874. Child's successor, Adams Sherman Hill, likewise did little to unite the teaching of writing with a philosophy of rhetoric, but he did succeed in building a composition program in the face of significant faculty resistance.

In the 1870s Latin and Greek were the dominant languages on college campuses, and Harvard's faculty, like faculties everywhere, was resistant to English studies. Hill was successful in overcoming this resistance and in instituting a required freshman composition course, English A, in 1885. Hill's influence extended beyond Harvard through his textbooks. The most popular of these, *The Principles of Rhetoric and Their Application*, was published in 1878 and was still in use in the 1930s. This text demonstrates the schism between the teaching rhetoric and a philosophy of rhetoric. Hill's text substituted manner for originality of matter. He borrowed directly from the Scottish rhetoricians Blair, Campbell, and Whateley, simply putting their ideas in more accessible form. While his material was not original and therefore did not profit from new philosophical insights, Hill adopted a dogmatic tone that contributed to the popularity of his text. Pronouncements such as "From the point of view of clearness, it is always better to repeat a noun than to substitute for it a pronoun which fails to suggest that noun"[22] admit no ambiguity and reassure uncertain students and instructors.

Hill's dogmatic tone may have increased the popularity of his text, but it did little to unite philosophy with composition pedagogy. In fact, it worked in the opposite direction. Until very recently teachers of composition at all levels have received no formal training. College composition instructors may have themselves taken a freshman English course, but they had no direct instruction in composition pedagogy, and the same has been true for secondary and elementary school teachers. For example, in 1952 Harold Allen could find only five graduate-level courses on composition in this country, and not all of the five were offered regularly.[23] What composition teachers learned, therefore, came through what I have called the informal curriculum.[24] This informal curriculum, a combination of self-sponsored reading, orientation meetings, and conversations with other instructors, depended heavily upon textbooks. Hill therefore influenced composition pedagogy much more substantially than would have been the case if composition pedagogy had developed its own philosophical and intellectual foundations. Instead, composition instructors, pressured by "time and expediency," clung gratefully to pronouncements about usage and emphasized these in their classes because they discouraged student questions, making teaching easier.

Hill's text was not alone in allowing "time and expediency" to create the current-traditional model of composition pedagogy. There was, in addition, the ongoing resistance of Harvard faculty. When English A became a required course in 1885, the rest of the Harvard curriculum was adopting the German university model of electives, so the one required course stood out. Further, college enrollments expanded over 60 percent during the 1890s, so this requirement directed a high proportion of Harvard's resources toward composition instruction. Predictably, this allocation of resources disgruntled faculty and administrators, leading Harvard's Board of Overseers, in 1891, to appoint a committee to investigate English A.

This committee, composed of three people from outside the academic community, issued the first of three "Harvard Reports." This report proposed a simple solution to college composition: It should be taught by high schools. The report stated:

It is obviously absurd that the College—the institution of higher education—should be called upon to turn aside from its proper functions and devote its means and the time of its instructors to the task of imparting elementary instruction which would be given even in ordinary grammar schools, much more in those higher academic institutions intended to prepare select youth for a university course.[25]

The committee went on to recommend that admission requirements be raised to eliminate students underprepared in composition and to suggest that if schools did not devote more time to teaching writing, they could not expect their students to be accepted at Harvard. While this report may have helped solve Harvard's immediate problems, it had a negative long-term effect on composition instruction in this country.

Harvard's prestige led many other colleges to follow the recommendations of this and the other Harvard Reports. Not only did colleges emulate the position that they should have little responsibility for composition instruction; they also accepted the Committee's narrow definition of writing. This definition was characterized by statements such as it is "little less than absurd to suggest that any human being who can be taught to talk cannot likewise be taught to compose. Writing is merely the habit of talking with the pen instead of with the tongue."[26] This narrow view also emphasizes mechanical correctness in writing above all else. The 1892 report contains many negative comments about students' poor usage and gives special attention to neatness and handwriting. Because composition instructors had no coherent philosophy against which to evaluate such statements, these limited views gained currency and shaped ensuing instruction.

Since a narrow view of writing dominated college composition pedagogy and fostered the development and maintenance of the current-traditional model, it is not surprising that composition pedagogy in secondary and elementary schools followed the same direction. Secondary schools took seriously Harvard's warning that they must prepare students to write mechanically correct papers. Texts used in secondary schools mirrored Hill's *Principles of Rhetoric* in their emphasis on dogmatic statements about correctness, and common school teachers, like their college counterparts, relied on the informal curriculum of texts for their training in the teaching of writing. The nagging Miss Fidditch commonly described as hounding composition classes with details of mechanical correctness can trace her ancestry to the Harvard Reports.

The colossus of current-traditional instruction developed, then, not out of a clearly articulated philosophical tradition but in the absence of same. A convergence of administrative, demographic, and prestige concerns created the climate in which composition instructors turned their attention to issues of form, style, and correctness. The aphilosophical emergence of the current-traditional model has been matched by an equally aphilosophical maintenance of it. The extent to which other models have and have not been allowed to coexist or have been partially included by the current-traditional model has resulted from aphilosophical concerns.

One of the earliest challenges to current-traditional instruction emerged in the 1890s. Fred Newton Scott, professor of rhetoric at the University of Michigan from 1889 to 1927, attempted to develop a philosophy of composition pedagogy by drawing on linguistics, psychology, and sociology as well as rhetoric.[27] In trying to foster a fuller conception of rhetoric, one that gave it intellectual breadth as well as social importance, Scott portrayed writing in terms of function rather than mere correctness. According to one of his students, Scott saw correctness as necessary but not the chief purpose of writing. Rather, he "looked on words as a cabinet maker looks on his tools—things that just must be right and unabused throughout or the work will be bad."[28] Although Scott had some brief successes during the reform period of the 1890s, Kitzhaber explains that "most of his ideas were too new, his recommendations for change too fundamental to be generally accepted. Rhetorical instruction fell in behind the Harvard group instead."[29] According to Kitzhaber, composition pedagogy in this country "until well into the 1930s became, for all practical purposes, little more than instruction in grammar and the mechanics of writing, motivated almost solely by the ideal of superficial correctness."[30] The reform movement of the 1890s was followed by a conservative, science-oriented shift in the early decades of this century, and Scott's model could not flourish in this hostile climate.

Had Scott's challenge been successful, the current-traditional colossus might never have reached its current status. Lacking an intellectual base, the current-traditional model fed on Harvard's prestige and grew out of proportion to other models. Scott's work did, however, provide the basis from which models of future generations developed. The contemporary model that owes most to Scott's work has been variously termed "rhetorical" (by Fulkerson), "discipline-centered-rhetoric-based" (by Woods), and neo-Aristotelian or classicist (by Berlin). Richard Young's whole paradigmatic critique of the current-traditional approach derives from his concept of rhetoric, both classical and modern, as including invention as one of its central parts.

Fulkerson describes the rhetorical approach as claiming that "good writing is writing adapted to achieve the desired effect on the desired audience. If the same verbal construct is directed to a different audience, then it may have to be evaluated differently."[31] For Woods the discipline-centered-rhetoric-based approach manifests itself in texts that "reproduce the features of classical rhetoric . . . [that offer] a fully developed alternative to classical theory."[32] Berlin explains neo-Aristotelian as "primarily concerned with the provision of inventional devices,"[33] and notes that few textbooks adhere closely to this model. Young describes the desired rhetoric as one that "begins with the perception of a social problem and ends with changes in an audience's beliefs and behaviors."[34] Throughout Scott's work, three dimensions—communicator, audience, and language—receive continuing attention, and this emphasis laid the foundation for the contemporary rhetorical model of composition pedagogy. Scott even placed mechanical correctness in a rhetorical context in his textbook: "Presented as a means of meeting definite social needs more or less effectively, of winning attention and consideration, the various devices of grammar and rhetoric make an appeal to self-interest which pupils can understand."[35] Scott's attempt to reconnect the teaching rhetoric with a philosophy of rhetoric failed to succeed because it competed with an aphilosophical and mechanical model in a period when the growing dominance of science reinforced mechanics over philosophy.

Another factor contributing to the eclipse of Scott's model was the separation of rhetoric from English departments, a separation to which Scott himself contributed. Scott sought to create a separate department of rhetoric at the University of Michigan, and in 1903 he succeeded. This move was emulated on many campuses during the next few decades, and in 1914 these shifts were institutionalized by the formation of the Speech Association of America. The majority of these new departments of rhetoric were motivated by the resentments of rhetoricians who felt snubbed and/or overpowered by their colleagues in literature.

Composition pedagogy remained in English departments, isolated from the classical rhetoric that could give it intellectual depth. This separation not only impoverished the philosophical basis of composition pedagogy, but it also contributed to major distinctions between speaking and writing. Composition pedagogy and rhetoric remained distant from one another until the early 1960s.

Writing instruction in the common schools followed a similar pattern. Texts emphasized mechanical correctness, and all but a few exceptional teachers proffered formulaic advice about topic sentences and five-paragraph themes to their students. Compounding philosophical limitations were time constraints which sandwiched writing instruction into a curriculum crowded with language and literature studies. As recently as 1968, a study of exemplary English programs revealed that only 15.7 percent of class time was spent on writing instruction, and most of that was devoted to correcting completed papers.[36] The teaching of writing in secondary schools shared with college classes the liabilities of separating philosophical and teaching rhetorics.

Rhetoric reentered college English departments during the 1940s via the literary criticism developed at the University of Chicago by Richard S. Crane and Richard McKeon. Subsequent to this reentry, a philosophical rhetoric began to exert influence on composition pedagogy. One of the first manifestations of this influence appeared in 1957 in Richard Weaver's textbook, *Composition*, which brought classical rhetoric's enthymeme and topics to the teaching of writing.[37]

This text was followed in 1962 by *Rhetoric: Principles and Usage*. Authors Albert P. Duhamel and Richard E. Hughes made their intentions explicit by stating: "Perhaps the most significant difference between our book and those currently used in composition and rhetoric courses is our attempt to introduce the art of rhetoric as a systematic body of knowledge."[38] Accompanying this text and Edward P. J. Corbett's *Classical Rhetoric for the Modern Student*, which followed in 1965,[39] was a growing intellectual ferment among a small number of composition instructors. The Rhetoric Society of America was founded in 1968 by directors including Edward P. J. Corbett, Wayne Booth, William Irmscher, Ross Winterowd, Richard Larson, Robert Gorrell, Richard Hughes, Harry Crosby, and Owen Thomas. For these individuals and their peers, the reintegration of classical rhetoric and composition pedagogy offered a successful challenge to the current-traditional model.

One offshoot of the revival of classical rhetoric was the development of a modern rhetoric of composition pedagogy. The most notable example appears in the tagmemic theory of Kenneth Pike and his associates. *Rhetoric: Discovery and Change*, the text Pike wrote with Alton Becker and Richard Young,[40] demonstrates how tagmemic linguistics can be used with effect in composition classes. Although the nine-cell matrix of particle, wave, and field combined with contrast, distribution, and variation of tagmemics draws on modern physics, it owes a great deal to Aristotle's topics.

For the majority of composition instructors, however, this reintegration and the resulting scholarship made little difference, and the current-traditional colossus continued its dominance. This lack of effect derived, in large measure, from the training of these composition instructors. The educational expansion of the 1960s gave way to constriction in the 1970s, and secondary and elementary teachers trained in the 1960s were the last group hired in significant numbers. The innovative programs and courses in rhetoric introduced by people such as members of the Rhetoric Society of America had little influence on a stable and aging population of teachers. Courses in the teaching of writing instituted in the past decade have produced college composition instructors who make the intellectual traditions of rhetoric and composition available to future generations of instructors, but the paucity of teaching positions at all levels prevents rapid adoption of this model.

Because training in the rhetorical model has been unavailable to the majority of composition instructors in this country, the informal curriculum has continued to serve as the dominant means of transmitting composition pedagogy. This means that textbooks continue to educate most writing instructors. The small number of textbooks representing the rhetorical tradition and their marginal commercial success demonstrate the relatively small impact of this approach. A second edition of *Rhetoric: Principles and Usage* was issued in 1967, and the book was out of print ten years later. A text such as *Classical Rhetoric for the Modern Student* remains in print, not because it is widely used by composition instructors, but because it is used in courses for graduate students in composition and rhetoric. The rhetorical model of composition pedagogy is not one easily adopted by instructors relying entirely on their own resources. To be effectively assimilated, it requires grounding in an intellectual tradition, something not available in the informal curriculum.

In his discussion of forms of invention, Richard Young separates the tagmemic approach from the rhetorical, explaining:

classical invention is concerned with finding arguments likely to induce psychological changes in the audience; prewriting, on the other hand, is concerned with the discovery of ordering principles and with changes in the writer. Tagmemic invention is concerned with both. It conceives of invention as essentially a problem-solving activity, the problems being of two sorts: those arising in one's own experience of the world and those arising out of a need to change others.[41]

To make this claim, Young minimizes the ethos of classical rhetoric and emphasizes the individual's experience in tagmemic invention. He also creates two other categories of invention: dramatistic (based on Kenneth Burke's work) and prewriting (to be discussed below). As long as these four—rhetorical, tagmemic, prewriting, and dramatistic—are described as systems of invention, there is no problem, but they are frequently extended to delineate models of composition pedagogy. David Harrington et al., for example, discuss composition texts in terms of Young's four categories, and this discussion wavers between emphasis on invention and immersion in a whole model.[42] For example, in the discussion of texts that adapt principles of classical rhetoric to the teaching of writing, Harrington et al. include not only works such as those by Duhamel and Corbett, but also books "that adapt principles of classical rhetoric for the teaching of writing."[43] This adaptation includes everything from overviews of principles of invention to a book in which "invention survives, lurking in a chapter on 'Development'."[44]

The range of Harrington's inclusions suggests the confusion that results when approaches to invention are substituted for pedagogical models, and this confusion has contributed to the maintenance of the current-traditional model. As Harrington et al. describe it, for example, some texts have adapted principles of classical rhetoric to devices for paragraph and essay development.[45] The focus on paragraph and essay signals a concern with form, an issue much more important to the current-traditional model than to classical rhetoric.

Prewriting, another of Young's categories of invention, has likewise been appropriated by the current-traditional model. As originally described by D. Gordon Rohman,[46] prewriting uses journal writing, meditation, and metaphorical thinking to stimulate writing. The logical pedagogical model for prewriting is the expressivist approach. As Fulkerson describes it, expressivists emphasize the writer and cover a wide range, "from totally accepting and nondirective teachers, some of whom insist that one neither can nor should evaluate writing, to much more directive, experiential teachers who design classroom activities to maximize student self-discovery."[47] Further, expressivists "value writing that is about personal subjects . . . [and] desire to have writing contain an interesting, credible, honest, and personal voice."[48]

The most obvious source of the expressivist model is the Dartmouth Conference of 1966. This meeting of American and British educators on the teaching of English brought new theories to this country. As Arthur Applebee puts it, "What the British offered the Americans was a model for English instruction which focussed not on the 'demands' of the discipline but on the personal and linguistic growth of the child."[49] The American educators present at this conference were profoundly affected, and their consequent activity helped shape the expressive model of composition pedagogy.

William Woods places the expressivist approach in his "student-directed" category and explains it in terms of a "maturationist" theory of development:

[H]umankind has in it the seeds of its perfection, which will flower if allowed to grow naturally, uninhibited and unharmed by social or environmental constraints. . . . [A]ll aspects of the communication triangle are treated as extensions of the writer's experience. . . . Teaching methods guided by this theory encourage such activities as observing, recording, expressing, listening, and reacting.[50]

As this description makes clear, the roots of the expressivist model of composition pedagogy extend past the Dartmouth Conference to the progressive education movement during the first decades of this century. John Dewey, generally credited with giving voice to what became known as the progressive movement, emphasized the learner's experience, interest, and motivation and encouraged teaching that centered on the student rather than on the discipline. Dewey's views influenced many teachers, but the groups shaping the English curriculum, groups such as the Committee of Ten (established in 1892) and the National Conference on Uniform Entrance Requirements in English (active at the turn of the century), operated from the current-traditional model.

The Dartmouth Conference, then, gave new vigor to a progressive movement that had lain dormant for several decades, and it targeted the insights of the progressives toward English instruction specifically. When seen from this perspective, the expressive approach is less tied to the 1960s and is more directly related to larger currents in education. Because the expressive approach has not always been identified with a major educational and intellectual tradition (and sometimes even when it has), it has been subject to appropriation by the current-traditional approach.

One of the terms most commonly appropriated from the expressivist approach is "prewriting." As originally conceived, prewriting denoted methods of enabling writers to explore their own minds. When appropriated by current-traditionalists, however, prewriting has come to mean any activity that occurs at the beginning stages of writing. Accordingly, many current-traditional textbooks include sections on prewriting, but what these sections contain has nothing in common with prewriting as described by expressivists. For example, one text describes prewriting as asking students to make a list of topics they intend to include in their writing. This activity, much closer to outlining than to the kind of exploration described by Rohman, demonstrates the confusions that can result when a practice of one approach is appropriated by practitioners of another approach.

These three approaches—current-traditional, rhetorical, and expressivist—are categories on which theorists such as Young, Woods, Fulkerson, and Berlin agree. There is, however, a fourth category which nearly every theorist expresses differently. Fulkerson borrows Abrams's term "mimetic" to describe instruction that emphasizes correspondence with reality. According to Fulkerson, one manifestation of this approach "says that a clear connection exists between good writing and good thinking. The major problem with student writing is that it is not solidly thought out."[51] The pedagogical solution to this problem is to emphasize the teaching of reasoning and logic as a basis for good writing. Another manifestation of the mimetic approach as Fulkerson describes it is to assume that students do not write well because they do not know enough. Mimetic solutions to this problem include (a) encouragement of more research during the early stages of writing, (b) emphasis on discovery procedures, (c) having students read authors who take different perspectives on the same topic. The result will be writing that is closer to the "real situation."

William Woods's discipline-centered-logic-based approach has much in common with Fulkerson's mimetic category. The emphasis as Woods describes it is on "the art of straight thinking."[52] Texts in this category emphasize the "reciprocal or 'dialectical' relationship between thought and language, the ways in which thought travels back and forth . . . moving from observation to classification, and from generalization back again to specification, in the process of developing and sequencing ideas."[53] Woods explains that texts following the logic-based approach rarely give much space to audiences for writing or to processes of writing, but they focus considerable attention on the dialogue between language and thought in writing.

James Berlin assigns the term "New Rhetoricians" to his version of this fourth category, explaining that it presumes that "knowledge is not simply a static entity available for retrieval. Truth is dynamic and dialectical, the result of a process involving the interaction of opposing elements. It is a relation that is created, not pre-existent and waiting to be discovered."[54] In this view, then, writing aids discovery because writers use language to converse with themselves and thereby discover new ideas. Berlin shares Wood's view that Ann Berthoff's *Forming/Thinking/Writing*[55] exemplifies the New Rhetoricians' approach, but he puts the Young, Becker, and Pike text in the same category. And he argues that audience plays a significant role in the New Rhetoricians' approach. The roots of this fourth approach— New Rhetoricians', mimetic, or logic-based—lie in logic, and the paucity of texts in this category suggests the limited number of instructors who use it. Of the major theories of composition instruction, the New Rhetoricians' logic-based approach is the least widely employed. Perhaps this is because the long-standing split between philosophical and teaching rhetorics has reduced logic's accessibility to composition instructors.

Throughout this discussion I have avoided describing "the writing process" as a model of composition pedagogy. The term "writing process," derived from descriptions of what writers do as opposed to the written products they produce, does not describe a model so much as a way of proceeding within that model. Elements of the writing process, whether they are called prewriting, drafting, and revising or incubating, writing, and reworking, can be adapted to any model discussed here. Indeed, many currently available textbooks graft writing process terminology onto current-traditional, rhetorical, and expressive models.

This grafting has the benefit of reducing emphasis on products in writing, but it also exemplifies one of the problems with current models of composition pedagogy. As the preceding discussion has shown, there is little agreement about the terminology for or exact shape of any of these models. These models can and have been stretched almost beyond recognition because of the continuing separation of the teaching rhetoric from a philosophy of rhetoric. While articulating the shape of models helps reduce vulnerability to the charge of mindlessness, the fact of articulating does not develop a philosophy.

Likewise, attempts to circumvent the issue by drawing on the theoretical foundations of another discipline will only confuse the issue. Richard Young's use of science's "paradigm," for example, finally confounds more than it helps because this term cannot be used accurately with reference to composition studies. Moreover, using such borrowed terminology weakens the models to which it is being applied. Fitting a borrowed term onto an aphilosophical model involves two translations, one from the borrowed field to composition, and a second within the model itself. Just as translations of translations (the King James Bible from the Latin Vulgate, for example) lose accuracy, so models of composition pedagogy lose their integrity when philosophies of another discipline are applied.

When models lose their integrity, they develop fissures into which foreign organisms intrude, and this explains why it has been so easy for each of the models discussed to borrow from one another and why it is so difficult to find a textbook that adheres to one model exclusively. Another result of operating with aphilosophical models is that arguments about central questions become clouded by extraneous issues. Among the questions facing composition pedagogy recently have been those of grammar instruction, Black English, and remedial studies. Each of these has been dominated by issues of time and expediency because the philosophical basis of existing models remains uncertain.

Grammar instruction, for example, has been dismissed by many theorists and researchers as useless for improving the quality of

*"time + expediency"
rather than philosophical
considerations*

writing,[56] but it has remained prominent in composition pedagogy, particularly in the current-traditional model. And there are those who take the position that grammar instruction actually does lead to improved writing. What has been lost in this debate is attention to the relationship between language and reality, to ways of knowing the world. Instead, issues of time (teaching grammar is or is not a waste of time) and expediency (grammar instruction does or does not produce better writing) have been argued.

Discussions of Black English have occupied considerable energy in composition pedagogy, and these discussions have likewise strayed from central questions of what constitutes knowledge and the relationship of thought to language. The Black English debate stems from the pragmatic issue of how composition instructors should treat nonstandard dialects. Linguists such as William Labov have demonstrated that nonstandard dialects such as Black English follow a definite grammar of their own. Those who use Black English, therefore, are not erratic or illogical; they simply follow a different system than do users of the standard dialect. An ensuing debate among composition instructors has wrestled with how to respond to nonstandard dialects.

Some people argue that children's concepts of reality are tied to their home dialects and that teachers, especially teachers of composition, need to acknowledge the importance of such dialects. This view is elaborated in a publication of the Conference on College Composition, *Students' Right to Their Own Language*.[57] Opponents, however, argue that students who use Black English will not be able to succeed in a world that assigns negative connotations to dialects other than standard English.

Likewise, following the model of the Harvard Reports, definition of and response to remedial studies have been shaped almost entirely by questions of time and expediency rather than by philosophical considerations of how students might best arrive at knowledge. Economic incentives, more than philosophical considerations, govern schools' policies. Open admissions programs of colleges in the 1960s resulted from an expanding economy and led to expanded remedial programs, particularly in writing. Secondary schools emulated this expansion by introducing elective programs in writing, among other things. The economic constriction of the late 1970s and early 1980s led to a general shrinking in education and in writing courses particularly. Colleges began to define their missions more narrowly, excluding remedial instruction. Secondary schools likewise retreated from electives to the former pattern of combining composition with language and literature study.

This dominance of time and expediency in composition pedagogy will continue as long as models of instruction fail to have a philosophical basis. Developing such a basis does not require scrapping all current models; it simply means asking different questions about them. These questions should include issues such as thought-word-thing relationships, abstraction, definition, and logic. Put another way, when the teaching rhetoric and philosophy are united, the following questions will become central to each model:

1. What relationship exists between language and reality?
2. What relationship exists between thought and language?
3. How does this model define "truth" or "knowledge"?
4. What system of logic does this model employ to arrive at "truth"?

When such questions are asked and answered, models of composition pedagogy will become more unified and thereby more effective.

FOOTNOTES

1. Charles Silberman, *Crisis in the Classroom* (New York: Random House, 1970).

2. Richard Fulkerson, "Four Philosophies of Composition," *College Composition and Communication* 30 (December 1979): 347.

3. Meyer Howard Abrams, *The Mirror and the Lamp: Romantic Theory and the Critical Tradition* (New York: Oxford University Press, 1953).

4. Fulkerson, "Four Philosophies of Composition," p. 343.

5. Ibid., p. 344.

6. William F. Woods, "Composition Textbooks and Pedagogical Theory 1960-1980," *College English* 43 (April 1981): 396.

7. Daniel Fogarty, *Roots for a New Rhetoric* (New York: Russell and Russell, 1959), p. 118.

8. Richard Young, "Paradigms and Problems: Needed Research in Rhetorical Invention," in *Research on Composing: Points of Departure*, ed. Charles R. Cooper and Lee Odell (Urbana, Ill.: National Council of Teachers of English, 1978), p. 31.

9. Fogarty, *Roots for a New Rhetoric*, p. 117.

10. Ibid., p. 120.

11. Ibid., p. 122.

12. James Berlin, "Contemporary Composition: The Major Pedagogical Theories," *College English* 44 (December 1982): 770.

13. Ibid., p. 775.

14. Ibid., p. 775-76.

15. Fulkerson, "Four Philosophies of Composition," p. 347.

16. Ibid., p. 345.

17. Woods, "Composition Textbooks and Pedagogical Theory 1960-1980," p. 393.

18. Robert Connors, "Composition Studies and Science," *College English* 45 (January 1983): 1-20.

19. Berlin, "Contemporary Composition: The Major Pedagogical Theories," p. 766.

20. Fogarty, *Roots for a New Rhetoric*, p. 120.

21. Charles W. Eliot, *Educational Reform: Essays and Addresses* (New York: Century, 1898), p. 2.

22. Adam Sherman Hill, *The Principles of Rhetoric and Their Application* (New York: Harper, 1878), p. 84.

23. Harold Allen, "Preparing the Teachers of Composition and Communication— A Report," *College Composition and Communication* 3 (May 1952): 3-13.

24. Anne Ruggles Gere, "Teaching Writing Teachers," *College English* 47 (January 1985): 58-65.

25. *Reports of the Visiting Committees of the Board of Overseers of Harvard College* (Cambridge, Mass.: Harvard University Press, 1902), p. 119.

26. Ibid., p. 155.

27. Fred Newton Scott and Joseph Villiers Denney, *Elementary English Composition* (Boston: Allyn and Bacon, 1900).

28. Shirley Smith, "Fred Newton Scott as a Teacher," *Michigan Alumnus*, 1933, p. 279.

29. Albert Kitzhaber, "Rhetoric in American Colleges 1850-1900" (Doct. diss., University of Washington, 1953), p. 114.

30. Ibid., p. 120.

31. Fulkerson, "Four Philosophies of Composition," p. 346.

32. Woods, "Composition Textbooks and Pedagogical Theory 1960-1980," p. 396.

33. Berlin, "Contemporary Composition: The Major Pedagogical Theories," p. 769.

34. Young, "Paradigms and Problems," p. 42.

35. Scott and Denney, *Elementary English Composition*, p. iv.

36. James R. Squire and Roger Applebee, *High School English Instruction Today* (New York: Appleton, 1968), p. 42.

37. Richard M. Weaver, *Composition: A Course in Writing and Rhetoric* (New York: Holt, 1957).

38. Richard E. Hughes and Albert P. Duhamel, *Rhetoric: Principles and Usage* (Englewood Cliffs, N.J.: Prentice, 1962), p. v.

39. Edward P. Corbett, *Classical Rhetoric for the Modern Student* (New York, Oxford University Press, 1965).

40. Richard Young, Alton Becker, and Kenneth Pike, *Rhetoric: Discovery and Change* (New York: Harcourt, 1970).

41. Young, "Paradigms and Problems," p. 39.

42. David V. Harrington, Philip M. Keith, Charles W. Kneupper, Janice A. Tripp, and William F. Woods, "A Critical Survey of Resources for Teaching Rhetorical Invention," *College English* 40 (February 1979): 641-61.

43. Ibid., p. 643.

44. Ibid., p. 644.

45. Ibid.

46. D. Gordon Rohman, "Pre-Writing: The Stage of Discovery in the Writing Process," *College Composition and Communication* 16 (May 1965): 106-112.

47. Ibid., p. 345.

48. Ibid., p. 345.

49. Arthur Applebee, *Tradition and Reform in the Teaching of English: A History* (Urbana, Ill.: National Council of Teachers of English, 1974), p. 229.

50. Woods, "Composition Textbooks and Pedagogical Theory 1960-1980," p. 397.

51. Fulkerson, "Four Philosophies of Composition," p. 345.

52. Woods, "Composition Textbooks and Pedagogical Theory 1960-1980," p. 396.

53. Ibid., p. 408.

54. Berlin, "Contemporary Composition," p. 774.

55. Ann Berthoff, *Forming/Thinking/Writing* (Montclair, N.J.: Boynton/Cook, 1978).

56. See, for example, Richard Braddock, Richard Lloyd-Jones, and Lowell Schoer, *Research in Written Composition* (Urbana, Ill.: National Council of Teachers of English, 1963).

57. "Students' Right to their Own Language," special issue of *College Composition and Communication*, Fall 1974.

CHAPTER IV

Composing Processes: An Overview

PATRICIA BIZZELL

What Is "Composing"?

Composition scholars agree that the composing process exists or, rather, that there is a complex of activities out of which all writing emerges. We cannot specify one composing process as invariably successful. Current research in the field is beginning to draw a detailed picture of these composing processes.

"Composing" usually refers to all the processes out of which a piece of written work emerges. During composing, the writer may spend some time musing, rereading notes or drafts, or reading the texts of others, as well as actually putting words on the page herself. In composition research, "writing" usually refers precisely to the scribal act. One focus of composition research examines the extent to which composing occurs during writing, as opposed to the composing that takes place while other tasks, such as those I just listed, are being performed.

Simply to acknowledge that composing processes exist is something of a gain for modern composition studies. My undergraduate students would like to deny this premise: they prefer the fantasy that when they finally become "good writers," they will be able to sit down at the desk and produce an "A" paper in no more time than it takes to transcribe it. Nor are my students alone in this fantasy of instant text production. It is part of a more general notion in our culture, a sort of debased Romantic version of creativity wherein verbal artifacts are supposed to be produced as easily and inevitably as a hen lays eggs. This more general fantasy affects Americans' judgment of political orators, for example; we value as "good speakers" those who can think on their feet, apparently producing eloquence in no more time than it takes to utter the words.

The classical rhetoricians knew better. Greek and Roman teachers of effective writing and speaking elaborated a five-stage composing process: invention, or finding ideas; arrangement, or putting the ideas into persuasive order; style, or dressing the ideas in persuasive language; memory, or memorizing the text of the speech thus prepared; and delivery, or delivering the speech with the most

I would like to thank Bruce Herzberg and David Bartholomae for their careful reading of drafts of this chapter.

effective use of voice, gesture, and so on. No one supposed that brilliant orators simply opened their mouths and let it flow.

Many of my students, however, have not encountered anything like the classical composing process in school. Until very recently, most language arts instruction in American schools had lost a sense that composing requires complex processes. Instead, students brought their finished products to the teacher for correction and evaluation. The composing of these products was something students had to manage on their own. Whatever processes they used remained a "black box" to the instructor: the assignment went in at one end, and out came the final paper at the other.

Given that classical rhetoric did emphasize process, how is it that we have inherited such a product-oriented pedagogy? The history is too long to recount here in detail, but let me summarize by saying that over the centuries rhetoric was shorn of four of the five classical stages of composing. In the Renaissance, Ramist rhetoricians, because they sought to develop a purely objective discourse in which to conduct the researches of the new science, redefined invention and arrangement as matters of logic. Rationality, rather than persuasiveness, would be the new standard for judging the soundness and order of ideas. Much later, as English departments were formed in late nineteenth-century American colleges, their avowed focus on literature—on texts to be read—made the study of memory and delivery unnecessary (these elements continued to be studied in the departments of speech which, not coincidentally, split off from English departments at about this time).

As a result of these changes, the study of rhetoric came to focus on only one stage in the classical composing process: style. The tasks of the English department were to analyze the style of canonical literary works, for the purpose of interpreting these works' enduring human values; and to analyze the style of student essays, for the purpose of correcting their errors and encouraging the writers toward the beauties discovered in the canonical works. From the students' viewpoint, the English department thus devoted to the study of style certainly encouraged the fantasy that there are no composing processes. Only finished products were treated in class, whether the accomplished works of literary masters or the mediocre ones of the students themselves. Evidently one could not learn how to compose more effectively, since this was never taught. Evidently one either possessed the inborn ability to produce good texts, or one was out of luck: a cat can't lay eggs.

Rediscovering Composing

Dissatisfaction with this product-centered pedagogy has arisen periodically at least since the early twentieth century in the Progressive Education movement. But a surge of interest in composing developed in the 1960s. It probably received its single greatest impetus from the change in the school population that began to be evident at that time. To summarize this change crudely: more and more students were unable to bring to their teachers essays that needed only stylistic revision. More and more students were producing essays full of errors that were supposed to disappear in the earlier grades and of ideas so ill considered as to call into question the students' cognitive development. Drastic action seemed called for to help these student writers to improve.

It was largely in response to the perceived new needs of students—and teachers—that composition studies began to emerge in the 1960s as an area of specialization within English studies. Literary critics, too, were dissatisfied with the New Criticism's focus on style and began the theoretical debates over a replacement paradigm that have continued to the present. The entire discipline of English studies, in other words, has been undergoing some radical changes. But while literary scholars have focused on problems of reading literary texts, composition scholars have turned to examining writing, the process of composing texts, and particularly the texts of student writers and others who are not literary masters.

Most of the research that shapes our current knowledge of composing has been published since 1970. Composition specialists in the 1960s saw themselves primarily as teachers of writing, not as researchers. Nevertheless, their work has strongly influenced current research, not only in what it tells us about composing but also in the professional agenda it establishes for composition studies.

These first of the modern scholars in composition found themselves at odds with the academy from the beginning. Many academics (not to mention administrators and parents) assumed that the solution to the problem of student writing was simply to correct the ever-more-numerous errors, until by dint of the drill students finally learned not to splice commas, split infinitives, and so on. This assumption informed many early professional decisions made by senior academics about their colleagues in composition. For instance, if teaching grammar need be the only content of the writing class, writing teachers would not require advanced academic training. It became customary (as it still is to this day) to staff the bulk of a school's writing courses with teachers reassigned from other disciplines, voluntarily or not, with graduate students, or with people no longer actively seeking terminal degrees and teaching part-time by choice or necessity. These writing teachers found themselves garnering little professional respect, except, perhaps, that due the person who undertakes a necessary but unpleasant job that nobody else wants. Their senior colleagues assumed, moreover, that there was no serious scholarly work to be done in the field of composition studies, so that the way to professional advancement lay in escape from the writing classroom.

But writing teachers became increasingly convinced, on the basis of their classroom experience, that the initial assumption on the need for grammar drills simply was wrong. Attending closely to the problems students had in writing their papers, rather than merely to the problems that appeared in their finished products, writing teachers became convinced that students needed a better understanding of the whole process of working on a piece of writing, to give adequate time to the task and to make the time spent more productive. To gain this understanding, writing teachers began to work through this process along with their students and to try to determine what contributed to a successful, or unsuccessful, writing process.

Some early fruit borne by such study was the model of composing introduced by Gordon Rohman and Raymond Wlecke.[1] Rohman and Wlecke found that successful college-level writers typically traverse three stages in composing: pre-writing, writing, and editing. Most significant here is the concept of "pre-writing," that is, idea-generating activities that provide essential preparation for drafting. This was perhaps the first intimation that we needed to study a whole complex of composing processes, of which the actual writing of the paper was only one. Moreover, Rohman suggested that pre-writing activities such as journal keeping and meditation could be taught—that composing processes, rather than grammar drills, could become the actual content of the writing course.

Some academics opposed such activities, however, on grounds that they were not likely to foster the writing of good academic expository prose. This objection was met with even stronger resistance from writing teachers. During this same era, the academy itself began to seem discredited, in the eyes of many students and teachers, by political developments in the nation at large. For one thing, the academy was reluctant to incorporate new methods of responding to these developments, preferring its traditional subjects and methods of inquiry. For another, this reluctance was seen as enforcing discriminatory social sorting, with white middle-class men being educated for positions of power and all others being disenfranchised. Academic expository prose, the mastery of which was a prerequisite for traditional academic work, was implicated in the indictment of the academy as an institution of political oppression.

Hence, many writing teachers came to argue that students could not write good academic expository prose because academic expository prose was bad in itself—it was verbose, indirect, and impersonal to the point of hypocrisy. Instead of forcing students to master it, and the concomitant complexities of formal Standard English, writing teachers began to believe that they should be helping students to free themselves from its baleful influence if ever their writing were to improve. Students should forget their anxieties about correctness, stop trying to sound like someone else, and work to discover and refine their own personal, authentic writing styles.

The study of composing thus came to serve the liberation of each student's personal style, a way of writing that would clearly and sincerely convey her perspective on the world, as uniquely valuable as the student's own humanity. As I have tried to suggest, a combination of professional and historical circumstances made the development of a pedagogy of personal style something of a political crusade for many writing teachers. By fostering students' own styles, instead of forcing conformity to an oppressive institutional standard, writing teachers could feel they were making their own contribution to the reform of oppressive academic and political institutions.

Since the standard for judging a personal style could come only from within the student, who alone could certify its ability to represent her perspective on the world, the pedagogy of personal style aimed mainly to remove barriers to students' perceptions of what they had achieved in their writing. Close-reading, a technique of literary New Criticism, in which many writing teachers were trained, could be adapted for this purpose. Working as a group, teacher and students focused on student writing as the principal text for the course, and by detailed analysis helped each student writer to see whether her choice of words adequately expressed her thoughts. Given the original political agenda of personal-style pedagogy, this process typically worked to eliminate oppressive vestiges of academic writing. A student's personal style was to be characterized by comfortable use of the first person; by focus on a topic the student knows at first hand, typically personal experiences rather than academic subjects; and by exposition relying far more heavily on a detailed account of the writer's perceptions and feelings than on analysis and generalization. Peter Elbow's influential textbook, *Writing Without Teachers*, emphasizes the open-endedness of the composing processes necessitated by the search for a personal style.[2]

The pedagogy of personal style thus established that composing processes are complex and often lengthy and, hence, that a substantial phenomenon exists for scholarly study. The Rohman-Wlecke model of composing has been faulted for its linearity, that is, for assuming that the successful writer typically moves through the composing process without backtracking or omitting any stage. But, in general, personal-style pedagogy, with its emphasis on rewriting, encouraged the view of composing processes as recursive, which has been confirmed by contemporary research.

In addition to these influential assumptions about composing, personal-style pedagogy helped shape contemporary research through its assumptions about what should go on in the writing classroom: that students and teacher should democratically discuss each student's work, with the teacher acting not as authoritative director but as knowledgeable collaborator and with the goal being each student's accomplishment of self-selected writing tasks. Students should not be sidetracked in their search for personal styles by emphasis on standards of correctness set by others, such as the rules of formal Standard English. The teacher's main function, in addition to participating in the class writing workshop, should be to protect students from the academy's oppressive requirements.

Since the great majority of composition scholars have adhered at some time to personal-style pedagogy, it is not surprising that its pedagogical assumptions, as well as its assumptions directly bearing on composing, have influenced our sense of what research projects are worth undertaking. Moreover, this influence is not pernicious, both because all research can only occur under the guidance of assumptions and because these assumptions have guided us toward some fruitful research. It might not be too much to say that we owe all our current knowledge of composing to the early decisions of beleaguered composition scholars to resist the pedagogical agenda being set for them by senior academics, namely teaching grammar, and to seek a pedagogy more responsive to student needs. This pedagogy, in helping students develop their personal styles, brought their composing processes into the classroom and hence into the domain of scholarly inquiry. Moreover, the emphasis of this pedagogy on the personal, on the creative power of the individual writer's mind, helped to legitimate voices silenced in the traditional English classroom, voices of women, ethnic minorities, and other oppressed groups, and so did help to make the academy more responsive to contemporary political issues.

Under the influence of personal-style pedagogy, the first school of thought on composition research, which continues to flourish, encouraged the study of what goes on inside the individual writer's head. Such research is now often referred to as cognitive analyses of composing, because it has borrowed some methods and assumptions from the social sciences. The work of this school has been valuable, as I will explain below; unfortunately, however, until recently, composition research was limited to work in this school by personal-style pedagogy's assumptions about the individual nature of writing ability.

The problem was—and still is, to some extent—that personal-style pedagogy sees the political conflict in schools as between an oppressive institution and individual creative talents. In this view, what the student writer needs to do is to strip away all "outside" influences, such as academic standards of correctness, in order to get down to the thoughts and language that are uniquely, authentically hers. The kind of first-person narrative elicited in personal-style classes was assumed to be such "authentic" writing. The problem with this assumption, however, is illustrated by the fact that this "anti-academic" writing is actually a well-recognized belletristic essay style in itself, as exemplified in writers such as George Orwell and E. B. White, favorites for personal-style classroom reading. To heighten the irony, this style comes much more easily to white middle- and upper-class students than to others, thus preserving in personal-style pedagogy the very social discrimination it sought to combat.

What this example illustrates, however, is not the culpability of writing teachers for failing to free themselves from class-based attitudes, but rather the impossibility of doing so. No one uses language autonomously. One's speaking, reading, and writing are always shaped by one's social and cultural background and by the political relations this background creates with audiences of similar or very different backgrounds. This shaping is as much a matter of what the writer knows as of what she does. For example, a student may fail to produce an acceptable personal-style essay because she comes from a social group that does not value the sort of intense introspection such an essay calls for. Hence, she may either be simply too unfamiliar with introspection to produce it, or too wary with classmates (and teacher) from other social groups to produce it for them to read. As I have argued elsewhere, research into the social and cultural contexts from which the writer's knowledge comes and in which she is addressing an audience is as necessary to our understanding of composing as is research into what goes on in the writer's head.[3] Recently, more research into these contexts of composing has been forthcoming, as I will explain below.

Cognitive Analyses of Composing

The contemporary moment of research on composing may be said to begin with the work of James Britton and Janet Emig. Working independently, but aware of each other's work, Britton and Emig developed strikingly similar pictures of students' composing processes. Perhaps the greatest insight they share is that composing processes vary with the kind of writing the student is doing. Britton distinguishes three kinds: "poetic," which produces literary artifacts; "expressive," in which the student explores a subject and her own feelings about it, for an audience of herself or an intimate friend; and "transactional," in which the student seeks to convey information or argue for a position, for an audience of the teacher in the role of examiner.[4] Emig names two kinds of writing: "reflexive," very similar to Britton's expressive; and "extensive," very similar to Britton's transactional.[5] Britton and Emig agree that student writers' composing processes typically are most truncated and least successful in transactional/extensive writing and most elaborated and most successful in expressive/reflexive writing. Britton and Emig conclude that students should be offered far more opportunities in school for expressive/reflexive writing.

Britton and Emig formed these conclusions about composing by looking at student work, not literary masterpieces. Britton and his colleagues read about 2000 essays by British schoolchildren between the ages of eleven and eighteen. Emig interviewed eight American high school seniors while they composed and produced a case study of one of these writers. This methodology has been widely influential, without being followed to the letter. Although not all researchers base their conclusions on a sample of student essays or on case studies, there is general agreement that composing is best investigated by looking at writers at work.

Emig's and Britton's conclusion, that students need more opportunities in school for expressive/reflexive writing, has also been widely influential, even when their terminology is not used. Indeed, this conclusion formed one of the assumptions of the pervasive pedagogy of personal style. The work of Emig and Britton was thus welcomed because it appeared to provide empirical justification for personal-style pedagogy's political indictment of academic writing. Britton and his colleagues, however, do not see the conflict in terms of academic writing versus individual styles, although their language is sometimes misleading. Rather, it is a battle between the language-using practices of the privileged social class and those of other social classes attempting to gain legitimacy in school. The underlying political agenda of Britton et al. is thus much more radical than that of personal-style pedagogy, calling for a class-based reversal of what constitutes good style rather than for a democracy of styles.

Preferring a focus on the personal, American composition research developed first along lines indicated by Emig, to explore what goes on in the individual writer's head. Some researchers have attempted to make the examination of working writers more rigorous by borrowing methodology from the social sciences. Composition scholar Linda Flower and her colleague, cognitive psychologist John R. Hayes, have pioneered the use of protocol analysis, a cognitive psychology research technique, for studying composing. Flower and Hayes ask writers to describe their thought processes aloud while they are composing. The transcript of what they say is the protocol, which the researchers then analyze for regular features of a composing process.

The Flower-Hayes model divides composing into three main parts: one, the "task environment," subdivided into "rhetorical problem" and "text produced so far"; two, the "writing process," subdivided into "reviewing" (further subdivided into "revising" and "evaluating"), "translating," and "planning" (further subdivided into "generating," "goal-setting," and "organizing"); and three, the "writer's long-term memory." "Task environment" encompasses the immediate context of a composing situation, such as a school assignment for which a written product must be completed; "long-term memory" encompasses the larger social context for composing to be found, for example, in the writer's knowledge of genre. In the Flower-Hayes model, however, these contexts of composing are treated largely as a ground or frame for the main area of interest, namely the "writing process" (note the much greater number of subdivisions in this part of the model). "Writing process" encompasses activities taking place inside the writer's head.[6]

The most influential arguments propounded in the Flower-Hayes model are, first, that the writer can "access" task environment and long-term memory and switch from one writing subprocess to another at any time while composing: in other words, the composing process typically is recursive, not linear. For instance, the writer typically does not plan first and, that done, go on to write without ever reconsidering her plans. Second, although there is no single natural order in which composing activities do or should occur, there is a sort of natural relationship among them such that some activities are, or should be, subordinated to other activities: in other words, the composing process typically is hierarchical.

The Flower-Hayes model seeks to be comprehensive, that is, to describe all possible composing behaviors, although Flower and Hayes have been careful to point out that not every act of composing will—or should—employ every possible behavior. But in spite of this model's important arguments, which I just mentioned, it can be critiqued precisely on grounds of its claim to comprehensiveness. The problem is that some composition specialists have been prompted by this claim to attempt to explain the differences between successful and unsuccessful writers in terms of how fully they make use of the cognitive activities described in the model. Such research might lead to use of the Flower-Hayes model as a Procrustean bed for students' necessarily diverse composing processes.

For example, some researchers influenced by the Flower-Hayes model have argued that poor writing results from neglecting the recursive quality of the composing process, as did the poor writers in Pianko's study who failed to pause for reflecting on what they were writing.[7] Other researchers have held that poor writing results from misranking activities in the process hierarchy. The poor writers

"recursive process"

studied by Sondra Perl accorded inordinate importance and time to editing for errors in grammar, spelling, and mechanics.[8] The single most important factor in successful writing, Perl has argued, is to allow for the recursive quality of composing by rereading the text as one produces it and waiting for a "felt sense" of structure to emerge and guide planning.[9]

The new importance given to the recursive quality of composing has led some researchers to focus exclusively on revision. Nancy Sommers has argued that the whole composing process, rightly understood, is a process of revision in which the writer does not simply polish her style but, more important, develops her ideas. "Revision" comes to mean the whole complex of activities of rereading, evaluating, and making small-scale and large-scale changes in the text as one produces it. Unsuccessful writers, Sommers argues, do not so understand revision, saving it for the end of the composing process and using it only to make small-scale changes such as in word choice.[10] It follows that the most effective writing pedagogy will be that which creates a climate for continual revising in the classroom, as described, for example, by Lil Brannon.[11]

Interest in revision and a desire to correct some problems with protocol analysis by adapting Emig's case-study method for research on composing have led researchers such as Carol Berkenkotter[12] and Mimi Schwartz[13] to follow the progress of a single text through multiple revisions. This research has emphasized that successful writing, whether by accomplished professionals or beginning students, emerges from recursive composing processes. There must be adequate time for rethinking; a willingness to respond to hunches, word associations, and other seemingly random techniques to trigger revision; and a recurring strong sense of the audience for whom one is writing.

Schwartz, Donald Graves, and others have argued that these factors influence revision even in very young children's writing.[14] Children have a natural proclivity for composing, according to Glenda Bissex and other researchers into the genesis of writing ability.[15] Graves argues in his influential book *Writing: Teachers and Children at Work* that it is vitally important for schools not to stifle children's natural desire to write by constraining them with assignments they are not interested in and intimidating them with constant corrections.[16] Rather, children should be given many opportunities to write on topics they choose and offered help with any aspect of composing only when such help seems necessary to the successful completion of a particular writing project and when it can be offered in such a way as not to make the child feel that she is no longer in control of her own writing. Although Shirley Brice Heath, David Olson, and others have argued that students' readiness to develop their writing in school is greatly influenced by their social and cultural backgrounds, most researchers into children's writing agree that Graves's pedagogy is the most helpful for all students.[17]

It is interesting to note how these various kinds of cognitive research on composing, like the work of Britton and Emig, echo some assumptions of personal-style pedagogy. The work of Pianko, Perl, and Sommers leads to the conclusion that something very like personal-style pedagogy is still the best: the main classroom activity is group revision of student texts, students rewrite to achieve their own expressive goals rather than to satisfy academic requirements, and any insistence on formal correctness is taboo. Graves recommends a similar pedagogy for elementary-school children, with the additional personal-style assumption that the resources they will call on in writing are mainly innate abilities, not knowledge gained in school. Thus, the kind of pedagogy emerging from current cognitive research on composing is open to the same objection that was leveled against personal-style pedagogy, namely, that this new pedagogy does not lead to mastery of academic writing. Personal-style pedagogues, as I noted earlier, were inclined to answer this charge by arguing that mastery of academic writing was undesirable anyway. Those advocating the new pedagogy, however, generally argue that it offers the best route to eventual mastery of academic writing and any other kind of writing the student chooses to do. This view is still open to debate; we have no research evidence that students educated according to this pedagogy develop into more accomplished academic writers than those educated by other means, though the student excerpts typically quoted in works advocating this pedagogy suggest they are accomplished at other kinds of writing. The fact is, however, that curricula designed according to this pedagogy generally do not teach academic writing directly, whatever abilities may be expected of students afterwards.

Research on the Social and Cultural Contexts of Composing

Although, as I suggested earlier, the first contemporary school of thought on composition research focused on the individual writer's mind, more recently a second school has developed to research the social and cultural factors that influence the individual writer's performance. These researchers have been motivated in part by a reluctance to accept the conclusion, forced by personal-style and cognitive-based analyses of composing, that differences in individual performance are due to differences in individual talent. This reluctance sprang from the scholars' observation that performance differences seemed to correlate with social groups; it seemed logical, therefore, to assume that social and cultural, as well as individual, factors influence

context in composing

composing. Moreover, poor performance seemed to correlate with relatively less privileged social groups. Retaining a sympathy with these groups consistent with some assumptions of personal-style pedagogy, these scholars wished to save them from the stigma of personal failure and to seek a pedagogy specific to their needs.

For many of these researchers, mastery of academic writing has become once more an acceptable goal of composition pedagogy, but not as it was traditionally taught. Once, the course teaching academic writing simply laid down its laws, and those who would not or could not conform simply left the academy. Now, composition scholars seek to serve these students particularly—the ones who have trouble mastering academic writing—so as to give them equal access to the knowledge generated and maintained by the academy. Some scholars may hope that, if academic writing is still a weapon of political oppression, students who master it may be able to turn the weapon against the oppressors. At any rate, many students are now asking for help in mastering academic writing, and writing teachers are responding, just as we responded fifteen years ago when they asked for help in mastering nonacademic, personal styles.

Another influence on the interest in social and cultural contexts of composing has been the new interest in classical rhetoric among composition specialists. Classical rhetoric began to be recovered for English studies in the 1960s, when new collections of original classical texts became available and E. P. J. Corbett's influential *Classical Rhetoric for the Modern Student* suggested contemporary pedagogical applications.[18] At first, classical rhetoric's most important contribution was its multistage composing process, particularly its emphasis on invention, which reinforced the movement in personal-style pedagogy to develop "pre-writing" or idea-generating techniques.

The classical model of composing has been faulted on grounds of excessive linearity. C. H. Knoblauch and Lil Brannon have blamed classical rhetoric, not as recently rediscovered but as embedded in American schooling since the nineteenth century, for influencing teachers to vitiate new pedagogical techniques, such as those encouraging personal style, by inserting them into a curriculum dominated by this linear model of composing.[19] In this way the techniques become mere moments in a rigid progression of stages of composing, rather than, as they should be, periodically useful tools in an open-ended and recursive process. But there is more to the story of classical rhetoric's relevance for the modern student.

As composition specialists have begun to turn to research on the contexts of composing, they have become aware that perhaps the most important contribution of classical rhetoric is precisely its focus on context. Classical rhetoric assumes that the function of writing is not to express oneself but to effect change in the human community in which one lives. Hence, the ability to suit one's style to the particular audience, rather than addressing all in one "personal" register, becomes art, not hypocrisy. Classical rhetoric invites discussion of the social and political uses of writing in ways that personal-style pedagogy, for all its political agenda, never could.

As composition specialists' interest in the contexts of composing has emerged, two seminal theorists have been Ann Berthoff and Mina Shaughnessy. They take two very different approaches, without much reference to each other, but both insist on the crucial connection between individual writer and "outside world." Berthoff has made this point in the strongest terms: human beings use language to make sense of themselves and their world.[20] Hence, if we want to understand composing, we must look at that world with which the writer is in a dialectical relationship, as well as at the writer's individual talents. Berthoff does share some assumptions with personal-style pedagogy concerning all students' innate meaning-making powers. But because she also looks at the context of composing, the world in which and on which they work, she realizes that student writers can be taught to make more personally satisfying use of their meaning-making powers in language—that is, she favors a more directive pedagogy than the personal-style, one that offers what she calls "assisted invitations" to composing. These "invitations" aim not to liberate student writing from the influence of others' styles, but to make students constructively self-conscious about the resources available to their own writing in their society's repertoire of styles. For example, instead of merely keeping a personal journal, Berthoff's students might be encouraged to maintain a "double-entry notebook" in which they periodically reread and critique their own earlier observations. Thus they are made students of their own language-using practices.

While Berthoff's approach is intended, I believe, to be universally applicable, that is, to describe the universal human experience with making meaning in language, Shaughnessy confined her study specifically to the academic community.[21] In her analysis of successive drafts of papers by extremely unskilled college writers, Shaughnessy has found attempts at meaning making where there appears to be no order at all. She understands the composing process as a socialization process, in which gradually bringing one's writing into line with the discourse conventions of one's readers also brings one to share their thinking, their values, in short, their world view. Shaughnessy has argued that student writers are least successful when most ignorant of academic discourse conventions: how the academic audience evaluates evidence, what allusions strike it as elegant, what personae it finds credible, and so on. Shaughnessy has suggested a philosophical critique of personal-style pedagogy in her repudiation of the "honest face" persona for student writers. Nowhere, including the academy, does clear, sincere self-expression win assent unaided.

Shaughnessy's work gave composition specialists a new perspective on student writing problems. Her analysis allows us to retain the best element of personal-style pedagogy, namely, its sense that students' relationship with the academy is agonistic and requires our mediation if social justice and common humanity are to be served. But she also allowed us to step back from the position that bad student writing was caused by the imposition of bad academic standards on natural creativity. Rather, if no writing is autonomous, if all writing is situated in some language-using community, then bad student writing, according to Shaughnessy, should be understood as the output of apprentices or initiates into the academic community. The pedagogy they need is not one that excoriates academic discourse, but rather one that mediates their introduction to it while remaining respectful of the language-using practices they bring to school.

Research into the social, cultural, and political influences on composing, particularly as they bear on students attempting to master academic writing, has taken several directions, exploring writing across the curriculum, basic writing, collaborative learning, and reading/writing connections. Questions which remain problematic for this research include the extent to which social, cultural, and political factors determine composing as opposed to merely influencing it, and the pace at which students should be urged toward mastery of academic writing. Assumptions from personal-style pedagogy can be seen playing their part in this school of research, as much as in the cognitive research that this school often seeks to correct or oppose. For example, recommendations for workshop classrooms in which students pursue self-selected writing goals often emerge from this research, as my brief overview will show. Nevertheless, the emphasis on contexts of composing is an essential and unique contribution.

Writing across the curriculum began as a pedagogical movement in Great Britain in the late 1960s. It was fostered by James Britton, Nancy Martin, and their colleagues in response to the discovery, made in the course of their composing process research, that students wrote very little outside the English classroom. Believing that students would write better if given more opportunites to write in school, particularly opportunities for expressive writing, the British researchers published a series of pamphlets explaining how to integrate expressive writing into a wide range of academic disciplines. In effect, these pamphlets argue for teaching a composing process which would begin with expressive writing, for example in class journals, and only later issue in finished academic essays. The British researchers envision a classroom in which much student writing and talking do not issue in finished work at all, but are nevertheless essential for their heuristic value.[22]

Toby Fulwiler[23] and Lil Brannon and C. H. Knoblauch[24] are among the American composition scholars who have adapted for American colleges the work of Britton et al., which is aimed at elementary and secondary level students. In arguing for the efficacy of a journal-centered composing process in college-level academic disciplines, these proponents of writing across the curriculum have focused the British methods more directly toward the production of finished essays, while maintaining that better papers grow from personal interest in the topic that students develop through their journals. This pedagogy, too, has argued that student composing processes may be idiosyncratic and no single composing process can be assumed to be successful for everyone.

Other American work in writing across the curriculum moves away from this focus on the individual writer to look more directly at the academic context and its demands. Composition scholars such as Elaine Maimon have sought to respond to Shaughnessy's call for a taxonomy of academic discourse conventions.[25] Maimon's focus is not merely on formal features of texts, such as laboratory report format. Rather, she analyzes the intellectual framework suggested by the laboratory report and asks: What do the discourse conventions reveal about how scientists define and interact with the world? What kind of thinking does this kind of writing ask students to do or actually make them do as they write? Maimon's work suggests that there may be epistemological constraints on composing. A writer's varying degrees of success with different kinds of writing may not be due to a simple dichotomy of personal writing (good) versus academic writing (bad). Rather, the different kinds of thinking demanded in different disciplines may cause the student's composing process to vary as a function of the different distances between these ways of thinking and that with which the student is originally comfortable.

Thus these two different approaches to writing across the curriculum typically issue in different pedagogies. The journal-centered approach, once again, endorses something very similar to personal-style pedagogy. The classroom is a workshop, students generate their own writing topics and stylistic goals, and emphasis on correctness is avoided. The teacher is likely, however, to encourage writing projects that involve something like traditional academic inquiry—for instance, a topic requiring library research. Moreover, it is not unusual for such a writing course to be linked with a course in some other discipline, so that the students prepare their papers for that course with the aid of the journal-centered pedagogy of the writing course. Typically, however, journal-centered pedagogy spends relatively little time on formal academic expository writing.

In contrast, the approach centered on academic discourse conventions gives first priority to mastery of academic writing and the formal Standard English it employs. Students may well be encouraged to begin from journals and other forms of pre-writing associated with personal-style pedagogy, but they will be urged along more quickly to the production of finished academic essays. Students will be helped to meet academic English standards in the final stages of composing, on grounds that to do so is to observe what counts as polite behavior in the community they are seeking to enter. The classroom atmosphere is likely to be more directive, with the teacher actively seeking to explain academic writing conventions and to demystify the kinds of thinking they make possible.

The academic context has particularly marked effects on students who are least familiar with its discourse conventions and ways of thinking—the students known as "basic writers" who are at the very beginning stages of being able to produce successful academic writing. Much research on the composing processes of basic writers has focused on the extent to which their difficulties are due to the academic context. Mike Rose has argued that a truncated or blocked composing process can result from overly rigid internalization of advice given in writing instruction, rather than from some deficiency in the student's innate ability to compose.[26] David Bartholomae, extending the work of Shaughnessy, has explained the discourse of basic writers as an approximation of the academic discourse whose conventions and world view are unfamiliar to them, rather than merely as a tissue of errors.[27] These readings of the work of basic writers suggest that their composing processes must include a considerable amount of trial-and-error experimentation as they gradually discover how to use academic discourse for their own purposes.

Teaching academic discourse to basic writers has become a particularly sensitive issue because their difficulties with academic writing tend to be a function of the social distance between the academy and their home communities. That is, basic writers typically come from less privileged social groups, where the language-using practices are most unlike those of the academy, which reflect the practices of the privileged groups in our society. Hence, basic writers appear to be in more danger than others of being alienated from their home communities by mastery of academic discourse. Literacy researchers Walter Ong[28] and James T. Farrell[29] have argued in favor of such alienation or assimilation, on grounds that the ways of thinking enabled by the language-using practices of such students' home communities are cognitively inferior to those of the academy. Other scholars, however, see such arguments as unjustly enforcing the social privileges of academic writing.[30] We do not know whether academic ways of thinking are in fact cognitively different from, or superior to, those of other communities; nor do we know to what extent assimilation is unavoidable for basic writers.

As research on writing across the curriculum and on basic writing has emphasized students' adapting to new ways of thinking, many composition researchers have been led to focus on the extent to which learning to compose is a socialization process, a process of initiation into the discourse community's world view. Such a focus immediately brings to the foreground the extent to which composing is a collaborative process. More broadly, the ways we "compose" experience are culturally conditioned. More particularly, all writers are influenced in their composing processes by other writers, other writing, more experienced mentors, and so on. For the student, these are the influences of academic discourse, teachers, and peers. Kenneth Bruffee, a specialist in the "collaborative learning" of writing, has explored these influences and concludes that students who understand something of the academic world view and its discourse are often more effective than teachers in mediating other students' introduction to the academy.

Bruffee has developed a method of training students to tutor their peers that helps them all to become conscious of what they already knew about academic discourse and to improve their knowledge through attention to their own composing processes. Bruffee's writing workshop resembles the personal-style classroom in procedure, with the difference that the main goal is not discovery of one's inmost honest feelings, but rather articulation of a public voice that will allow participation in the academic intellectual community.[31] The greatest contribution of work on collaborative learning is to emphasize that composing is always in some sense a social process.

Intellectual socialization may be accomplished not only by interacting with people, but also by encountering the writing of others. Thus research on connections between reading and writing also speaks to our knowledge of composing processes. That the writer must be able to read her own text while composing it, we know from such work as that of Sommers and of Flower and Hayes. But Anthony Petrosky and Mariolina Salvatori have suggested that the ability to read the works of others also affects a writer's composing process. Petrosky argues that the successful reading of a literary text is a "transaction" in which the reader must work to make the text meaningful in terms of her own experience, a view influenced by reader-response literary theory. Writing from these perceived correspondences between personal and literary experience helps student writers to elaborate their composing processes where improvement is most needed: in the linking of adequate illustrations to the generalizations that frame their arguments.[32] Similarly, Salvatori has argued that student writers develop intellectually more complex composing processes as they learn to link moments of reading comprehension into larger patterns of meaning and to relate these in turn to their own experience for comparison or critique.[33] In effect, for these researchers, the texts of others become collaborators in the students' composing processes, stimulating critical reflection on composing in much the same way as do peer tutors or the conventions of academic discourse itself, self-consciously viewed.

What We Know: Curricular Implications

We know that the act of composing through writing is a complex process. Although we are beginning to identify characteristic moments or stages in this process, we cannot say exactly what are the relationships of these stages one to another. We can say that we know such relationships exist, that is, the composing process is hierarchical, and also that they are not necessarily ordered serially, that is, the composing process is recursive. We cannot say that there is one composing process invariably successful for all writers, for all purposes. Rather, we know that composing processes vary both as the same writer attempts different kinds of discourse and as different writers attempt the same kind of discourse, and that such variations may be necessary to success in composing. The current state of our knowledge of composing permits the limited generalizations that successful composing results more often from attention to the thinking required by a piece of writing than to its adherence to standard conventions of grammar, spelling, and so on; and that successful composing results more often from a process that allows for rereading, rethinking, and rewriting than from one in which time limitations or other pressures force a rush to closure. I believe that we can also conclude—although this is perhaps more debatable—that "successful" composing results in writing that participates actively in the language-using practices of a particular community, without slavishly imitating them.

This limited understanding of composing processes nevertheless permits some broad recommendations on curriculum. First, learning to write requires writing. Students cannot be expected to master such complex processes if they only practice them two or three times in a school term, or without a teacher's guidance. It follows, then, if students are to be writing frequently and receiving frequent responses from the teacher, that classes in which writing is taught (whether in English or some other discipline) must be kept small. The teacher must be able to get to know the students in order to respond consistently to the thinking they develop in their writing. Moreover, if the emphasis in writing is to be on developing thinking, it follows both that the curriculum should be structured to encourage recursive composing processes and that institutionalized testing of student writing should not set a counteragenda for the writing class, such as mastering a certain number of features of formal grammar.

But in this small class in which students are writing and rewriting frequently, what should they be writing? What should the classroom activities be? These questions, it seems to me, are more open to debate. Some answers can be found in the Position Statement on teaching composition recently promulgated by the Commission on Composition of the National Council of Teachers of English.[34] This document suggests that students should be encouraged "to make full use of the many activities that comprise the act of writing," presumably including various pre-writing and editing techniques as well as the actual drafting of papers. The document also states that writing assignments should reflect the wide variety of purposes for writing, including expressive writing, writing across the curriculum, and writing that would have a place in "the world beyond school." The writing classroom, according to the document, should be organized as a workshop in which students write for each other, as well as for the teacher, and in which writing is used as "a mode of learning" rather than merely "reporting on what has been learned." To accomplish these ends, class size should not be larger than twenty students, and student writing should be the principal text. Tests should allow students "to demonstrate their writing ability in work aimed at various purposes" and should encourage the development of students' self-critical abilities.

The recommendations on class size, testing, and teaching a full range of composing activities, which would necessitate much attention to substantive revision, may be the most politically sensitive of the recommendations, since they at once ask the public for more money for education (more teachers to keep class size small) and deny the public the kind of testing in writing skills that it seems to desire. Yet current research suggests that it is essential to implement these recommendations if student writing is to improve.

It is not equally evident, however, that for good writing to ensue students must always write for each other and make their own writing the principal text. If the curricular goal is to foster mastery of academic discourse, such a classroom organization will not be very productive unless many of the students have already achieved the desired goal and so can teach the others. But it appears that today's students typically do not have enough prior knowledge of academic discourse conventions to help each other to mastery of them. More guidance from the teacher and more reading materials that illustrate and elucidate these practices may be needed (without, however, returning to the traditional, authoritarian classroom).

The Position Statement may be recommending what amounts to a personal-style classroom because the value of this approach is widely acknowledged among composition specialists, while the goal of mastering academic discourse is more problematic. The Commission also finesses the issue of academic discourse by taking a pluralistic view of the kinds of writing assignments it recommends, all the way from personal-style pedagogy's favored expressive writing to some kind of business or technical writing (for "the world beyond school"). In fact, there is no consensus on what kinds of writing students should be doing. Recent anthologies of college student writing, published as textbooks, suggest that personal-style essays still enjoy an edge; indeed, if they did not, there would be no point in publishing such anthologies.[35] But, as I suggested earlier, various kinds of academic writing are mounting a strong challenge. I believe, however, that it is salutary for teachers and students to discuss the problem of what constitutes "good" writing. Thus there is no way to escape the fact that course content choices, with the kinds of writing they valorize, will have political consequences with which we must deal.

Indeed, perhaps the most important conclusion to be drawn from this overview of research on composing is that research results alone not only should not dictate a curriculum, they cannot dictate it. Notice how persistently composition researchers have interpreted their results in light of personal-style pedagogical assumptions, whether about classroom organization or political agenda. But we could not do otherwise. Scholars writing up their research, like students struggling with their first essay assignments, must work within the language-using practices of a particular community, which are in turn shaped by its social, cultural, and political circumstances. The challenge is to be an active participant, to change the community in light of the values that make one's commitment to education professionally and personally meaningful.

FOOTNOTES

1. D. Gordon Rohman, "Pre-Writing: The Stage of Discovery in the Writing Process," *College Composition and Communication* 26 (May 1965): 106-12.

2. Peter Elbow, *Writing Without Teachers* (New York: Oxford University Press, 1973).

3. Patricia Bizzell, "Cognition, Convention, and Certainty: What We Need to Know about Writing," *PRE/TEXT* 3 (Fall 1982): 213-44.

4. James Britton, T. Burgess, N. Martin, A. McLeod, and H. Rosen. *The Development of Writing Abilities (11-18)* (London: Macmillan Education, 1975).

5. Janet Emig, *The Composing Processes of Twelfth Graders* (Urbana, Ill.: National Council of Teachers of English, 1971).

6. Linda Flower and John R. Hayes, "A Cognitive Process Theory of Writing," *College Composition and Communication* 32 (December 1981): 365-87.

7. Sharon Pianko, "A Description of the Composing Processes of College Freshman Writers," *Research in the Teaching of English* 13 (February 1979): 5-22.

8. Sondra Perl, "Composing Processes of Unskilled College Writers," *Research in the Teaching of English* 13 (December 1979): 317-36.

9. Sondra Perl, "Understanding Composing," *College Composition and Communication* 31 (December 1980): 363-69.

10. Nancy Sommers, "Revision Strategies of Student Writers and Experienced Adult Writers," *College Composition and Communication* 31 (December 1980): 378-88.

11. Lil Brannon, Melinda Knight, and Vera Neverow-Turk, *Writers Writing* (Montclair, N.J.: Boynton/Cook, 1983).

12. Carol Berkenkotter and Donald Murray, "Decisions and the Planning Strategies of a Publishing Writer, and Response of a Laboratory Rat—or Being Protocoled," *College Composition and Communication* 34 (May 1983): 156-72.

13. Mimi Schwartz, "Two Journeys through the Writing Process," *College Composition and Communication* 34 (May 1983): 188-201.

14. Donald Graves, "An Examination of the Writing Processes of Seven-Year-Old Children," *Research in the Teaching of English* 9 (Winter 1975): 227-41; Linda Leonard Lamme and Nancye M. Childers, "Composing Processes of Three Young Children," *Research in the Teaching of English* 17 (February 1983): 31-50.

15. Glenda L. Bissex, *Gnys at Work: A Child Learns to Write and Read* (Cambridge, Mass.: Harvard University Press, 1980).

16. Donald H. Graves, *Writing: Teachers and Children at Work* (Portsmouth, N.H. and London: Heinemann Educational Books, 1983).

17. Shirley Brice Heath, *Ways With Words: Language, Life, and Work in Communities and Classrooms* (Cambridge, Eng.: Cambridge University Press, 1983); David R. Olson, "The Language of Instruction: The Literate Bias of Schooling," in *Schooling and the Acquisition of Knowledge*, ed. Richard C. Anderson, Rand J. Spiro, and William E. Montague (Hillsdale, N.J.: Lawrence Erlbaum Associates, 1977), pp. 65-90. For a dissenting view, see Margaret Donaldson, "Speech and Writing and Modes of Learning," in *Awakening to Literacy: The University of Victoria Symposium of Children's Response to a Literate Environment: Literacy before Schooling*, ed. Hillel Goelman, Antoinette A. Oberg, and Frank Smith (Exeter, N.H. and London: Heinemann Educational Books, 1984), pp. 174-84.

18. Edward P. J. Corbett, *Classical Rhetoric for the Modern Student*, 2d edition (New York: Oxford University Press, 1971).

19. C. H. Knoblauch and Lil Brannon, *Rhetorical Traditions and the Teaching of Writing* (Montclair, N.J.: Boynton/Cook, 1984).

20. Ann E. Berthoff, *The Making of Meaning: Metaphors, Models and Maxims for Writing Teachers* (Montclair, N.J.: Boynton/Cook, 1981).

21. Mina P. Shaughnessy, *Errors and Expectations: A Guide for the Teacher of Basic Writing* (New York: Oxford University Press, 1977).

22. Nancy Martin, editor, *Writing across the Curriculum: Pamphlets from the Schools Council/London Institute of Education W.A.C. Projects* (Montclair, N.J.: Boynton/Cook, 1984).

23. Toby Fulwiler, "The Personal Connection: Journal Writing across the Curriculum," in *Language Connections: Writing and Reading across the Curriculum*, ed. Toby Fulwiler and Art Young (Urbana, Ill.: National Council of Teachers of English, 1982), pp. 15-32.

24. C. H. Knoblauch and Lil Brannon, "Writing as Learning through the Curriculum," *College English* 45 (September 1983): 465-74.

25. Elaine Maimon, "Maps and Genres: Exploring Connections in the Arts and Sciences," in *Composition and Literature: Bridging the Gap*, ed. Winifred Bryan Horner (Chicago: University of Chicago Press, 1983), pp. 110-25.

26. Mike Rose, "Rigid Rules, Inflexible Plans and the Stifling of Language: A Cognitivist Analysis of Writer's Block," *College Composition and Communication* 31 (December 1980): 389-400.

27. David Bartholomae, "The Study of Error," *College Composition and Communication* 31 (October 1980): 253-69.

28. Walter J. Ong, "Literacy and Orality in Our Times," in *Composition and Literature: Bridging the Gap*, ed. Horner, pp. 126-40.

29. James T. Farrell, "I.Q. and Standard English," *College Composition and Communication* 34 (December 1983): 470-84.

30. See rebuttals to Farrell by Karen Greenberg, Patrick Hartwell, Margaret Himley, and R. E. Stratton in *College Composition and Communication* 35 (December 1984): 455-77.

31. Kenneth A. Bruffee, "Collaborative Learning and the 'Conversation of Mankind,' " *College English* 46 (November 1984): 635-52.

32. Anthony R. Petrosky, "From Story to Essay: Reading and Writing," *College Composition and Communication* 33 (February 1982): 19-36.

33. Mariolina Salvatori, "Reading and Writing a Text: Correlations between Reading and Writing," *College English* 45 (November 1983): 657-66.

34. Commission on Composition of the National Council of Teachers of English, "Teaching Composition: A Position Statement," (Urbana, Ill.: National Council of Teachers of English, 1983). I should note that as a member of the Commission, I participated in the drafting of this document and endorsed its publication.

35. See, for example, William E. Coles, Jr., and James Vopat, editors, *What Makes Writing Good: A Multiperspective* (Lexington, Mass. and Toronto: D. C. Heath and Co., 1985); Nancy Sommers and Donald McQuade, editors, *Student Writers at Work: The Bedford Prizes* (New York: Bedford Books of St. Martin's Press, 1984).

CHAPTER V

The Writer's Knowledge: Theory, Research, and Implications for Practice

GEORGE HILLOCKS, JR.

Over the past twenty-five years studies related to the teaching of composition have dealt with so many diverse aspects of composition instruction that one is tempted to suppose that no coherent view of them is possible. However, if we ask what kinds of knowledge writers bring to bear on the composing process, a coherent view emerges. Studies of the composing process seek to discover the kinds of knowledge writers use as they write. Studies of instruction examine how writers best learn particular kinds of knowledge and how and to what extent that knowledge affects writing. This essay will examine four major types of knowledge that appear to be important in composing.

In the past fifteen years many studies have been concerned with what might best be called production activity. While these studies have been important because they have drawn attention to various aspects of the composing process (for example, prewriting, activity during pauses, rate of writing, what writers do when they stop), they also raise an important question which has largely gone unrecognized. Generally, these studies indicate that prewriting times are quite short: one minute for Pianko's remedial writers[1] to 4.18 minutes for Stallard's "good" writers.[2] They indicate almost no "prefiguring" (Emig's term) such as notetaking or outlining. At the same time, they differ on how much writers have in mind of what they will write when they begin writing. Emig claims that "most of the elements that will appear in the piece are present."[3] Mischel indicates that her single subject, Clarence, "seemed to have a great store of small, manageable topics" such as "learning to play the guitar" and "my first year of high school."[4] While such topics are not inherently short, Clarence appears to have written about them rapidly and adequately in a forty-five-minute session, suggesting that he had most elements in mind. Pianko claims that none of her subjects had a "complete conception of what they were going to write when they began writing."[5] Perl reports that when her subjects used one of four strategies, they began to write with an "articulated sense of where they wanted their discourse to go."[6]

Several researchers indicate that their subjects compose at a steady, rapid rate. Pianko, for example, reports a rate of over nine words per minute for both her remedial and traditional groups.[7] Stallard reports just under nine words per minute for his "good writers" but almost 13.5 words per minute for his randomly selected writers.[8] That comes to two typewritten pages an hour for Pianko's writers, a bit less for Stallard's good writers, and a whopping three typewritten pages an hour for Stallard's randomly selected writers. (By comparison, Hemingway is said to have set himself a *daily* goal of about two typewritten pages—500 words.)

How can such rapid composing be explained? None of the researchers indicates that the students were simply writing whatever random phrases came to mind. All of them apparently wrote connected, intelligible discourse. The evidence suggests that the writers in these studies did indeed begin with the major substantive elements in mind or thought of them soon after rephrasing the topic question in writing. Further, it suggests that the writers had some form in mind early in the writing, if not during the prewriting period. They appear to write rapidly and generally know when they have reached a conclusion. They all appear to write steadily to what they regard as a stopping place. Thus, although Stallard claims that, when asked, his subjects were unanimous in stating they had not considered form or organization, one suspects that form must have been a subconscious element in the writing, sometimes dictated by the content itself. For example, in writing about an "experience observed," as in Pianko's topic, a writer selects "an experience," thereby automatically imposing time boundaries and conceiving a beginning, middle, and end—certainly aspects of form in Aristotle's terms.

We can hypothesize tentatively that the writers observed in the studies cited above made use of two kinds of knowledge: substantive and formal. By substantive knowledge, I mean knowledge of facts, opinions, events, beliefs, and so forth. By formal knowledge, I mean knowledge of lexical, syntactic, rhetorical, and discourse forms used to express substantive knowledge (and perhaps to store it in memory). Cognitive psychologists discriminate between two other types of knowledge: declarative and procedural, sometimes called knowledge of *what* and knowledge of *how*. Declarative knowledge allows us to identify phenomena and to name or recall information stored in memory. By contrast, procedural knowledge comprises the ability to produce, transform, or instantiate that knowledge. My daughter was once required by her third-grade teacher to write a limerick. She could identify a limerick and its parts but could not produce one. She had declarative knowledge of limericks but not the procedural knowledge which would enable her to write one.

It is possible, then, to think of four major types of knowledge which come to bear on writing. Declarative knowledge of substance can be thought of as the data base of any piece of writing—the facts, opinions, beliefs, and images incorporated in the discourse, whatever its form and purpose may be. Procedural knowledge related to substance permits the recall, ordering, and transformation of substantive knowledge. At one level, as Bereiter and Scardamalia have argued, procedural knowledge includes knowing how to conduct a memory search for relevant information without the prompting of a conversational partner.[9] At higher levels, as suggested by a variety of experimental studies, procedural knowledge includes such strategies as classifying data and generalizing about it. Declarative knowledge of form involves the ability to identify forms, then parts, and their relationships. Procedural knowledge of form is the ability to produce examples of particular forms.

Although we might wish for more precise definitions of these types of knowledge, they serve as useful categories to examine existing research on both process and instruction in composition. In addition, they provide a matrix of questions for future research. The remainder of this paper will examine each category before turning briefly to their interactions and recommendations for practice.

Declarative Knowledge of Substance

Increasingly, researchers involved in reading comprehension have recognized the importance of prior knowledge in the comprehension of texts. They distinguish between world knowledge of the kind that comes with increasing experience and domain-specific knowledge that comes with levels of expertise within content areas. Two decades ago, researchers and practitioners generally assumed that meaning lay within the text and that the reader's role was to retrieve that meaning by decoding the words and understanding their relationships. Current theory, however, hypothesizes that successful comprehension involves an amalgam of retrieving meaning by decoding (bottom-up processing) and by bringing prior knowledge to bear even on the decoding process as well as on inference making (top-down processing). For skilled readers these act as complements.[10]

In effect, readers construct meaning for themselves in the context of what they already know and believe.[11] When we know, for example, that turning a faucet releases water from its spigot, we are likely to assume the release of water when we read that a character turned a faucet even though the text does not state that water was released. As Spiro points out, "In the process of comprehending discourse, what is understood and stored frequently includes not only what is directly stated, but also what seems to follow from that information."[12] What seems to follow, of course, is dependent on what the comprehender knows. Schema theories of cognition elaborate these ideas and provide plausible explanations of how prior knowledge is activated and how it operates on the emerging interpretation of texts.[13]

Not only does prior knowledge influence inference making, but a number of studies indicate that it affects the degree of comprehension and retention. Langer, for example, found that the degree of topic-specific background knowledge was highly related to measures of comprehension and retention of passages.[14] Voss reports comparable findings in a study which presented subjects with a text describing one half-inning of a baseball game. The text presented the standard events of the game as well as information not related directly to the game, for example, weather conditions. Prior knowledge of baseball was related to recall and to success on completion items based on the text. More interesting, subjects with high levels of prior knowledge "recalled more information directly related to the goal structure of the game, whereas there was little performance difference of the groups in recalling information unrelated to the game. Low-knowledge individuals tended to recall the teams, weather, and first batter coming to bat, but recall of subsequent events of the game was infrequent and not systematic."[15]

However, although a number of studies examine the effects of topic-specific knowledge on reading comprehension, very few examine the effects of such knowledge on writing performance. Voss and his colleagues asked people with high and low levels of knowledge about baseball to generate "their own segment of a baseball game."[16] They found that subjects with high levels of knowledge about baseball generated texts which provided "better descriptions of the actions and related state changes" than those who had low levels of knowledge.[17] Langer studied the responses of high school students to social studies writing assignments, two of which, she says, required a "thesis/support" structure while two required a "comparison/contrast" structure. She examined the specific knowledge of each student on the writing topics prior to their writing by presenting "the students with each of the three concept words just before distributing the writing assignments; students were asked to write everything that came to mind about those words."[18] Raters then judged the responses, providing three "knowledge" scores: (a) a count of total responses to the stimulus words; (b) a score, based on a three-point scale, reflecting the highest level of organization in the student's response; and (c) a combined measure of the first and second. Langer then correlated these knowledge scores with holistic scores assigned the student compositions. While the resulting correlations were significant, they are low (.04 to .09), suggesting that prior knowledge accounts for surprisingly little of the variance in holistic scores. Most correlations of knowledge scores with other writing measures (words per clause and coherence scores) are not significant.

The most interesting finding of the study is that when the assignments were grouped according to whether they required a thesis/support structure or a comparison/contrast structure, the knowledge scores correlated with holistic scores differentially. Correlations between the first knowledge measure, the "simple count of total responses," and holistic scores for the thesis/support topics were significant ($r = .26$ and $.33$, $p < .05$). However, correlations between the second measure of prior knowledge (organizational level) and holistic scores were quite low and not significant for thesis/support compositions. The reverse was true for comparison/contrast themes. That is, the measure of organizational level of prior knowledge correlated more highly ($r = .39$ and $.68$) with holistic scores than did the simple count of responses ($r = .03$ and $.15$).

While these findings evade clear explanation, they do suggest the importance of different kinds of prior knowledge for different writing tasks. Organizational level of prior knowledge accounts for nearly half the variance in holistic scores for one composition. It may be that the differences would be more clear cut if the measure of knowledge were more systematic and if the composition tasks were more carefully structured to require thesis/support. (One of these permits what Langer calls a " 'free floating' associational response.")

Additional systematic research is necessary to determine the range of effects substantive knowledge has on various features of writing, at various age levels, and in different occupational groups.

Procedures for Analysis of Substance

By procedures for the analysis of substance, I mean those procedures that writers appear to bring to bear on substantive knowledge which permit the recall of data, the formulation of new generalizations, the development of criteria necessary to contrast, and so forth. Research has not provided a clear analysis of such procedures as they relate to text production. Available research, however, strongly indicates that such skills are important to effective writing. Further, we may speculate from existing research that these procedures may form a continuum from lower- to higher-level skills, with some dependent upon others.

Bereiter and Scardamalia have considered a number of these procedures (which they call production factors) including memory search, recognizing appropriate information, evaluating it, and making a decision to use or not to use it.[19] They begin by assuming that discourse production is directed by schemata which specify the kinds of things present in a given discourse and their relationships. They argue that when children come to school, they have learned schemata for conversation but not for written discourse. The result is that what they write is about the length of a conversational turn. In a series of experiments, they show that youngsters have in memory far more information on a topic than they write. In one study, for example, they asked children in grades four and six to say as much as possible about the topic. When the children stopped, the researchers used what they call "contentless prompts" (requests to write more without any specific suggestion of what to write). The initial prompting to say "as much as possible" tripled the amount written in comparison to the first study. When the children were urged to say even more, they wrote about as much as they had before the prompt. When contentless prompts had apparently exhausted what the children could recall, the researchers asked specific questions. The answers indicated that the children had far more information. Bereiter and Scardamalia conclude that children, having learned the schemata for conversation but not for written discourse, need a conversational partner to initiate memory searches until they learn how to stimulate memory searches without a partner.

Accordingly, they instituted a study using a procedure developed by Anderson[20] in which they asked students in grade six to list all the single words that might be relevant to a topic before they wrote. Students followed this procedure for twelve one-hour sessions in which they wrote on a variety of "expository and opinion" topics. On the posttest compositions experimental group students wrote twice as much as did control group students, used three times as many uncommon words, assumed to be an indication of more varied content, and in opinion essays wrote an average of three arguments on an issue as compared to two for control students. However, there were no significant differences in quality between compositions written by students in the two groups, an interesting finding in light of the usual finding that, in student writing, length correlates significantly with quality ratings.[21] Bereiter and Scardamalia speculate that had the students used some criteria in conjunction with their memory search—such as persuasiveness or significance—the improved access to memory should have resulted in improved quality.[22]

At any rate, Bereiter and Scardamalia conclude from these and other studies that children must and can learn to do memory searches. The memory search appears to be a basic procedure in working with data. The application of criteria such as relevance and importance probably can be taught directly, as other criteria have been taught.[23]

A number of studies have used instruction in which students have practiced what are best described as strategies of inquiry. Typically, this kind of instruction presents students with sets of data (for example, objects to be described, cases to be analyzed, facts related to a given problem requiring a solution). The instruction presents a problem for discussion and writing, the solution to which involves a particular strategy or set of strategies (for example, description of a univalve seashell so that a reader can pick out the shell from among many;[24] analysis of a relatively simple ethical problem by identifying the relevant ethical principles, exceptions, obligations, and consequences;[25] analysis of the facts related to problems such as pollution or a prison uprising with a view to developing generalizations and appropriate support and eventually an argument in favor of some solution[26]).

In one such study Hillocks, Kahn, and Johannessen examined the effects of two different approaches to teaching extended definition.[27] Such definitions are to be found in any serious research and analysis, for example, in the work of philosophers (Aristotle in *The Nichomachean Ethics*), literary critics (Northrop Frye, *The Anatomy of Criticism*), and sociologists (Riesman, *The Lonely Crowd*). Extended definitions have the function of differentiating the concept under consideration (the definiendum) from similar but different concepts. To differentiate, they typically place the definiendum in a class, illustrate it with specific examples, discriminate it from similar concepts by showing what criteria the definiendum must meet, and illustrate the criteria by providing examples which do or do not fulfill the criteria. For example, Aristotle defines courage as a state of character having to do with feelings of fear and confidence. He indicates several criteria which discriminate true courage from seeming courage, such as the following: (a) the actor must be aware of the danger to be confronted and must have cause to fear it; (b) the action must be undertaken with an honorable motive; (c) it must be freely chosen, as opposed to forced. Each of these criteria is explained and illustrated by examples which clarify the criteria by revealing in a specific manner the difference between what Aristotle believes is and is not courageous.

Intuitive analysis of such definitions suggests that writing a definition involves such complex strategies as the following: (a) recalling or generating examples of the definiendum for analysis; (b) generating examples of similar concepts; (c) identifying the essential features of the definiendum by contrast with examples of similar but different concepts; and (d) generating criteria which discriminate the definiendum from similar concepts.

Conventional instruction in writing definitions provides examples of extended definitions along with the explanations of the parts of the definitions. It then requires students to produce definitions exhibiting those features. The question one is forced to ask is whether such instruction in itself can help students to write effective definitions. A variety of informal classroom trials indicated that more than knowledge of form was necessary.

Hillocks, Kahn, and Johannessen devised and tested instruction which provided practice in certain of the strategies or procedures listed above. The instructional procedures included giving students sets of scenarios each related to a concept to be defined: courageous action and freedom of speech. Each scenario presented actions which might or might not illustrate the definiendum. For example, one scenario described a soldier wandering in enemy territory without being aware that he was in enemy territory. Another described a soldier flying into a rage, charging the enemy with a grenade launcher, and wiping out a machine gun nest. Students, working in small groups, were asked to decide whether the main action in each was courageous and to generate a criterion by which the particular action could be included in or excluded from the category of courageous action. Following the examination of all incidents, the teacher conducted a discussion of the incidents and led the class in devising a definition of courage which included several criteria and examples. Students then wrote their own definitions of courage. Similar procedures were followed with the scenarios related to freedom of speech. In the following activity students planned a definition of one of several concepts without the aid of any examples. This sequence of instruction emphasizes strategies (c) and (d) above: identifying essential features of the definiendum by contrast and generating criteria. To some extent it encourages generating examples of the definiendum, but it does not provide any means for helping students learn procedures for generating concepts and examples similar to but different from the definiendum. That may be the most difficult step of all.

Despite this possible failing, the instruction emphasizing procedures for comparing, contrasting, and generating criteria yielded significant pretest to posttest gains, over twice those for students receiving conventional instruction which focused on model definitions. Similarly, other studies which involved students in using procedures for examining data exhibit consistently high gains. My meta-analysis of experimental treatment studies, which grouped such treatments together under the category of inquiry, indicates that their gains are significantly higher than any other focus of instruction examined, with the experimental groups gaining a mean of .56 standard deviations more than their control counterparts.[28] Knowledge of procedures for dealing with the substance of writing (the data) clearly cannot be ignored.

Declarative Knowledge of Form

By declarative knowledge of form I mean the kind of knowledge which permits the identification or recall of forms and their parts, whether those be syntactic, generic, or rhetorical forms. Traditionally, instruction in composition in English-speaking countries has focused on form. Teachers of grammar have asked their students to identify parts of speech, parts of sentences, types of sentences, and types of clauses. Books on writing have provided model compositions such as the model paragraph with its topic sentence and development by illustration, detail, and up to nine or ten more methods of development. The conception of learning to write underlying this kind of instruction is that if one knows the appropriate forms, one can use them and that knowing them is largely the ability to identify them and their parts.

Evidence about the efficacy of such instruction appears, at first, to be contradictory. The evidence coming from studies of classroom instruction has shown for decades that the study of traditional school grammar and, more recently, transformational grammar does not improve writing significantly.[29] My own meta-analysis of experimental treatments indicates that instruction which emphasizes grammar study stimulates almost no improvement in composition. In fact, when examined against almost any other systematic effort to improve composition, instruction in grammar results in significantly less improvement. Sometimes, grammar study, especially when coupled with thorough marking of mechanical and usage errors which often accompanies it, results in losses for the students. Their writing is weaker after such treatments than before.[30] We can surely speculate that in order to avoid criticism, students begin to write fewer, shorter, and simpler sentences, with the result of less developed content.

Evidence about teaching model compositions in schools is somewhat more positive. The use of models is significantly more effective than teaching grammar and more effective than free writing, but less effective than other available approaches. What we do not know is the contribution it might make to quality in conjunction with the development of other kinds of knowledge. In addition, we do not know what aspects of generic or rhetorical form have psychological validity. That is, outside simple stories, we do not know which formal elements play a role in guiding the comprehension or production of discourse.

Cognitive psychologists have explored the structure of simple stories with a view to examining the organization of story knowledge and its use in comprehension. From the point of view of an English teacher or literary critic, the stories they have worked with are minimal, and their main questions have been what are the features a text must have before it can be considered a story and what minimal features must be included in a "good" story. Several definitions of a story have been developed. One which has been used in examining story production as well as judgments about what stories contain is that by Stein and Glenn.[31] This definition posits a two-part structure consisting of a setting and an episode. The setting includes information about place and characters. The episodes must consist of (a) an initiating event which brings about or may be an internal response; (b) an internal response which reveals the character's emotional response or plans; (c) an attempt in which the character puts the plan into action; (d) a consequence revealing the result of the character's actions; and (e) a reaction indicating the character's response to the consequence. In a later study, Stein and Policastro recognize that texts may be classified as stories when the character formulates no plan and makes no attempt under one of two conditions. In the first, there must be "absolutely no chance of initiating goal-directed behavior" as with stories in which some natural disaster prevents a character from forming or carrying out plans. In the second, "where there is the possibility of initiating goal-based behavior, the text would have to contain some type of intentional action and outcome or some explanation for the lack of goal-directed behavior" for the text to be classified as a story.

Stein and Policastro use a set of what I call minimal texts exhibiting the presence or absence of these features as well as the features posited as essential by other definitions. They found that the more features incorporated into a text, the more likely it would be judged a story (as opposed to not a story) and the more likely it would be judged a "really good" story by both students and teachers.[32] Studies of story comprehension and recall indicate that children best remember information that falls into the major categories and that when they retell the story and add new information, it tends to be inferred from the given information and falls into one of the main categories (for example, internal response). Other studies indicate that when the normal story schema is disordered, children recall it less well and tend to reorder it in the sequence of the story schema.[33] Finally, a few studies indicate that as children grow older, their original stories are more likely to contain the elements of the story episode.

In short, evidence that knowledge of form guides both comprehension and production of narrative texts is increasing. These findings are in accord with the assumptions underlying traditional programs in rhetoric. Even in the ancient academies of Greece and Rome, the study of rhetoric involved not simply the reading, but the memorization of exemplary texts. Research examining the effects of direct instruction on the structure of texts, however, shows only very weak effects for the study of sentences (grammar) and only somewhat stronger effects for the study of model pieces of writing. Why this is the case is open to speculation.

Although I have grouped the study of grammar and model pieces of writing in the same category, their limited effectiveness is probably due to entirely different problems. The study of grammar provides knowledge relevant to composing only at the syntactic level—nothing about analysis of the data base, nothing about text plans, nothing about audience; perhaps we cannot expect it to influence any higher-level operations in writing. Evidence from many studies indicates that composing takes place at various levels of abstraction. The work of Hayes and Flower,[14] for example, suggests that the transcription of specific sentences generally comes as the result of many other operations (for example, generating, organizing). Competent writers do not simply generate sentences. They generate them after thinking about content, purpose, audience, and so forth.

In an interesting study, Matsuhashi found evidence to suggest that sentences may be planned ahead in large semantic chunks without specific lexical content.[35] Bereiter, Fine, and Gartshore conducted an experiment with fourth and sixth graders in which they concealed what writers were writing at certain intervals and asked them to say aloud the word they had in mind to write.[36] They found that the youngsters' "forecasts" of words averaged five or six words and tended to end with a clause, suggesting as does Matsuhashi's study, that syntactic arrangements of lexical content may take place one clause at a time, although guided by larger semantic chunking of some kind. (The length of the forecast is about what we would expect from what we know about short-term memory.) In addition, Bereiter, Fine, and Gartshore found minor differences between words forecast and those actually written. Most of these differences (78 percent) were stylistic and tended to be in the direction of more formal written English. Most of the remaining changes involved the addition of words. Both kinds of changes suggest the presence of an editorial process which occurs *after* the planning of the specific syntactic unit and during the time the structure is committed to writing—clearly, a kind of last-minute editing process. If these findings are correct, it is little wonder that the kind of grammar traditionally taught in schools has little effect on the way anyone writes.

In addition, the traditional study of school grammar concentrates on the identification of parts of speech and their functions in sentences, parts of sentences, and types of sentences. Students spend time studying sets of relatively simple sentences, the content of which has little relationship to anything, in order to pick out the nouns, verbs, adjectives, or adverbs, or to identify the subjects and predicates, participles or infinitives, adjective, adverbial, or noun clauses. There is evidence that after years of intensive study of such grammar, students cannot recognize the parts of speech in running prose. But assuming students could learn to recite the definitions and apply them successfully, is there any reason to believe that such knowledge might result in more effective text plans, in more specific and interesting content, or even in more effective sentences? Because the study of traditional grammar does not help students to generate various syntactic structures for use with the same semantic content or help them to evaluate the alternative structures available, we can hardly expect more effective sentences to result from the instruction. The best we can hope for is an enhanced ability to copyread and punctuate according to conventional usage. A study by Elley and colleagues over three years of instruction, contrasting traditional grammar study, transformational grammar study, and no grammar study, shatters even that modest hope. At the end of each of the three years of instruction and at the end of a fourth year, there were no significant differences among the mean quality ratings for compositions written by students in the three groups—not even among the mean subscale scores for mechanics.[37]

The traditional study of model compositions is more powerful than the study of grammar and somewhat more effective than the widely recommended use of free writing, but its effects are not significantly greater than those for free writing. Why such study is not more effective is less clear, especially given the increasing evidence that schemata appear to guide the production of stories. It may be, however, that while children learn procedures for instantiating a story schema in conversations through the promptings of conversational partners, they do not have the opportunities to learn the procedures for producing the standard expository forms espoused by so many school writing programs. Perhaps conversations do not elicit information in ways that reflect the forms thought to be important in non-narrative writing.

Typically, writing programs do not teach such procedures but simply the identification of forms and their parts. For example, teachers show students pieces of writing which include introductions with thesis statements and plans, with several paragraphs developing the points in the plan, and with a conclusion of some kind. Textbooks and teachers then ask students to produce their own compositions displaying similar features. Teachers may even go to some length to find topics likely to be of interest. However, neither they nor the textbooks teach students *how* to generate and evaluate a thesis statement, a plan, or how to select and evaluate the data to support the thesis. Students are left to do that on their own.

The same problems pertain to the use of essays in the typical college freshman reader, with one added difficulty. The essays presented in college readers are generally rich and complex belletristic essays prized more for sophistication of rhetoric and style than for content. They are often so rich and complex that freshmen can barely understand them, let alone internalize the structure well enough to allow it to influence their own writing.

Procedures for the Use of Form

By procedural knowledge for the use of form I mean that knowledge which permits writers to manipulate forms and their parts. Declarative knowledge of form allows their identification and perhaps their definition. A person may have declarative knowledge of a musical instrument, its parts, and how it works but may lack the procedural knowledge to play it effectively. In composition this distinction between declarative and procedural knowledge is still hypothetical, but considerable evidence suggests that the distinction is real.

A case study by Calkins examines a young girl as she gains what appears to be the procedural knowledge requisite to instantiating a form. At the beginning of the school year, Andrea, a nine-year-old, is writing a book about a homesick Chinese girl, adding three to four hundred words per day at the rate of 15.5 words per minute, a rate somewhat faster than Stallard's randomly chosen high school seniors.[38]

On October 3 of the school year, Calkins says, the teacher asked the children to "bring something to school which you know and care about." After interviews with other children, the teacher asked them to write a story. Calkins reports that the teacher "hoped this time Andrea's title and first lines (lead) would be focused and show a point of view. But Andrea wrote the title, 'The Bird's Nest,' and began a long-winded explanation of how she found the nest under a tree (with no birds nearby), brought it to school, and remembered trying to fly when she was younger." Andrea's teacher asks, "Is your story really 'The Bird's Nest?' What's important about that nest?"[39] When Andrea tries to erase the title, the teacher suggests crossing it out, but Andrea gets a clean sheet and begins again, this time eliminating the material about finding the nest. However, the teacher draws a line under what Andrea has written and says, "See if you can say it differently." Andrea writes two more leads for a total of three: (a) "Once when I was very little I got a hank to fly so I tryed jumping of things and tryed to float up and across I tryed and tryed til my father made me and my sister big cardboard butterfly wings"; (b) "I always wanted to fly, but whenever I tried, I always fell Kaboom!"; (c) "Kabboom! That hurt! Why can't I fly."[40] Andrea decides she likes the third one best, but says she doesn't know why.

For the next five months, Andrea goes through a process of writing out several leads before choosing a best one. She learns to apply the same strategy to developing internal parts of the composition. At this stage, Andrea writes more slowly. "She often averages only six to eight words a minute and writes only one hundred words in a sitting."[41]

Calkins claims that the externalized process of writing out several possibilities and choosing one becomes internalized. By March, Andrea is writing 15.5 words a minute once again, as in September. She produces leads such as the following (about washing her dog Caspar) "with very little revision"; " 'Come on, Caspar,' I firmly say. The dog squats down. I drag her by the collar." In March, Andrea is quoted as saying, "It's easier for me to start a piece of writing now. I have a better idea for topics which will work, and the leads come to me easily."[42]

These changes from September to March are fascinating. Even more interesting is the question of why they take place. Calkins attributes the changes to learning to revise, a process which she says is self-learned, a matter of learning strategies for developing alternatives and making deliberate choices. Calkins implies that making the appropriate choice develops from some innate sense in the child.

But the evidence available is open to other interpretations and hypotheses. Early in September Andrea demonstrates the mastery of the mechanics of writing. The evidence suggests that she is precocious, cooperative, and eager to please. She clearly has worked hard on her story of Lin-Su, producing words at a rapid rate for several minutes a day over several days and over nineteen pages. Early in October, Andrea's stories exhibit the conventional schema of stories examined by Stein and Glenn and others. Her first lead for the piece on learning to fly introduces the protagonist, tells the protagonist's goal (to fly) and two attempts to do so. The second lead reiterates the goal and the attempt and supplies a consequence. The third lead reiterates the consequence eliptically (Kaboom!) and moves to the final category of the story schema, the reaction, which expresses the character's emotional and cognitive responses to the consequence. On the basis of a number of studies, Stein and Trabasso state that "under most conditions, the story teller, listener, or reader constructs a representation of events corresponding to the real-time order of occurrence rather than to the narrative time sequence."[43] Andrea's set of leads about learning to fly follows the real-time order predicted by the story schema. The same is true for the set of "leads" she produced for "My Dog's Heartworm Pill." Indeed, Calkins herself comments that "each lead is deeper into the sequence of events in Andrea's story."[44]

When Andrea's teacher encourages her to "say it differently" and when she approves a new lead, she is encouraging Andrea to invert the conventional form. In effect, Andrea uses the plot that Horace and the neoclassicists would have said begins *in medias res*, in the middle of things. Despite the fact that Andrea uses the new form successfully in October, for several months she has difficulty; her words come slowly and are far fewer at a given setting. But by March her writing speed is back to 15.5 words a minute. And she produces *in medias res* leads "written with very little revision." Andrea has learned to begin with a statement of an attempt, a consequence, or response. She has learned to work in the exposition about settings and goals later. This new form appears to supply the criteria she needs to guide her quickly to leads which meet the teacher's approval. In March the teacher does not draw a line and ask Andrea to "say it differently."[45]

Andrea might be said to know the *in medias res* form in October, but without direct instruction she does not learn to begin with an attempt, consequence, or reaction until the following March. At that point, she apparently has mastered the procedure, and she begins writing as fluently as she had at the beginning of the school year.

An important issue is whether or not procedures related to form can be taught directly. Calkins implies they cannot. Donald H. Graves states that the variability of each writer "demands a waiting, responsive type of teaching."[46] One suspects, however, that there are ways of helping children learn the *in medias res* opening that Andrea's teacher wanted without reducing the child's fluency for five months. One method might involve having children read and discuss stories with such openings, asking them next to suggest different "leads" for stories written according to the conventional story schema, asking them to revise one of their own stories to begin *in medias res*, asking them to assess the virtues of such openings, and so forth.

Certainly, research indicates that other procedural knowledge related to form can be taught directly. My meta-analysis of instructional treatment studies contains two categories of instructional foci which can be classified as teaching procedural knowledge related to form. One deals with syntax, the other with the whole piece of writing. Both were significantly more effective than the study of grammar, model compositions, and free writing.

The first includes studies of sentence combining and sentence construction. In sentence combining, students are given sets of preformed sentences and asked to combine them using some particular syntactic construction but cued so that the construction can be made with almost no knowledge of grammatical terminology.[47] These treatments have consistently shown increased t-unit and clause length as well as increases in quality. Sentence construction shows students various syntactic patterns (for example, final free modifiers) and helps them write similar constructions, but generating their own material to fill out the structure. A study of sentence construction by Faigley achieved larger gains than the usual sentence combining study.[48]

Although both kinds of instruction result in increased t-unit and clause length (and therefore, presumably, greater syntactic sophistication), length of syntactic structures alone is clearly not responsible for increases in quality. Several studies which correlate mean t-unit length and quality rating show correlations ranging from only .03 to about .09.[49] Thus, the mean length of t-units accounts for very little of the variance in quality ratings. Faigley, on the other hand, found relatively high correlations between the frequency and length of free modifiers, particularly final free modifiers, and quality ratings.

What, then, does systematic work on sentence combining contribute to quality? In commenting on the difficulty young writers have in revising a given sentence plan while retaining the intended semantic content, Scardamalia and Bereiter suggest that work in sentence combining may help students develop a hierarchy of syntactic structures which they can review more or less systematically to find a structure suitable to their purposes.[50] Shaughnessy, in writing about the syntactic problems she discovered in the writing of "basic" students at the college level, also suggests that practice in sentence combining might enhance the ability to select and use appropriate structures.[51]

The main procedure which sentence combining and sentence construction teach may be that of reviewing the possibilities available and selecting the best one, rather than settling on the first possibility that comes to mind. Although this explanation remains an empirical question, the effect that sentence combining and sentence construction have on quality is fairly well established. And, clearly, both focus on developing procedural knowledge about the use of syntactic structures.

The second focus of instruction which conveys procedural knowledge of form made use of criteria to guide the production and revision of texts. One of the most interesting studies in this category was conducted by Carol Sager with sixth graders.[52] Her treatments teach students to use four scales, one at a time, for judging the quality of narratives. The scales deal with elaboration, word choice, organization, and structure. Working with one scale at a time, students learned what features earn scores of 0, 1, 2, or 3. Small groups of students were then given a composition to score. In addition, however, they also had to suggest revisions and incorporate their revisions into the original. For example, when they received a composition rated 0 for elaboration, they were asked a series of questions which prompted them to generate a set of details that could make the bare-bones story they had received much more detailed and interesting. When members of the group had talked about a variety of details, they then each rewrote the story, incorporating the details they liked, and read their revised versions to the other members of their small groups. Students followed this procedure until they were adept at both scoring and revising the compositions. The effect size of this study was quite large.

The treatment in the Sager study involves the examination of models and the features which make them exemplary. In addition, however, students learn procedures for bringing weaker compositions into conformity with higher levels of quality. The questions or prompts which the children receive facilitate their thinking about how to rectify specific problems. Most important, the study demonstrates that criteria which children learn through applying the scales and through the revision exercises apparently become guides when they generate their own narratives.

My meta-analysis revealed several studies, at a variety of grade levels including college, that used sets of criteria, usually in the form of questions or prompts which were guides for revision. As a group these produced a large mean effect size. The key difference between these treatments and those in which students simply examine model pieces of writing appears to be the use of detailed criteria. Students receive extensive practice in applying the criteria. As a result, they appear to internalize them and use them to guide their own production. In the Sager study, particularly, the criteria virtually outline the procedures necessary to improve a given composition. For example, when students work with a bare-bones narrative about a relatively nondescript green Martian monster who lands in the USA, the prompts ask students to generate a list of specific places where the Martian might have landed, a list of reasons why the Martian might have landed, a list of thoughts people might have had when they saw the Martian, and so forth. This set of prompts asks students to generate more detail, particularly detail which helps to clarify causal links in the story. One can imagine sets of prompts which focus on developing the description of the monster or other aspects of the story. The result of using such prompts is that students learn to elaborate their own writing.

Types of Knowledge and Their Interaction

The types of knowledge outlined above are examined in separate categories partly for convenience and partly because the available research on instruction tends to focus on one type of knowledge at a time. Whether these types of knowledge are as clearly separable as I have suggested is an empirical question that researchers may profitably address. Even more important is the question of their interaction. Before we can provide an adequate answer to the question posed at the beginning of this paper (How is it possible for writers to compose relatively coherent prose at rapid rates?) it is necessary to know how knowledge of substance relates to knowledge of forms and how the kinds of procedural knowledge identified above relate to both.

The matrix in table 1 sets out a sample of the kinds of questions which appear to be important to developing a theory of instruction in composition. I have phrased the questions in terms of instruction, for example, Does instruction in recognizing one form affect the learning of another? They might have readily been phrased in terms of knowledge, for example, Does knowledge of one form affect knowledge of another? In fact, this distinction is a useful one, suggesting two different lines of research. The important point here, however, is that we must be concerned not only about what effect each type of knowledge has on writing, but also about what their interactions are. Available research suggests that the interactions are quite important. Our research on defining suggests, for example, that a combination of knowledge of form *and* the relevant procedures for analyzing available data is necessary for writing effective definitions.[53] But we do not know exactly what the relationship is. Faigley's work on sentence construction suggests that procedural knowledge related to the use of free modifiers affects the way students use available data. More interesting, it may affect *what* available data they use.[54]

Of the questions in the matrix, some are broadly focused while some are more specific. To generate research, the broad questions will have to be made specific. They will not affect practice, of course, until we begin to answer them.

The Writer's Knowledge and Instructional Practice

The available research strongly indicates the need for instruction which helps to increase the writer's knowledge, especially procedural knowledge related to form and to the analysis of data.

One kind of instruction, which I have called elsewhere *natural process* instruction, is based on the assumption that students already have or will develop the appropriate knowledge if teachers only give them the chance to write.[55] Teachers in the natural process mode often call themselves facilitators in order to avoid the image of the teacher standing at the front of the class handing out advice to passive students. The facilitator is in the classroom not to direct or lecture, but to support students as they grow toward independence. The facilitator's responsibility is to make possible the natural development of the child. In composition teaching, this stance results in a clearly identifiable pattern of classroom events. In the words of Robert P. Parker,

TABLE 1

A Sample of Questions about the Influence of Instruction in One Type of Knowledge Related to Composition on Other Types or Subtypes of Knowledge

	Data Base	Form	Procedures for Data Analysis	Procedures for Use of Form
Data Base	Does instruction in one data base facilitate the learning of another?	How does instruction in the recognition of forms affect the understanding of available data?	How does instruction in procedures of analysis affect the use of available data?	How does instruction in sentence construction affect the use of available data?
Form	How does instruction in the data base affect syntax or other aspects of form?	Does instruction in recognizing one form affect the learning of another?	How does instruction on analytic procedures inherent in a form affect use of the form?	How does instruction in sentence combining affect the recognition of conventional sentence forms?
Procedures for data analysis	How does instruction in the data base at the level of recall or recognition affect the use of procedures for analysis?	How does instruction in recognizing a form (e.g., extended definition) affect ability to analyze (e.g., define another concept)?	How does instruction in procedures for one type of data analysis affect the learning of another type?	How does instruction in using comparison/contrast forms affect the ability to compare/contrast new data sets?
Procedures for use of form	How does instruction in the data base affect students' abilities to use forms they know?	How does instruction in recognizing a form affect ability to use the form?	How does instruction in procedures for devising and supporting generalizations affect the ability to use organizational forms?	Does instruction in procedures for using one kind of form facilitate learning procedures for use of another?

Writing demands usually to be preceded by a period of exploratory talk about what students have chosen to write on, a time in which ideas and the language to express them can be generated. It demands also the freedom for students to choose the forms suitable to their material and their purposes. . . . Writing is learned by doing it and sharing it with real audiences, not by studying and applying abstract rhetorical principles in exercises which the teacher alone will read and judge.[56]

A number of studies have examined the natural process approach to teaching writing.[57] All tend to assume with Parker that preliminary talk, a period of free writing (usually without assigned topics), sharing what is written with peers, redrafting, and so forth will result in a writer's being better able to write on some other occasion. Most reject the study of form, the use of criteria, and structured lessons in the analysis of data. Such instruction, they believe, will inhibit young writers. Available research does not bear out the contentions of the natural process advocates. Their own research reveals weaker effects than any focus of instruction other than grammar.

Although the research is incomplete, it does provide clear direction for practice. We know that the teaching of traditional grammar has virtually no impact on the quality of writing and cannot be expected to have. We know that free writing when it is disconnected from knowledge related to data and form is of little use, even when coupled with peer feedback. We know that the traditional study of model pieces of writing has effects somewhat greater than free writing. We know that the most effective approaches to teaching writing involve students in learning how to examine and analyze data and how to use formal knowledge.

After reading two limericks to the class, my daughter's third-grade teacher asked the class to write a limerick. After similar preparation, she later asked the class to write a fable. My daughter could do neither. Had her teacher known what we know today, perhaps she would have recognized that in order to produce such forms independently children need more than the knowledge that allows them to identify the forms. Before asking children to write a fable, for example, she would have asked them to read several fables over a period of time and then asked them to generalize about the form, particularly the relationships among the key elements (for example, the animal characters usually represent some abstract human characteristic, often an undesirable one such as greed or excessive pride). She might have asked students to revise or complete inadequate fables using techniques suggested by Sager, asking them to think of morals, elaborations of how a prideful mouse might act, what such a mouse might say in a given situation, and so forth. She might then have asked children to think of human characteristics that annoy them (for example, "saying bad things about you behind your back," "thinking you're better than anyone else"). She might have asked children to think of animals that might be used to represent each such characteristic: a hypocritical cat, canary, or giraffe; an egotistical monkey, ant, or toad. The teacher might then have asked youngsters to work in groups listing foolish things an egotistical monkey, ant, or toad might do, what might happen as a result, what the animal might learn, and so forth. In short, before making the writing assignment, the teacher would help students develop the substantive, formal, and procedural knowledge necessary to writing a fable. Finally, she would have provided opportunities for students to share their ideas and writing before producing a finished draft.

The fable, of course, is one form that most people never write outside school. But the instruction involved in helping students write effective fables is parallel to that involved in helping them learn to write effective reports, analyses, or arguments. Until curricula in composition begin to prepare students with the necessary types of knowledge, improvements in student writing will continue to come slowly and painfully. While we still have much to learn about the composing process, the writer's knowledge, and how it comes to bear on process and product, we know enough to make important changes in composition curricula now.

FOOTNOTES

1. Sharon Pianko, "A Description of the Composing Processes of College Freshman Writers," *Research in the Teaching of English* 13 (February 1979): 5-22.

2. Charles K. Stallard, "An Analysis of the Writing Behavior of Good Student Writers," *Research in the Teaching of English* 8 (Fall 1974): 206-218.

3. Janet Emig, *The Composing Processes of Twelfth Graders* (Urbana, Ill.: National Council of Teachers of English, 1971).

4. Terry Mischel, "A Case Study of a Twelfth Grade Writer," *Research in the Teaching of English* 8 (Winter 1974): 303-314.

5. Pianko, "A Description of the Composing Processes of College Freshman Writers."

6. Sondra Perl, "The Composing Processes of Unskilled College Writers," *Research in the Teaching of English* 13 (December 1979): 328.

7. Pianko, "A Description of the Composing Processes of College Freshman Writers."

8. Stallard, "An Analysis of the Writing Behavior of Good Student Writers."

9. Carl Bereiter and Marlene Scardamalia, "From Conversation to Composition: The Role of Instruction in a Developmental Process," in *Advances in Instructional Psychology*, vol. 2, ed. Robert Glaser (Hillsdale, N.J.: Lawrence Erlbaum Associates, 1982).

10. Marilyn J. Adams, "Failures to Comprehend and Levels of Processing in Reading," in *Theoretical Issues in Reading Comprehension*, ed. Rand J. Spiro, Bertram C.

Bruce, and William F. Brewer (Hillsdale, N.J.: Lawrence Erlbaum Associates, 1980), pp. 11-32.

11. Rand J. Spiro, "Constructive Processes in Prose Comprehension and Recall," in *Theoretical Issues in Reading Comprehension*, ed. Spiro, Bruce, and Brewer, pp. 241-78.

12. Ibid., 241.

13. David E. Rumelhart and Andrew Ortony, "The Representation of Knowledge in Memory," in *Schooling and the Acquisition of Knowledge*, ed. Richard C. Anderson, Rand J. Spiro, and William E. Montague (Hillsdale, N.J.: Lawrence Erlbaum Associates, 1977); David E. Rumelhart, "Schemata: The Building Blocks of Cognition," in *Theoretical Issues in Reading Comprehension*, ed. Spiro, Bruce, and Brewer, pp. 33-58.

14. Judith A. Langer, "Relation between Levels of Prior Knowledge and the Organization of Recall," in *Perspectives in Reading Research and Instruction*, ed. M. Kamil and A. J. Moe (Washington, D.C.: National Reading Conference, 1980).

15. James F. Voss, "On Learning and Learning from Text," in *Learning and Comprehension of Text*, ed. Heinz Mandl, Nancy L. Stein, and Tom Trabasso (Hillsdale, N.J.: Lawrence Erlbaum Associates, 1984), p. 201.

16. Ibid.

17. Ibid., p. 202.

18. Judith A. Langer, "The Effects of Available Information on Responses to School Writing Tasks," *Research in the Teaching of English* 18 (February 1984): 31-32.

19. Bereiter and Scardamalia, "From Conversation to Composition."

20. Valerie Anderson, Carl Bereiter, and David Smart, "Activation of Semantic Networks in Writing: Teaching Students How to Do It Themselves" (Paper presented at the annual meeting of the American Educational Research Association, Boston, 1980).

21. See, for example, Ellen W. Nold and Sarah W. Freedman, "An Analysis of Readers' Responses to Essays," *Research in the Teaching of English* 11 (Fall 1977): 164-74; and Murray F. Stewart and Cary H. Grobe, "Syntactic Maturity, Mechanics of Writing, and Teachers' Quality Ratings," *Research in the Teaching of English* 13 (October 1979): 207-215.

22. Bereiter and Scardamalia, "From Conversation to Composition."

23. Carol Sager, "Improving the Quality of Written Composition through Pupil Use of Rating Scale" (Doct. diss., Boston University, 1973).

24. George Hillocks, Jr., "The Effects of Observational Activities on Student Writing," *Research in the Teaching of English* 13 (February 1979): 23-25.

25. William J. McCleary, "Teaching Deductive Logic: A Test of the Toulmin and Aristotelian Models for Critical Thinking and College Composition" (Doct. diss., University of Texas, Austin, 1979).

26. Lynn Q. Troyka, "A Study of the Effect of Simulation-gaming on Expository Prose Competence of College Remedial English Composition Students" (Doct. diss., New York University, 1973).

27. George Hillocks, Jr., Elizabeth Kahn, and Larry Johannessen, "Teaching Defining Strategies as a Mode of Inquiry: Some Effects on Student Writing," *Research in the Teaching of English* 17 (October 1983): 275-84.

28. George Hillocks, Jr., "What Works in Teaching Composition: A Meta-analysis of Experimental Treatment Studies," *American Journal of Education* 93 (November 1984): 133-70.

29. Richard Braddock, Richard Lloyd-Jones, and Lowell Schoer, *Research in Written Composition* (Urbana, Ill.: National Council of Teachers of English, 1963).

30. Vernon A. Adams, "A Study of the Effects of Two Methods of Teaching Composition to Twelfth Graders" (Doct. diss., University of Illinois, 1971).

31. Nancy L. Stein and Christine G. Glenn, "An Analysis of Story Comprehension in Elementary School Children," in *New Directions in Discourse Processing*, ed. Roy O. Freedle (Norwood, N.J.: Ablex Publishing Corp., 1979), pp. 53-120.

32. Nancy L. Stein and Margaret Policastro, "The Concept of a Story: A Comparison between Children's and Teachers' Viewpoints," in *Learning and Comprehension of Text*, ed. Mandl, Stein, and Trabasso, p. 126.

33. Nancy L. Stein and Tom Trabasso, *What's in a Story: An Approach to Comprehension and Instruction*, Technical Report No. 200 (Champaign, Ill.: Center for the Study of Reading, University of Illinois at Urbana-Champaign, 1981).

34. John R. Hayes and Linda Flower, "Identifying the Organization of Writing Processes, in *Cognitive Processes in Writing: An Interdisciplinary Approach*, ed. Lee Gregg and Erwin Steinberg (Hillsdale, N.J.: Lawrence Erlbaum Associates, 1980), pp. 3-30; Linda Flower and John R. Hayes, "The Dynamics of Composing: Making Plans and Juggling Constraints," in *Cognitive Processes in Writing*, ed. Gregg and Steinberg, pp. 31-50.

35. Ann Matsuhashi, "Pausing and Planning: The Tempo of Written Discourse Production," *Research in the Teaching of English* 15 (May 1981): 113-34.

36. Carl Bereiter, Jonathan Fine, Sondra Gartshore, "An Exploratory Study of Microplanning in Writing" (Paper presented at the annual meeting of the American Educational Research Association, San Francisco, 1979).

37. W. B. Elley, I. N. Barham, H. Lamb, and M. Wyllie, "The Role of Grammar in a Secondary School English Curriculum," *Research in the Teaching of English* 10 (Spring 1976): 5-21.

38. Stallard, "An Analysis of the Writing Behavior of Good Student Writers."

39. Lucy M. Calkins, "Case Study of a Nine Year Old Writer," in Donald H. Graves, *A Case Study Observing the Development of Primary Children's Composing, Spelling, and Motor Behaviors during the Writing Process* (Durham, N.H.: University of New Hampshire, 1981), p. 245.

40. Ibid., p. 246.

41. Lucy M. Calkins, "Andrea Learns to Make Writing Hard," *Language Arts* 56 (1979): 575-76.

42. Calkins, "Case Study of a Nine Year Old Writer," p. 259.

43. Stein and Trabasso, *What's in a Story*, p. 15.

44. Calkins, "Case Study of a Nine Year Old Writer," p. 250.

45. Ibid., p. 259.

46. Graves, *A Case Study Observing the Development of Primary Children's Composing, Spelling, and Motor Behaviors during the Writing Process*, p. 29.

47. Frank O'Hare, *Sentence Combining: Improving Student Writing without Formal Grammar Instruction*, Research Report No. 15 (Urbana, Ill.: National Council of Teachers of English, 1973). ED 073 483.

48. Lester Faigley, "The Influence of Generative Rhetoric on the Syntactic Maturity and Writing Effectiveness of College Freshmen," *Research in the Teaching of English* 13 (October 1979): 197-206.

49. George Hillocks, Jr., *Research on Written Composition: New Directions for Teaching* (Urbana, Ill.: National Conference on Research in English, 1986).

50. Marlene Scardamalia and Carl Bereiter, "The Development of Evaluative Diagnostic, and Remedial Capabilities in Children's Composing," in *The Psychology of Written Language: A Developmental Approach*, ed. Margaret Martlew (London: John Wiley and Sons, 1983).

51. Mina P. Shaughnessy, *Errors and Expectations* (New York: Oxford University Press, 1977).

52. Sager, "Improving the Quality of Written Composition."

53. Hillocks, Kahn, and Johannessen, "Teaching Defining Strategies as a Mode of Inquiry."

54. Faigley, "The Influence of Generative Rhetoric."

55. Hillocks, "What Works in Teaching Composition."

56. Robert P. Parker, "From Sputnik to Dartmouth: Trends in the Teaching of Composition," *English Journal* 68 (September 1979): 36.

57. See, for example, Adams, "A Study of the Effects of Two Methods of Teaching Composition"; James F. Gauntlett, "Project WRITE and Its Effect on the Writing of High School Students" (Doct. diss., Northern Arizona University, 1977); Evans Alloway, Joyce Carroll, Janet Emig, Barbara King, Isabella Marcotrigiano, Jeffrey Smith, and Willa Spicer, *The New Jersey Writing Project* (New Brunswick, N.J.: Consortium Project of Rutgers University, Educational Testing Service, and Nineteen New Jersey Public School Districts, 1979). ED 178 943.

CHAPTER VI

Problems in Process Approaches: Toward a Reconceptualization of Process Instruction

ARTHUR N. APPLEBEE

The traditional approach to writing instruction in American schools has been prescriptive and product-centered. At the sentence level, instruction has emphasized correct usage and mechanics; at the text level, it has emphasized the traditional modes of discourse (narration, description, exposition, persuasion, and sometimes poetry). In this approach, instruction usually consists of analyzing classic examples of good form, learning the rules that govern those classic examples, and practicing following the rules (either in exercises of limited scope or by imitating the classic models). In turn, success in writing has been measured by the ability to incorporate those rules into one's own writing. Warriner's *English Grammar and Composition*[1] is the archetypal example of this approach to the teaching of writing, and (in its many editions) it is the most widely used composition text today.

The 1970s and 1980s, however, have seen a major change in accepted approaches to writing instruction. In direct opposition to the focus on the final written product, there has been a groundswell of support for "process approaches" to learning to write. While research has emphasized the thinking strategies underlying the processes of composing a text, exactly what process approaches mean in classrooms varies somewhat from one teacher to another. In general, they are marked by instructional activities designed to help students think through and organize their ideas before writing and to rethink and revise their initial drafts. Instructional activities typically associated with process approaches include brainstorming, journal writing, focus on the students' ideas and experiences, small-group activities, teacher/student conferences, the provision of audiences other than the teacher, emphasis on multiple drafts, postponement of attention to editing skills until the final draft, and elimination or

The research reported here was supported in part by a grant from the National Institute of Education. The views expressed do not necessarily reflect the policy or position of the funding agency.

deferment of grading. For convenience in instruction, process activities are often partitioned into stages such as prewriting, drafting, revising, and editing, usually with the caveat that the processes are recursive rather than linear, complex rather than simple.

The Research Base

The current vogue for process-oriented approaches is one of those oddities in education, a clear instance of research driving practice. Process studies are often traced to Emig's examination of the writing processes of eight high school seniors,[2] though as early as 1963 Braddock, Lloyd-Jones, and Schoer noted the need for such studies in the course of their extensive review of research in writing instruction.[3] Emig's seminal work was followed by a flood of similar studies, emphasizing the essentially heuristic, problem-solving nature of writing about new material.[4] Most studies of writing processes have been case studies of individual writers completing relatively difficult or unfamiliar tasks set by the investigator. Across the multitude of specific results, several general findings have been evident:

1. Writing involves a number of recursively operating subprocesses (for example, planning, monitoring, drafting, revising, editing) rather than a linear sequence.

2. Expert and novice writers differ in their use of those subprocesses.

3. The processes vary depending upon the nature of the task. More recent studies have suggested that the processes also vary depending on the instructional context,[5] personal history,[6] and knowledge the writer has about the topic.[7]

The first two findings have an older research history and have been the most influential. They provided a new way to think about writing in terms of what the writer does (planning, revising, and the like) instead of in terms of what the final product looks like (patterns of organization, spelling, grammar). And descriptions of the difference in the writing processes of expert and novice have offered an easy prescription for instruction: to reform the teaching of writing, teach young writers the processes observed in studies of experts. This relatively direct leap from descriptions of what writers do to prescriptions for the teaching of writing lies at the heart of process-oriented approaches. But as we shall see later, the prescription is seriously inadequate.

The Classroom Response

Arising as a radical response to an overemphasis on the final written product, process approaches in their various manifestations have become the conventional wisdom, at least among leaders in the teaching of English. The journal literature for the past decade has been dominated by suggestions on how such approaches can be best implemented, and influential programs such as the National Writing Project have helped make the works of such scholars as Emig,[8] Britton,[9] and Moffett[10] more widely known. During the early 1970s, process-oriented approaches were received enthusiastically because they focused on the child during a generally child-centered era; during the later 1970s and 1980s, they continued in favor as national attention focused on the "writing crisis" and the need for fostering "higher-order" reasoning skills. In one sense, such approaches were the only apparent avenue of reform, and reform was clearly needed.

As process-oriented writing instruction has become more widely accepted, our research and practical knowledge have also deepened to the point where it is timely to stand back and assess the weaknesses as well as the strengths of process approaches. In this chapter, I will address the success of process approaches against three criteria: (a) How widely have they been adopted? (b) When adopted, how successfully are they implemented? and (c) When implemented, do they lead to noticeable improvement in students' writing? I will evaluate process-oriented instruction against each of these criteria in turn and will find it seriously wanting on two of the three counts. Rather than a call for abandoning the work of the past decade, however, my argument will be that writing processes in general, and the nature of process-oriented instruction in particular, have been underconceptualized. In the first flush of enthusiasm, process-oriented instruction was embraced simplistically and naively; in the next wave of reform, we must carry it toward a more sophisticated maturity. If we do not, we may find our colleagues abandoning process approaches entirely in favor of the traditional emphasis on the rules of good writing. Why stress this more difficult task of reconceptualization above a return to a simpler rule-governed approach to writing instruction? I will argue that properly implemented process approaches are more effective in fostering good writing and breadth of form, and also in encouraging more reasoned and disciplined thinking about the topics themselves.

How Widespread Are Process Approaches to the Teaching of Writing?

There is no question that process approaches now dominate the professional literature on the teaching of writing, just as they do the concerns of the various authors in the present yearbook. Yet there is almost always a gap between educational theory and educational practice, and process approaches are no exception. To examine this question, as well as to develop a better understanding of the context within which process approaches are being implemented, I want to turn now to recent studies of the status of writing instruction.

For the past six years, my colleagues and I have been engaged in a series of studies of learning to write in American schools. The work began with the National Study of Writing in the Secondary School, which sought simply to describe the contexts and conditions in which writing was taught. As the study progressed, our emphasis has gradually shifted from description toward the development of more effective approaches.[11] The results of those studies provide the first step in my argument about the problems in process approaches to writing instruction.

The National Study examined writing instruction and learning to write from a number of perspectives. The study included year-long case studies of writing in all ninth- and eleventh-grade classes in individual schools; a national survey of the uses of writing in composition, literature, science, social science, foreign language, mathematics, and business education classes; analyses of the assignments suggested in the most popular textbooks in each of those subject areas; case studies of the development of writing skills in individual children during the secondary school years; and case studies of individual science and social studies teachers who were using writing in unusual and interesting ways. The results from the various substudies converged to provide a remarkably consistent portrait of students' experience in learning to write.

WHERE STUDENTS WRITE

Though we usually think of the English class as the place where students learn to write, less than half of their writing is done at the behest of the English teacher. This is an important and often neglected fact; it means that in thinking about the factors influencing what students learn about writinng, we must move beyond the English class. If the requirements and expectations of the English class are too different from what they encounter in the rest of their experience, students will quickly decide that what they learn in English is irrelevant to the rest of their writing; the good approaches we teach them will quickly be forgotten.

There is considerable evidence that this is indeed what happens. Listen to Sarah, an eleventh-grade student whose work we studied in some detail, telling us about her writing for social studies:

Normally it will be a compare essay where we're supposed to compare two periods with several different things. I don't write an introduction to these, 'cause I rarely have time. So I'll just go in and I'll show the differences in very short paragraphs. For everything, for every topic he gave us, I'll show the differences and if I have time I'll add a little conclusion at the end which will tell what I really think.

Sarah is a very good student, and the approach she describes was tailored effectively to her audience. Writing in social studies, like most of the writing students are asked to do, is used primarily as a tool to assess what students have learned about the subject. In most classrooms, writing requires recitation of what the student has learned, whether from a textbook or from the teacher's lectures. The accuracy of that recitation is what matters—in Sarah's case, her ability to "show the differences in very short paragraphs." The student's own thinking remains an afterthought, to be added at the end if there is any time remaining.

Across subjects and grades, the typical writing assignment in American schools is a page or less, first-and-final draft, completed within a day (either in class, or taken home to finish up), and serving an examining function. Personal and imaginative writing have little place in most classrooms, which focus instead on various types of informational (or expository) writing. The particular kinds of informational writing vary from one subject to another. Science classes emphasize reports (often as write-ups of observations or experiments); social studies classes assign a mixture of summary and analysis; English classes place the most emphasis on analytic writing (usually in the context of literary criticism) and give some attention to personal and imaginative writing. Even within these broad categories of writing, however, each subject has its own accepted types of argument and rules of evidence that students must learn to orchestrate appropriately as they pass through the high school. These differences can lead to tensions and misunderstandings, such as those voiced by a highly successful science teacher:

There is a certain way in which papers have to be written in order to be published and I've tried to follow with some of [my students] this particular format and try to show them how this writing is different from others. Which brings out a point which was a problem to me a few years back. I had a student who went to the state competition, and won outstanding in the state. The scientific paper was well written, he had aspiration of being in science— this is his area—and he said he wanted to go into it. He was doing excellent . . . he could use subordinate clauses. . . . I thought there was nothing wrong with the way he was writing, his grammar, and everything else as far as English was concerned. Yet he was failing his English class in ninth grade because he was not creative. This young man did not want to be creative, he wanted to be scientific. So I think students need to know that there is more than one type of writing . . . and some learn to write poems while others would just as soon write a scientific paper and do quite well at it. And we never could convince this young man to be creative, and I believe he ended up failing freshman English.

Instruction in English was running at cross purposes to instruction in science, and neither subject (nor student) benefited from the conflict.

Given tasks of the sort I have been describing, what of process-oriented approaches to instruction? We found very few of them, in English or any other subject. The typical pattern of instruction was to give an assignment, allow the students to complete it, and then to comment extensively on the students' work. Perhaps the most striking statistic to emerge from the National Study was a simple measure of the time that elapsed between the point at which instruction turned toward a writing assignment and the point at which students were expected to be at work, pens on paper. This prewriting time averaged just over three minutes and was devoted almost exclusively to the inevitable classroom routines: writing the assignment on the board (or passing out dittoed copies), explaining requirements such as length and due dates, and answering the inevitable diversionary tactics: "Can I finish my report instead?" "Can I do it in pencil?" "I forgot my paper." Rather than starting with prewriting activities to think through new topics and develop ideas, the students were expected to plunge right in. When we looked at later stages in the writing process, the pattern was similar. Few papers went beyond a first draft, and even on the first drafts 60 percent showed no revisions of any kind. Peer response groups, editing sessions, the provision of broader audiences, deferment of grading—the panoply of process activities was used in the minority of classrooms. The National Assessment of Educational Progress found a similar result in its studies, reporting that only 7 percent of the seventeen-year-olds in their large samples engaged in a full spectrum of process-oriented activities.[12]

And given the topics that students were being asked to write about, this approach to instruction was eminently sensible. When writing is being used primarily to assess previous learning, when the teacher knows more than the students about what is being written about, and when the students' own ideas and experiences have little place, the appropriate instruction is simply to make an assignment and let the students write. Extended help before writing would short-circuit the evaluation function, while emphasis on drafting and revision would be largely irrelevant to the goals in the assignment. (Recall Sarah's comments about her introductions and conclusions in her writing for social studies: she could revise them to satisfy our sense of what a "good" essay should look like, but she has already very effectively addressed the needs of her teacher-audience in her first draft.)

My comments so far have been limited to secondary school

instruction, but the information that is available from elementary school and college suggests that similar patterns prevail. Graves found few writing activities of any sort when he examined elementary school instruction;[13] the National Assessment of Educational Progress found that younger students were even less likely than seventeen-year-olds to have engaged in any sort of extensive writing process;[14] and a variety of commentators have pointed out that the concern with process in the college writing curriculum may run wide, but does not run deep.[15]

On the first criterion, then, process-oriented writing instruction is failing; there has been no widespread movement toward process-oriented assignments in American schools and colleges. More importantly, given the nature of the writing that students are asked to do, a shift toward process approaches would be inappropriate without an accompanying (and more difficult) shift in the purposes for which writing is assigned at all.

There is one false note in the argument so far, and that stems from the fact that, on the surface at least, composition and grammar textbooks are changing. Though the textbooks analyzed in the National Study showed little concern with writing processes, since about 1984 the major grammar and composition series at both elementary and secondary level have included sections with such labels as "prewriting," "revising," and "editing," and have begun to incorporate activities similar to those that have dominated the journal literature for the past decade. If these textbooks are adopted in many school districts (and at the moment some of them seem to be doing quite well), they may lead to more widespread attention to process-oriented activities, at least within English language arts classrooms. The central question will then become one of how these approaches are implemented: What happens to process activities when they are embedded in the ongoing stream of instruction?

How Effectively Are Process Approaches Implemented?

I have already noted that process approaches began as studies of individual writers, rather than as studies of instruction. It is only in the past few years that anyone has thought to ask how well these approaches transfer from laboratory to classroom. In one series of investigations, Judith Langer and I have been studying excellent teachers who use writing in interesting and effective ways in a variety of academic disciplines.[16] We planned these studies as a way to develop a series of models of effective instruction, as well as a way to provide hard evidence that the effort involved in process-oriented writing instruction was worth the payoff in terms of student learning. Our biases are clear in our rather optimistic title: "Moving toward

Excellence: Writing and Learning in the Secondary School Curriculum." We are no longer so optimistic; rather than providing models of successful process-oriented approaches to writing instruction, the series of studies points to some serious problems in current conceptualizations of writing processes.

Some of the problems have their origin in the difficulties involved in translating our knowledge of what writers do into instructional approaches that make a difference in the classroom. Our work indicates that in many excellent classrooms the various process activities have been divorced from the purposes they were meant to serve. In the original studies of individual writers, the multitude of specific techniques that writers used to aid their planning, revising, or editing were strategies or routines that they orchestrated to solve particular problems. The choice of appropriate strategies was driven by the task at hand—not by a generalized conception of the "writing process" that the writers used in all contexts. The original studies of writing processes, however, did not have to address this point; they typically asked writers to undertake relatively difficult tasks, in which considerable overt planning, as well as considerable revision, was needed. The link between the processes that emerged and the problems faced was obscured by the similarity in the problems; researcher and writer both took the need for these processes for granted.

For the novice writer, however, faced with school tasks, understanding the problem and the means available for its solution is an important aspect of what is being learned. The novice must come to recognize not only that there is a range of prewriting, revising, and editing strategies available but that a writing task can be seen as posing problems for which those strategies offer particular solutions.

Process activities are not appropriate for all writing tasks, however, and even when such activities are needed, different tasks will pose different problems and require in turn somewhat different writing processes. Some tasks require much planning and organizing before the writer can begin; some require careful editing before being shared with a critical audience; some involve sharing of familiar experiences within well-learned formats and require no further process supports at all. Indeed, the universe of writing tasks, both in and out of school, is large and diverse. Essay exams require one set of approaches, research papers another. The journalist dictating a late-breaking story over the telephone writes in one way, the short story writer in another. In part because studies of writing processes have ignored this diversity, process-oriented instruction easily degenerates into an inappropriate and lockstep formula. If instruction is not conceptualized to make the link between process and product explicit and real, the approach is easily trivialized. Rather than suggesting a range of strategies for solving problems, process instruction will become just another series of practice exercises.

An example from our case study materials will help clarify this point. Dan Phillips is a science teacher who has made special efforts to stress writing in his science classes. He is a popular workshop leader and conference speaker, known for his practical and useful suggestions on using writing to improve science instruction. Excited about the kinds of activities we saw in his classroom, we chose Phillips for one of our early case studies.[17]

Phillips's approach contains many of the components characteristic of process-oriented instruction. Students compose tentative, exploratory pieces about both their reading and their in-class activities, often in the form of journal entries or learning logs. Phillips uses these because they "can help students think through the problems they meet in science. They are free to think on paper without fear of the teacher as examiner." At other points in a unit, Phillips assigns longer writings that pull together what they have been studying. Typically, these assignments include prewriting activities to help generate relevant ideas, sharing of rough drafts for peer response, and teacher comments on work in progress. After all of that, final drafts are submitted for a grade. At the end of a unit, Phillips may assign essays or examination questions that test what students have learned— but only about topics they have had a chance to think through (and make their own) in their earlier writings.

On the face of it, Phillips's approach is a model of process-oriented uses of writing, but our studies of his classroom uncovered some unsuspected problems in implementation. The major difficulties stemmed from a tension between the student-centered goals of the process activities and the underlying definition of what counts as knowing science. Phillips introduced the process activities as a way to help students learn what he wanted them to know about science; he had a clearly defined body of knowledge in mind, represented best by the textbook content. In this situation, most of the students quickly separated the process activities from the "product" (their final essays or reports) to which the activities were supposed to be leading. Cooperative and dutiful, they made their way through the sequence of learning logs, drafts, and response groups. But for the final draft, they turned to the textbook or to the best students in the class, to be sure they got the answers right.

Given their perception of what really counted as knowing science, most of the students found the process activities a hindrance rather than a help. As Jenny, a tenth grader, noted, "It's easier to paraphrase from a book then to write from observation notes." Michelle, another of Phillips's students, complained about an essay on meiosis and mitosis:

You put the definitions of meiosis and mitosis first. He likes us to write out little notes so you have something to start with, but I don't like to do that. . . . It's easier for me just to write it. I don't like to write little words out. I just like to write the whole thing.

Phillips would argue that Jenny and Michelle are short-circuiting the learning process, taking over other people's ideas instead of developing their own. And of course he is right—it is easier for them to "write the whole thing" only because they are lifting what they say from their notes and textbooks. On the other hand, the activity he is offering is really extraneous to the task—it is textbook knowledge that will finally be rewarded, not steps in the writing process. As Terry explained, "In science you can be wrong, and most of the time I am." And given that perception, the students find ways to avoid those wrong answers.

Phillips's classroom illustrates a common conflict between the institutional forces shaping instruction and the values implicit in successful process-oriented approaches to writing. This conflict centers around such traditional issues as curriculum coverage, teaching of requisite skills, and the importance of the student's own thoughts and opinions in the educational process. Process instruction takes time, which must come at the expense of other activities; process instruction stresses the student's role as author with something of value to say, reducing the teacher's role as transmitter of information; and process instruction focuses on the skills needed in the context of particular activities, rather than as part of a separate curriculum organized around the logic of the subject matter.

Does Process-Oriented Instruction Improve Students' Writing?

The third criterion for success is in some ways most important; if we are to champion process-oriented instruction, we should expect it to make a difference in students' writing. Here, the best evidence currently available comes from Hillocks's meta-analysis of the results of experimental studies of writing instruction published between 1963 and 1982,[18] referred to in chapter five of this volume. Hillocks describes four broad approaches to writing instruction and uses them to structure his meta-analysis. These approaches are (a) a traditional, product-oriented, teacher-centered mode of instruction (the presentational mode in his terminology), (b) individualized instruction (a mixed bag of approaches varying from tutorials to programmed materials), (c) natural process (a student-centered, activity-based version of process-oriented instruction), and (d) the environmental mode (a structured process approach that often involves inquiry-based learning and group problem solving). Hillocks uses his analyses to claim that process-oriented instruction is in fact less effective than other alternatives, in particular the "environmental" approach that he has advocated in his own studies.[19] Hillocks has been direct in his criticism, arguing that his results "contradict the assumptions, policy decisions, and recommendations of publicly funded agencies such as the National Assessment of Educational Progress [stressing process-oriented writing instruction]. . . . The experts, 'conversant with the state-of-the-art research' . . . were either not 'conversant' with the research summarized in the meta-analysis or chose to ignore it."[20]

Yet while I find Hillocks's review helpful, I interpret his results quite differently. First, I think his most important finding is that the search for alternatives to the traditional, product-centered mode of teaching writing has been well-motivated: each of the alternatives considered in his meta-analysis leads to a greater gain in student writing achievement than do traditional approaches. Because of this finding, I interpret the problems sketched in earlier sections of this chapter as part of the process of developing a new instructional paradigm, rather than as part of a call for a return to older patterns of instruction. I am convinced that the movement toward process-oriented approaches to instruction has been a beneficial one, and Hillocks's results lend support to my convictions. That our first attempts to develop an alternative should be less than perfect should surprise no one, however, nor should Hillocks's results be cause for complacency—or for retreat.

Indeed, as we have seen, Hillocks interprets his findings as a condemnation of process-oriented approaches because he finds that classrooms using an environmental mode of instruction do better than those using a natural process mode. Hillocks's argument involves a semantic sleight of hand, however, that can produce a serious misinterpretation of what his data mean. The "environmental" mode that Hillocks champions is itself a version of process-oriented instruction and draws on the panoply of techniques he seems to be attacking. What differs in "environmental" instruction is that materials and problems are orchestrated by the teacher in order "to engage students with each other in *specifiable processes important to some particular aspect of writing*."[21] "Environmental" instruction is in fact a series of process-oriented activities structured to avoid at least some of the problems of implementation that I discussed in the previous section; rather than an alternative to the pedagogical trends of the past decade, it represents a natural extension of them. Indeed, "environmental" instruction in Hillocks's terminology might better be labeled "structured process" (in the seemingly obvious contrast to the "*natural* process" mode he does include).

Recast in this way, the results from Hillocks's meta-analysis reinforce those from the studies that Langer and I have been conducting: process-oriented approaches to instruction offer many advantages over the traditional, product-oriented modes of instruction that they are meant to replace; but these advantages cannot be fully realized without a more sophisticated conceptualization both of writing processes and of how to incorporate those processes into instructional programs. Hillocks's "environmental mode" of instruction represents a particular instance of how process-oriented activities can be used more successfully, but it ducks the more fundamental problem of reconceptualization; it represents one structured version of process-oriented instruction, rather than providing the principles from which a variety of successful constellations of activities could be generated.

The remainder of this chapter will provide a sketch of what the necessary reconceptualization will entail.

Reconceptualization of Process Instruction

Most instruction is based on the simple assumption that we can specify a curriculum by studying what experts do and teaching our students to do likewise. (Both product-centered and process-oriented approaches to writing instruction share this assumption; they differ primarily in their definitions of what aspect of expert behavior should be studied and of how best to organize the teaching that must follow.) I have argued so far that process-oriented approaches have been based on misconceptualizations of both parts of the assumption: they have misinterpreted what experts do and have failed to consider how processes might best be taught. I think the most critical task facing both research and practice in the teaching of writing is to develop more adequate conceptualizations of both of these aspects of writing instruction. Given this longer range agenda, what can we say about what these more adequate conceptualizations should include?

Many of the components of a more adequate view of writing processes have been sketched in earlier sections of this chapter.

1. Writing processes must be reconstrued as strategies that writers employ for particular purposes.

2. For different tasks, writers will use different strategies, and for some tasks these strategies may involve no more than the routine production of a first and final draft.

3. More extensive writing routines must be recognized as problem-solving heuristics appropriate to work-in-progress; they are unlikely to be so useful in writing about things (or in ways) the writer already knows well.

If writing processes were reconceptualized in these ways, certain

change in process / change in teaching

changes could be expected to follow in process-oriented instruction. The variety of process activities that now fills the professional literature would be recast as ways to teach students particular strategies for dealing with difficulties in their writing; progress would become a matter of broadening the repertoire as well as the range of situations in which students would recognize that particular strategies might be employed. In a given classroom, the kinds and extent of process-oriented activities would vary from task to task in response to the difficulties posed by each task. Some tasks would require extensive prewriting activities; some would involve help with drafting; some would go through a variety of revisions; some would be edited to share with others; some would emphasize competent first-and-final draft performance. Running through all of these variations would be an awareness, on the part of teachers and students alike, that there are many different kinds of writing and many different strategies for approaching each task; and both tasks and strategies would be varied in a principled way.

Reconceptualizing the nature of writing processes will carry us halfway toward a reconceptualization of process instruction; the remainder of the journey will require a reconceptualization of the nature of instruction itself.

In a recent review, Langer has argued that teachers' approaches to literacy instruction have remained remarkably stable throughout the twentieth century. As she describes it, literacy education in the United States

is structured around a relatively consistent notion of instruction, one that defines relatively clear roles for teacher and student. In this view, knowledge is conceptualized as a body of information to be transmitted from teacher to student; the role of the teacher is one of organizing that knowledge in as logical and efficient a manner as possible; and the role of the student is one of remembering what has been imparted. This view carries with it its own technology to organize the knowledge to be transmitted (textbooks and accompanying exercise material) and to monitor the success of the enterprise (through unit tests and the apparatus of standardized testing).[22]

The view that Langer is describing accords well with the teaching practices that we observed in the National Study, as well as with the implicit assumptions of the content area teachers who have been working with us in an attempt to broaden the role of writing activities in their classrooms. Such a view of literacy instruction, however, stands in immediate conflict with the needs of process-oriented approaches to the teaching of writing. In process-oriented approaches, the students' goals drive the instructional activity, the teacher stands in the role of collaborator rather than evaluator, and the outcomes are better thought of as procedural rather than declarative knowledge (that is, as knowing *how* rather than knowing *that*). Issues of curriculum coverage, of evaluation, and of the respective roles of teacher and learner, discussed earlier, evolve directly from these tensions. Put simply, process-oriented approaches may be by definition impossible to implement successfully, given traditional notions of instruction.

There are, however, alternatives. In our recent work, Langer and I have begun to describe the features necessary for successful implementation of process-oriented approaches to instruction, though we are still a long way from offering a fully developed alternative instructional model.[23] Building on studies of early language learning[24] as well as the work of the psychologist L. S. Vygotsky,[25] we have used the notion of *instructional scaffolding* as a way to describe essential aspects of instruction that are often missing in traditional approaches.

In this view, learning is a process of gradual internalization of routines and procedures available to the learner from the social and cultural context in which the learning takes place. Typically, new skills are learned by engaging collaboratively in tasks that would be too difficult for the individual to undertake alone but that can be completed successfully in interaction with parent or teacher. In this interaction, the role of the parent or teacher is to provide the necessary support, or scaffolding, to allow the child to complete the task and in the process to provide the child with an understanding of the problem and of the strategies available for its solution.

To take a very simple example, the linguist Michael Halliday has described some of the interactions between parents and child as his son Nigel learned how to tell stories. One incident occurred after a trip to the zoo, where Nigel had seen a goat trying to eat a plastic garbage can lid, which was then removed by the zookeeper:

Nigel: try eat lid
Father: What tried to eat the lid?
Nigel: try eat lid
Father: What tried to eat the lid?
Nigel: goat . . . man said no . . . goat try to eat lid . . . man said no

Then, after a further interval, while being put to bed:

Nigel: goat try eat lid . . . man said no
Mother: Why did the man say no?
Nigel: goat shouldn't eat lid . . . (shaking head) good for it
Mother: The goat shouldn't eat the lid; it's not good for it

Nigel: goat try eat lid . . . man said no . . . goat shouldn't eat lid . . . (shaking head) good for it.[26]

The simple story that Nigel is able to tell at the end of this episode became a favorite of his, repeated verbatim at frequent intervals over the next several months. The interaction between Nigel and his parents provided a powerful medium of instruction (though neither Nigel nor his parents were thinking of their conversation in those terms); through it, Nigel learned to tell this story and was able to use what he learned from this and similar interactions to tell other stories without his parents' help. The comments and questions offered by the parents provided an appropriate scaffold that enabled Nigel to complete a new and difficult task, first collaboratively and later on his own.

If we recognize the dialogue between Nigel and his parents as a powerful mode of teaching and learning, it suggests a number of features that will be essential in any reconceptualization of traditional models of instruction. Importantly, the task itself was one that Nigel claimed as his own: though the parents shaped and guided the story that resulted (and even planned the initial excursion to the zoo), Nigel wanted to tell the story and took pride of ownership in what he had done. In this context, the parents' questions and rephrasings provided the scaffolding or support that Nigel needed in order to complete the task. In talking with Nigel, the parents structured their questions around their own implicit sense of what a "good" account should contain; by answering the questions, Nigel arrived at a story that was better formed than he could have managed on his own. In the process, the questions provided him with strategies that he eventually internalized; he learned to identify *who* a story is about and *why* characters behave as they do without needing his parents' promptings. Finally, the whole episode builds on skills (dialogue and interaction) that Nigel had already mastered in order to develop a new skill (narrative monologue) for which he was ready.

When we move from the natural interactions between parents and children to formal classroom settings, the nature of the dialogue becomes of necessity more structured and premeditated. The scaffolding provided is embedded in the materials of instruction (textbooks, assignments, direct instructional activities) as well as in the more immediate interactions between teacher and student. Nevertheless, there are many continuities across these formal and informal contexts for language learning and a variety of features of Nigel's interaction with his parents that can usefully be preserved. In our studies of classrooms, Langer and I have described a number of aspects of effective instructional scaffolding.[27] Though not in themselves an alternative model of instruction, they suggest some of the features that a more comprehensive reconceptualization of teaching will require:

1. Student ownership of the learning event. The instructional task must allow students room to make their own contribution to the activity as it evolves, giving them a sense of ownership of what they are doing. In writing instruction, this means that writing activities must serve real language functions (informing, persuading, telling a story, or the like) beyond the simple desire to please the teacher.

2. Appropriateness of the instructional task. Tasks should build upon knowledge and skills the student already possesses, but should be difficult enough to allow new learning to occur. Sequence in instruction thus becomes as much a function of the psychology of the learner as of the logic of the subject matter. In Vygotsky's words, instruction should focus not so much on the ripe as on the ripening functions.[28]

3. A structured learning environment. The instructional interaction should provide a natural sequence of thought and language, thus presenting the student with useful strategies and approaches to the task. Through this structure, the student learns new skills in the process of doing the task in a context where the instruction provides the scaffolding or support necessary to make the task possible. This structure is at the heart of learning: it is the mechanism by which social knowledge is shared with young learners, enabling them to participate in their common culture and eventually to claim it as their own.

4. Shared responsibility. Tasks are solved jointly in the course of instructional interaction; the role of the teacher in this process needs to be more collaborative than evaluative. The teacher's task must be conceived as helping students toward new learning, rather than just as testing the adequacy of previous learning.

5. Transfer of control. Over time, as students internalize new procedures and routines, they should take a greater responsibility for controlling the progress of the task. Some tasks will simply be completed independently; others will evolve into dialogues in which teacher and pupil become more equal partners in the problem-solving effort. The amount of interaction may actually increase as the student becomes more competent, with the interaction shifting from simple questions or directives toward a more expert exploration of options and alternatives.

One of the most appealing features of these principles is that they provide a new way to think about familiar teaching routines, rather than demanding the wholesale abandonment of the past. *Any* teaching technique will be appropriate to the extent that it provides useful scaffolding for a particular task; and given a particular new problem facing a student, any technique chosen will be seen as only one of a variety of possible ways to address that same problem.

Given a model of instruction that incorporates these principles, a number of changes could be expected to follow in process-oriented approaches to instruction. Writing assignments would themselves be broadened to give scope for students' opinions and solutions rather than stressing material that has been presented and problems that have been solved in previous lessons. (Donald Graves[29] and others have argued that it is essential to let students choose their own topics; the point here is that such a teaching technique is *one* way to insure that students claim ownership for what they write, but there are many others.) Teachers' first and primary response to student writing would shift from evaluator of its quality or success to that of interested reader (and skilled editor), seeking to understand and clarify what the writer has to say. (Here too, a variety of popular activities, such as peer response groups, can be reinterpreted as alternative options for insuring such response.) Perhaps most importantly, teachers' attention would shift from what students know about writing toward the strategies and procedures students need to learn in order to carry out more sophisticated writing tasks. (Again, a variety of current activities can be reconstrued from this perspective: simply dividing a long assignment into parts, for example, becomes a strategy that writers can learn to use on their own when confronted with lengthy and difficult tasks.) As part of the focus on learning new strategies, the writing classroom would take on a shape and structure—a sense of purpose and direction—that process-oriented approaches have too often lacked. (Here, Hillocks's "environmental mode" of instruction reemerges, as one approach that can provide such a shape and structure—though it is only one among a variety of alternatives that can usefully be employed.)

Taken individually, these changes can be construed as simple clarifications and strengthenings of current practice. Taken together, however, these changes require a fundamental shift in what counts as learning in American schools. It would no longer be sufficient, or even particularly necessary, for students to be adept at reciting of their teachers' points of view. Instead, what would count as important would be their ability to solve new problems, to make sense on their own terms of what they have learned and to defend and elaborate upon their own ideas. Such emphases would accord well with the demands of the National Commission on Excellence in Education for the development of "skilled intelligence,"[30] and with the concerns of the National Assessment of Educational Progress with "reasoned and disciplined thought,"[31] But they do not accord well with the emphases in most classrooms, and therein lie both the promise and the danger in process-oriented approaches to the teaching of writing.

Footnotes

1. John E. Warriner, *English Grammar and Composition* (New York: Harcourt Brace Jovanovich, 1951).

2. Janet Emig, *The Composing Processes of Twelfth Graders*, Research Report No. 13 (Urbana, Ill.: National Council of Teachers of English, 1971).

3. Richard R. Braddock, Richard Lloyd-Jones, and Lowell Schoer, *Research in Written Composition* (Urbana, Ill.: National Council of Teachers of English, 1963).

4. For a review of these studies see Ann Humes, "Research on the Composing Process," *Review of Educational Research* 53 (Summer 1983): 201-16.

5. Anne Haas Dyson, "Learning to Write/Learning to Do School: Emergent Writers' Interpretations of School Literacy Tasks," *Research in the Teaching of English* 18 (October 1984): 233-64; J. D. Marshall, "Schooling and the Composing Process," in *Contexts for Learning to Write: Studies of Secondary School Instruction*, ed. Arthur Applebee (Norwood, N. J.: Ablex, 1984), pp. 103-119.

6. Susan Florio, "The Problem of Dead Letters: Social Perspectives on the Teaching of Writing," *Elementary School Journal* 80 (September 1979): 1-7; Shirley B. Heath, *Ways with Words: Language, Life, and Work in Communities and Classrooms* (New York: Cambridge University Press, 1983).

7. Judith A. Langer, "The Effects of Available Information on Responses to School Writing Tasks," *Research in the Teaching of English* 18 (February 1984): 27-44; George E. Newell, "Learning from Writing in Two Content Areas: A Case Study/ Protocol Analysis," *Research in the Teaching of English* 18 (October 1984): 265-87.

8. Emig, *The Composing Processes of Twelfth Graders.*

9. James N. Britton, *Language and Learning* (Harmondsworth, England: Allen Lane, Penguin Press, 1970).

10. James Moffett, *Teaching the Universe of Discourse* (Boston: Houghton Mifflin, 1968).

11. Arthur N. Applebee, *Writing in the Secondary School: English and the Content Areas*, Research Report No. 21 (Urbana, Ill.: National Council of Teachers of English, 1981); Applebee, "Writing and Learning in School Settings," in *What Writers Know*, ed. Martin Nystrand (New York: Academic Press, 1982); Applebee, ed., *Contexts for Learning to Write.*

12. National Assessment of Educational Progress, *Writing Achievement, 1969-1979*, Vols. I-III (Denver, Colo.: Education Commission of the States, 1980).

13. Donald Graves, *Balance the Basics: Let Them Write* (New York: Ford Foundation, 1978).

14. National Assessment of Educational Progress, *Writing Achievement, 1969-1979.*

15. See, for example, Josephine Keroes, "Anthologies of Prose Models and the Teaching of Composition" (Doct. diss., Stanford University, 1983).

16. Arthur Applebee and Judith Langer, "Moving toward Excellence: Writing and Learning in the Secondary School Curriculum," Proposal to the National Institute of Education (Stanford, Calif.: Stanford University, 1982).

17. For a fuller report on this case study, see J. D. Marshall, "Process and Product: Case Studies of Writing in Two Content Areas," in *Contexts for Learning to Write*, ed. Applebee, pp. 149-68.

18. George Hillocks, "What Works in Teaching Composition: A Meta-Analysis of Experimental Treatment Studies," *American Journal of Education* 93 (November 1984): 133-70.

19. George Hillocks, Elizabeth A. Kahn, and Larry R. Johannessen, "Teaching Defining Strategies as a Mode of Inquiry: Some Effects on Student Writing," *Research in the Teaching of English* 17 (October 1983): 275-84.

20. Hillocks, "What Works in Teaching Composition," pp. 161-62.

21. Ibid., p. 144, emphasis added.

22. Judith A. Langer, "Literacy Instruction in American Schools: Problems and Perspectives," *American Journal of Education* 93 (November 1984): 121.

23. Arthur Applebee and Judith A. Langer, "Instructional Scaffolding: Reading and Writing as Natural Language Activities," *Language Arts* 60 (February 1983): 168-75; Langer, "Literacy Instruction in American Schools," pp. 107-32; Langer and Applebee, "Language, Learning, and Interaction: A Framework for Improving the Teaching of Writing," in *Contexts for Learning to Write*, ed. Applebee, pp. 169-81.

24. See, for example, Jerome Bruner, "The Role of Dialogue in Language Acquisition," in *The Child's Conception of Language*, ed. Anne Sinclair, Robert J. Jarvella, and William J. M. Levelt (New York: Springer-Verlag, 1978); Michael K. Halliday, *Learning How to Mean* (New York: Elsevier North-Holland, 1977).

25. Lev S. Vygotsky, *Thought and Language* (Cambridge, Mass.: MIT Press, 1962); idem, *Mind in Society* (Cambridge, Mass.: Harvard University Press, 1978).

26. Halliday, *Learning How to Mean*, p. 112.

27. Applebee and Langer, "Instructional Scaffolding"; Applebee, *Contexts for Learning to Write*; Langer, "Literacy Instruction in American Schools."

28. Vygotsky, *Thought and Language*.

29. Donald Graves, *Writing: Teachers and Children at Work* (Exeter, N.H.: Heinemann, 1983).

30. National Commission on Excellence in Education, *A Nation At Risk* (Washington, D.C.: U.S. Department of Education, 1983).

31. National Assessment of Educational Progress, *Reading, Thinking, and Writing* (Denver, Colo.: Education Commission of the States, 1981).

CHAPTER VII

Evaluation and Learning

REXFORD BROWN

Most evaluations in education should never have been undertaken in the first place, are badly done when they are undertaken, and are misused or ignored when they are completed. Most people do not like to be evaluated; tests are viewed as jokes, bothers, or stomach wrenching trials, but they are seldom viewed as positive learning opportunities. This is so not only because evaluation has been separated from ordinary learning experience but because people sense various agendas at work in an evaluation. For instance, many evaluations are attempts to control someone's behavior; many satisfy political rather than educational needs or are undertaken primarily in the interests of bureaucratic "efficiency."

There are good reasons to be skeptical about the application of empiricist, positivist, objectivist, utilitarian, or behaviorist assumptions and methodologies to the social sciences in general and education in particular. People trained in the humanities are most sensitive to these. They accordingly tend to prefer evaluation models based on experience, intuition, and the belief that tacit knowledge can never be explicitly articulated.[1] (Perhaps it is more accurate to say they believe that explicit articulations of human skills so belie the complexity and richness of those skills that evaluations based upon them must always be incomplete, if not false.) Many humanists are uncomfortable with evaluations that quantify human experience or force experience into an almost mathematical rationalism. Thus, they have resisted behavioral objectives, systems analysis, standardized testing, and various evaluation procedures designed to provide information to managers. They prefer modes of evaluation that are qualitative rather than quantitative; context-rich rather than context-free; naturalistic rather than artificial; aimed at understanding specific cases rather than general "truths"; involving multiple points of view rather than a single point of view presumed to be "objective"; based on organic rather than mechanistic assumptions; and that aspire to credibility and persuasiveness rather than "certainty." Ernest House provides an excellent review of these and other distinctions among various approaches to evaluation in *Evaluating with Validity*, an excellent overview of the subject.[2]

I lean more toward the humanistic preferences as I have defined them above, although I have spent a lot of time working with evaluation models derived more from mathematics and the physical sciences. The bottom line for me is persuasiveness. Evaluations, qualitative and quantitative, are forms of argument; one uses particular forms of argument—particular kinds of evidence, beliefs, warrants, reasons, propositions, and so on—to win the assent of particular audiences. That assent will be won or lost depending upon the match between the values undergirding the evaluation and the values of the audience, as well as the ingenuity and weight of the argument.

In education, which involves people with different values, and therefore different notions about what constitues a fair or compelling evaluation, quantitative, managerially oriented models have ascended to prominence over the last half century in both research and practice. This ascendance has created great resentment among people whose models no longer have the status they once enjoyed. The prominence of quantitative models is clearly not due to any superiority they may have over others in representing specific or general truths; nor can it be due to any capacity these models may have to generate noticeable improvements in teaching, learning, or applied research.

Rather, the ascendancy of quasi-scientific, quantitative evaluation models is more probably explained by factors such as the increasing growth and bureaucratization of education, the increasing consolidation of schools and centralization of funding and power at state and federal levels, and the consequently increased "appropriateness" of econometric, statistical, and managerial tools for analyzing and evaluating such a vast public enterprise. Whatever the explanation for the present situation, many of its consequences have been destructive. Evaluators are cut off from evaluatees. We have needless animosities between professionals in different disciplines. And there is such distrust among people at different levels of the education hierarchy that few evaluations are credible to more than a handful of the people who must work collaboratively if there is to be any progress.

Evaluation problems are especially compounded when the subject being evaluated is writing. Most of the people who teach and practice writing are deeply uncomfortable with the ways in which writing is most frequently tested. They do not buy into the values undergirding standardized testing or district, state, and national assessments. They do not find the arguments employed in these evaluations sufficiently persuasive to justify the time and expense they require. They resist acting upon the results of such measures until they are coerced to do so by considerations extrinsic to the measures, such as threats to their job security.

At the same time, however, it is manifestly clear that most people who teach writing do not evaluate it with anything like the care and responsiveness suggested by the very humanistic tradition they invoke to criticize quasi-scientific testing and assessment models.[3] Many critics of testing, assessment, and evaluation evaluate their students day in and day out without thinking for a moment about what they are doing and why. If they did, they would see they are often having their cake and eating it too, invoking their humanistic values one moment and donning their positivist frocks the next. We like to teach John Stuart Mill the writer and ignore John Stuart Mill the radical empiricist.

I would like to begin, then, by looking closely at classroom evaluation. I will establish what I consider to be a productive paradigm for evaluating writing, and then I will move out from that model to models that are less educationally productive because they are serving purposes not as directly related to learning.

Editing Writing

Much of my time is spent editing manuscripts for publication, so it will not surprise you to learn that I believe professional editors can be ideal evaluators. Good editors have a sixth sense that enables them to know toward what ideal particular manuscripts are aspiring (animism intended). Their skill consists in knowing how to move a given manuscript toward its ideal form with or without the author's help (preferably with). They can do this because they have read a great deal, they know a lot about the audience for whom the manuscript is intended, they love language more than most people do, and they have mastered a craft. They attend to the *substance* of the manuscript, its *flow* or "readability," and its *force*.

When considering substance, editors are trying to determine whether the information presented is reliable according to the forms of argument and canons of evidence appropriate to the field of inquiry the writer has chosen (for example, science, history, literary criticism). Are the facts facts or opinions? Are the authorities authorities? Is the research method competent? Is the presentation balanced (if it needs to be)? Has the author presented the facts, ideas, or feelings in a fresh or insightful way? Is the paper thoughtful? Is the argument sound, the reasoning clear, the description recognizable or accurate either in a literal or analogical sense?

Many substance questions can be answered definitively. It can be shown that the facts are wrong, the logic is faulty, or the evidence is insufficient to support the conclusion. An editor can argue strongly, but perhaps not definitively, that the paper never rises above its sources or fails to convey original information or distorts facts, ideas, or feelings in ways that are disadvantageous in light of the paper's overall purpose. So, on the whole, substance is relatively easy to evaluate. Most teachers outside the field of English evaluate what few papers they require almost solely in terms of substance.

Flow, unlike substance, has something to do with one's "ear for prose," a difficult thing to describe to someone who does not have it. But it is more than a sensitivity to the aesthetic and musical aspects of language. Flow and readability are affected by the relative concreteness or abstraction of the language, the amount of jargon, the clarity of a point of view, the organization of the piece, peculiarities of syntax, passiveness or activeness, structure of argument, and so on. Voice is very important, too. A little wit, a smidgin of irony here and there, apt quotations—all can smooth or hinder flow and readability.

Many of these elements, like elements of substance, can be dealt with definitively. It can be shown that reorganization improves or removes clarity, for instance, that a different syntactical strategy removes or creates ambiguity, or that strong verbs and concrete words can make a point of view more obvious, if not more appealing. It can certainly be shown that faulty punctuation, sentence structure, and other "mechanical" problems can impede flow. Good editors attend to these things as a matter of course. Their treatment of mechanics differs from the treatment many of us saw in school, largely because editors view mechanical problems in the larger context of flow and readability, whereas teachers tend to view each mechanical problem in the context of a unit of instruction and a set of rules focused only upon that particular problem. Other aspects of flow and readability are harder to talk about. For instance, appeal or interest can strongly condition readability. Although it is hard to tell someone exactly how to make a manuscript more interesting, good editors find ways.

The force of a manuscript has to do with its impact upon an attentive reader. Editors have to look not only at the text but at themselves as readers of the text. My first reading of a manuscript is largely devoted to evaluating its force. As I read, I make little notations wherever my interest is piqued or begins to flag, wherever I have lost my way, learned something, been surprised or delighted, persuaded, or whatever. I am also thinking of my readers and guessing where they too will be engaged or turned off. Authors and editors may disagree about force, and it is difficult to resolve the disagreement unless they have worked together often and come to trust each other's judgment.

Editors evaluate substance, flow, and force simultaneously, since these factors interact and do not exist independent of one another. They do this always with one eye on the ideal form of the piece, a form they would rather show you then tell you about in the abstract. They seldom have the time to explain all their suggestions in terms of specific elements of substance, flow, or force. They relish heated but respectful arguments with authors, knowing that nine times out of ten these confrontations improve the manuscript.

Is editing a manuscript, as I have defined it, the same thing as evaluating it? I want to argue that it is an active, collaborative, and comprehensive kind of evaluation. Moreover, it illustrates the qualitative sense of objectivity that Scriven distinguishes from the quantitative sense most people associate with the term.[4] Qualitative objectivity has to do with making factual, defensible observations: either the editorial change clarifies or does not clarify the ambiguity; either the pruning cut promotes or does not promote strong branching. Most importantly, I have described engaged, rather than disengaged evaluation. The product being evaluated—perhaps even the person being evaluated—changes in the course of the evaluation. When the director works with the actor, when the dance master works with the dancer, when the woodworker stands by the apprentice at the lathe, learning and evaluation fuse. Pupil and teacher are apprentices to the work itself, which is what matters. If it does not matter, then neither should have taken up the project in the first place, and an evaluation of it has no meaning to them or to anyone else.

At its best, engaged evaluation is nonmanipulative. Although it is clear that the evaluator's knowledge, craft, and contribution are different from those of the evaluatee, they meet as equals over the work. The ideal editor says "Here is what I think will strengthen your manuscript; I have argued as strongly as I can for these judgments. Now you will have to follow through in your own way and to the best of your abilities." I speak only of the ideal editor, of course.

Ranking and Grading Papers

Another aspect of my editor's job is to decide which of several manuscripts I am going to publish. Having worked with authors in the above fashion, I may find that I have only so much room for an article, and I will have to decide which article goes and which stays. Sometimes, too, I am a judge in contests and have to pick the best essay or paper from many entries.

These kinds of evaluation are a step away from the hands-on evaluation I just described. Although they require a certain amount of engagement, they require disengagement, too, in the interest of considerations extrinsic to the paper and its ideal form. I have to move away from the concept of *this paper's ideal form* to the concept of *an* ideal form against which all papers of a certain kind are to be judged. This is the situation of the average English teacher who has assigned the same topic to thirty students (not advisable, but done all the time).

Each paper is looked at partly on its own terms, partly with reference to all the rest, and partly with respect to the ideal paper on that subject (seldom brought into consciousness for scrutiny). I suspect that one of the reasons we are not perfectly consistent in our judgments about papers is that we move about a lot within those three frames of reference. That is, if I am asked to grade the same set of thirty papers several times, I may not assign the same grade to a particular paper because the first time I read it I was thinking more about where it was relative to its own aspirations; the second time I read it, I was thinking more about how it compared to the two papers previous to it; and the third time I read it, I was thinking more about what an A, B, C, D, or F paper would look like.

You can see how this would present problems if you imagine someone making pruning cuts sometimes because the tree needs them, sometimes in order to make this tree look more like the trees around it, and sometimes in order to make the tree look like the tree depicted in a nurseryman's handbook. Although the tree is probably helped, it is never served quite so well as it is served when taken on its own terms. Nor are consistency or objectivity or fairness problems when each tree is given its due; that approach is inherently consistent, objective, and fair.

Teachers are put in a situation that is less than desirable because they have so many papers to read they cannot give each its due and because they are supposed to compare papers to one another and assign them grades, often in predetermined proportions (5 percent A, 10 percent B, 15 percent C, and so forth). These constraints force teachers away from the ideal form of engaged evaluation, force them (along with other influences) to attend to the most obvious aspects of a text, and guarantee a certain amount of inconsistency (not to be mistaken for subjectivity) and arbitrariness (where subjectivity is likely to make its move). Moreover, these constraints render the process somewhat less directly educational than it might otherwise be. It is a learning experience to work with an editor in the ideal fashion earlier described; it is not so much a learning as a social experience to receive a paper from a teacher with a few comments and a letter grade. Knowing that these exchanges have little educational value and understanding the social implications very well, most students quite sensibly throw such papers away.

These constraints are not obvious as constraints; indeed, the constraints have themselves come to be identified as the essence of classroom evaluation. Ask anyone and he will tell you that evaluation means ranking and assigning grades. But it need not mean those things at all. In fact, the ranking and assigning grades detract somewhat from our ability to do what I have described as the best kind of evaluation— evaluation that is also learning.

When teachers internalize constraints like these, behavior that might otherwise seem strange seems simply to be the way things are done. Thus, for instance, it may seem perfectly natural for teachers to tell students what to write and to assign the same topic to all students. But, when you think about it, it is strange that they do so. Can you imagine more deadly ways to spend an evening than to read thirty-five essays on the same topic, each of which was written by someone guessing what you want to hear? How can you possibly learn anything from them? And how can they possibly write papers that aspire to a personal ideal you could help them approach? It would be simpler for everyone if you just wrote the paper yourself, passed it out, and told them why you had written it that way.

Evaluation and the Grammar-Mechanics-Usage Knowledge Base

At every meeting of the National Council of Teachers of English there are several programs in which experts denounce the practice of substituting the teaching of grammar for the teaching of writing. Across the hall, someone is always denouncing writing tests that focus almost entirely on grammar. All the experts point to an immense body of research going back more than fifty years that demonstrates no clear relation between knowledge of grammar and ability to write. The more homespun experts point out that you can drive a car well without knowing auto mechanics, can ride a bicycle without knowing physics, and so on. English teachers take notes, return to their classrooms after the conference, and go on teaching grammar as they always have. The experts fume and grind their molars. "Why don't these people listen?" they ask each other. And they decide another speech or article on the subject must be needed.

The trouble is that English teachers teach and test grammar for so many practical, educational, psychological, and cultural reasons that reference to fifty years of negative research findings is insufficient reason for them to stop. Their behavior is overdetermined.

Not the least of the reasons they teach grammar is that it is easy to test. There are right and wrong answers and some time-honored curve balls; you can correct grammar tests with a key. It is much faster than reading papers, yet it definitely has *something* to do with language and with writing. Mechanics and usage can also be construed in such a way that there are mostly right and wrong answers to questions and short-answer tests can be quickly constructed and corrected. English grades and rankings can be based upon knowledge of a body of facts, definitions, laws, and principles as concrete as those in science and mathematics. This is perfectly reasonable and eminently practical in a field charged with responsibility for teaching the native tongue.

With grammar, mechanics, and usage tests as the "hard"

foundation for grades in English, it is inevitable that the English teacher would examine grammar, mechanics, and usage most closely in student writing, when such writing is required. This ties the textbook unit tests and short quizzes to the open-ended tests which student essays tend to become. Writing exercises become "field tests" to see how well students apply in a broader context the facts they have learned one at a time through drill and practice. One thinks of chemistry students learning about certain compounds and certain principles of reaction and then going to the laboratory to apply their knowledge. Writing assignments are English "labs" for many teachers. They tend to evaluate the laboratory performance not so much for itself as for what it reveals about basic knowledge brought to the laboratory.

This makes sense when one assumes that a subject area is defined primarily by its particular knowledge base. The teacher's job is then to convey that knowledge base through systematic, linear instruction of elements, relying primarily upon drill, practice, memorization, and tests that both require and reinforce drill, practice, and memorization. Goodlad's recent study of schooling confirms that this assumption and its necessary correlatives in practice define pedagogy in all subject areas.[5]

Now an observer of education over the last fifteen years might find it surprising that the "knowledge-base" pedagogy still thrives. Did that not go out in the 1970s when the great wave of "process" washed over all subject areas? Didn't science instruction change from an emphasis on *what a scientist knows* to what a scientist *does*? Didn't social studies shift from an emphasis on history to an emphasis on social inquiry? What about the new mathematics and literature as "language used imaginatively" and writing—especially writing: hasn't the "writing process" come to dominate discussion of the subject?

Well, yes and no. Yes, many theoreticians and leaders in all of the subject matter fields have talked more and more about process. (See National Assessment of Educational Progress objectives, 1968-1983, for an overview of these shifts in emphasis.) I think it has to do with some kind of broad social transformation or redefinition. But no, curriculum, pedagogy, and school organization have not changed appreciably as a consequence of these shifts toward process. That is partly why there is such a cry these days for "school reform." And one of the reasons why a pedagogy based heavily on short-answer testing of a knowledge base continues is that teachers believe (a) that they must be "professionals" and (b) that professionals are people who command an arcane knowledge base. Doctors know things the rest of us do not know; physicists know special things; all experts have their knowledge bases. As English teachers struggle to gain the status they deserve as professionals, they must stay with their bread-and-butter knowledge base, the knowledge base that makes otherwise confident people shy away from English teachers at cocktail parties. "I never did that good with grammar," stammers the corporate giant, humbled and abashed by the sudden memory of his fifth-grade English teacher. You do not give up power like that even when you are flying high; much less are you likely to when you feel besieged.

There are many more reasons why the evaluation of writing is conflated with, and often replaced by, evaluation of the grammar-mechanics-usage knowledge base. Here are some, in brief:

1. Grammar can be pretty interesting in its own right, especially to older students, and it provides a useful vocabulary with which teachers and students can talk about writing.

2. All the textbooks are full of grammar, mechanics, and usage material; the K-12 English curriculum is heavily defined in terms of this knowledge base; most commercial tests center on these things; and parents want them taught. How can a teacher resist this immense pressure and momentum?

3. Language can be powerfully erotic. Literature can be defined as language used erotically. What better way to tame the erotic energy unleashed by literature than by abstracting language, cutting it into little pieces, and never letting it bust loose?

4. Language has profound, intertwined personal and social dimensions. English teachers and testers are caught up in a social sorting system whether they know it or like it or not. Through their relations to students and their pedagogy they can help reproduce social inequities and perpetuate existing power relations. Writing teachers whose primary goal is to promote standard English at the expense of other dialects and codes, whose concern for usage and cosmetics is paramount, and who employ grammar as a means of promoting compliance and docility could be seen as important, if unwitting, agents of social repression.[6] The work of Jeannie Oakes[7] and of John Goodlad[8] in "A Study of Schooling" strongly suggests that grammar and usage pedagogy and emphasis differ greatly for students from different socioeconomic and ethnic backgrounds.

If writing teachers' behavior is influenced by personal ambivalence about language and about children from different races and backgrounds; by powerful pressure from curriculum, textbooks, and parents; by a strongly felt need for a "professional" knowledge base; by the weight of tradition and their own schooling and training; by the need to control large groups of students in small spaces (again, see Goodlad); by the logistical and economic constraints of mass education; and by the invisible but powerful shaping forces of cultural reproduction; and if all of these forces tend to encourage an emphasis upon grammar, mechanics, and usage while discouraging writing instruction and engaged evaluation—then it should come as no surprise that a speech or an article here and there about research findings will have no impact upon teachers' behavior. Their behavior under these circumstances would appear perfectly rational and "normal."

Tests from beyond the Classroom

COMMERCIAL NORM-REFERENCED TESTS

Although too many teachers focus upon the grammar-mechanics-usage knowledge base instead of upon writing, there is a sense in which they can "afford" to do so, while test makers outside the classroom cannot. For teachers at least have a great many other indicators of student progress than the results of their short-answer quizzes. Commercial tests that dwell exclusively on the knowledge base and are purported nevertheless to assess "written expression" put their publishers out on a limb; they can rightly argue that they are assessing what teachers most value, but they cannot lay claim to the rich educational context within which each teacher makes complex judgments. Accordingly, commercial tests should not be used for making judgments about particular students, and it turns out they are not.[9] Administrators do not appear to make much use of them either;[10] school boards, superintendents, the media, and the public seem to be the groups most interested in these tests. This tells us that they are not learning tools. They are *management* tools, inevitable features of our vast, multiply governed, hierarchical school system. They are a species of rationalization.

I can think of many objections to multiple-choice, norm-referenced, standardized tests that focus on the grammar-mechanics-usage knowledge base: the research upon which they rest is not compelling; they employ formats and text seen nowhere else in students' lives; the argument that performance on these tests "relates" to performance in essay situations is specious; they are often culturally biased; they focus too heavily upon lower-level cognitive skills; they do not offer serious learning opportunities; and they are too often misused and misrepresented. None of the arguments, even in its most elaborated and specific form, seems to impress the people who use them as indicators of school progress. Many people are convinced that standardized tests, though far from perfect, are good enough estimates of what is going on in the schools and school districts. The Dow-Jones average badly misrepresents the situation of specific stocks, portfolios, or companies, but it is mentioned every evening on the news. Numerous economic indicators are gross estimators open to flagrant misuse and multiple interpretations, but policymakers, the media, and numerous publics use them constantly. It is a reality of our times that social and economic indicators appear necessary, that all of them are by definition abstract, and most are technically problematic and controversial. Educators are not the only people afflicted by dissonance between the complex realities of their lives and the simplistic indicators used to judge the quality of their performance. We can complain about the dissonance and we can work ceaselessly to broaden the range and improve the quality of educational indicators;[11] but we should not be so naive as to believe we can make abstract social indicators go away as long as education remains a public responsibility and as long as someone is able to make a profit selling standardized tests.

Norm-referenced tests are sorting devices that enable us to arrange large numbers of data points on a scale; that is all they do. When schools or districts use commercial tests, they are "evaluating" only in the sense that they are ranking individuals and schools and tracking changes in these rankings. Nothing absolute can be determined about what the students know or how well the teachers teach; all one can know from these tests is that some students score higher than others, some schools' average scores are higher than others', and so forth. Granting that this is very limited information, one can nevertheless use it to ask questions the answers to which may one day positively affect the instruction a particular child receives. This is the hope that lies deep in the breast of every good policymaker. You can put aside entirely the fact that a test may be measuring the wrong things in the wrong way if the test results cause the right people to ask why the Anglo children are getting higher scores than the Hispanics or why rich schools have higher scores than poor schools or why reading scores are going up but mathematics scores are going down. Questions such as these have sparked important dialogues and have led to concrete actions, legal and otherwise, aimed at improving educational opportunities for all children. So while it may be true that commercial, standardized, norm-referenced tests do not substantially help the classroom teacher teach and evaluate writing, they may, under the best circumstances, make significant long-term contributions both to education and to social justice.

NONCOMMERCIAL TESTS AND ASSESSMENTS THAT INCLUDE ESSAYS

Tests developed by schools, districts, states, and even nations often resemble commercial standardized tests, suffer from their drawbacks, and hold the same promise to help or hurt people, depending upon the values underlying their use. I distinguish them from commercial tests because educators are usually more directly involved in their creation, they may be slightly more likely to influence teacher behavior, and they are more closely tied to the decision-making and policy processes, often because they were mandated by policymaking groups in the first place. I have written elsewhere about the potentially damaging effects of minimum competency tests,[12] as have lots of other people.[13] I have also written in praise of comprehensive, challenging statewide testing and assessment programs that provide richer data than commercial tests, more direct and useful feedback to schools, and opportunities for teachers to improve their evaluation and teaching skills.[14] Here I want to focus on one aspect of good noncommercial assessments—essay evaluation—that bears on classroom teaching and moves me back a bit closer to where I began.

Knowing that multiple choice tests cannot suffice to assess writing, finding that when essay scores are coupled with test scores the results are better estimates of performance, and noting that if tests require writing, teachers may be more likely to assign it, many districts and states have incorporated essays into their assessments. They do not evaluate them; they *score* them. But some of the things they do in scoring essays may be of interest to teachers and can be useful in the classroom.

The primary aim of scoring is to rank papers according to some unspecified sense of their quality or to various prespecified features or traits they display. Since large numbers of papers are involved, readers must move fast and must be trained to be relatively consistent in the scores they assign. The writers are anonymous and do not receive any feedback on their papers, except possibly their score and what the score suggests about the kinds of problems they might have.

Holistic scoring involves ranking papers (all on the same topic) according to an impression each paper makes as a whole.[15] Before the scoring begins, readers who are leading the scoring select from the pool the papers that represent levels of quality. If they are using an eight-point scoring system, they select, by consensus, papers representing each of eight scale points. They train readers by having them review these papers and score new papers. When readers have so internalized the standards implicit in the scale papers that they are all assigning the same score to the same papers (plus or minus 1 point), the scoring commences in earnest. As they score, readers are asking themselves "Is this paper in the top half or the bottom half, given the papers I've read? Is it in the top half of the top half?" and so on, until they zero in quickly on a score. Periodically, readers regroup and retrain to maintain consistency.

Notice two things about this kind of holistic scoring. First, quality is not articulated; you know it when you see it. It does not lie in spelling or word choice or organization or grammar; it lies in all of these things and more. Readers who concentrate on one or two features instead of the whole generally fail to fit in with the other readers and drop out of the scoring.

Second, quality is defined only in terms of the papers at hand. If all the papers are poorly written, a holistic scoring will nevertheless arrange them on a scale from best to worst. It is not an evaluation technique, it is a *scaling* technique; this is its strength and its weakness.

Most people take one of two approaches to dealing with the weakness. The first is to define quality writing before looking at the pool and then select scale papers with reference to these prespecified criteria. This is called "modified holistic scoring." The modification is made in order to be able to say something about the papers besides "some papers are better than others" and in order to promote consciousness about the nature of quality writing. However, I can not see how you can strengthen holistic scoring in this regard without weakening its integrity as a scaling instrument. For if the pool of papers is indeed lousy and you nevertheless select papers for each of your prespecified scale points, you have either established lousy ideal scale points or lied to yourself about the quality of the papers you have placed in the top categories.

The other approach people take is to describe the papers at each scale point after the scoring is over: the best papers had these characteristics, the middle papers had those characteristics, and the worst papers showed these kinds of problems. Personally, I prefer this approach because it allows you to say that the entire pool was somewhat disappointing and does not force you into disingenuous judgments. On the other hand, the first approach livens up the scoring session by forcing people to define quality writing, so it is a good training device. I guess you pay your money and make your choice.

Holistic scoring makes no sense as a classroom evaluation technique, but it can be an interesting pedagogical tool. When you give twenty-five students the opportunity to score a batch of student papers and then argue about their scores and about what makes for good writing, you get a very lively and profitable week's worth of learning.

Two other approaches to essay scoring dominate the scene in district and state assessments. Both are versions of holistic scoring in which the aim is to zero in on specific features of the papers. The first, analytic scoring, aims to provide more information about papers by having them scaled on numerous dimensions, usually including organization, spelling, ideas, mechanics, and wording. These dimensions are popular because they correspond to teachable units and because research has shown that they (plus a factor called "flavor") account for much of the variance among scorers' judgments.[16] Some of us are apparently more influenced by mechanics, some of us by flavor, some of us by ideas, and that is why we do not agree about quality.

This may seem to provide better feedback to students, but consider the nature of the feedback: "Your paper was rated high on organization, medium on ideas, and low on mechanics," for instance. Is this really helpful? It is really management information likely to be translated into curricular terms, for example, "Your teachers seem to be stimulating kids to think of good ideas, but you need to put more stress on teaching organization skills." I do not like the sound of that, mostly because these supposedly helpful categories are still very abstract and embrace a multitude of sins. Analytic scoring presents an illusion of greater specificity that often makes it more appealing to teachers. However, the greater appeal is costly, not only in terms of dollars (it takes more time to score each paper) but in terms of reliability. It turns out that it is harder to get consistent scoring of several factors than it is to get consistent scoring of a single quality factor.

It can be argued that we will never get much agreement about the quality of a paper as long as the criteria (for example, those used in analytic scoring) are extrinsic to the writer's intentions. In making this argument, Hirsch recommends an Aristotelian rather than a Platonic approach to evaluation: judge a paper according to its implicit intentions, its particular *telos*, and you will get more agreement about its success in fulfilling its mission.[17] This is what people try to do in another version of holistic scoring called primary trait scoring.

The primary trait of an essay is the *telos*, the major intention behind the communication. If my task is to write a sick friend in the hospital to cheer him up, you can tell whether I succeeded or not by pretending to be the sick friend and asking yourself if my letter would cheer you up. If it would, then my letter is a success regardless of other criteria by which it might be judged. If it would not—if it elaborated upon the fatal possibilities of the disease, for instance—it could not be judged a success, however beautifully it might be composed.

The trick lies in being able to specify the rhetorical intention implicit in a given writing task and in being able to imagine a number of ways in which it might be realized or fail in its attempt. This is not easy. I have friends, for instance, to whom I might write a letter detailing the fatal possibilities of their disease, who would find my dark humor more amusing than solicitous or sentimental letters they might receive from more tactful friends. In designing criteria for successful letters, then, we would have to somehow take that into account, and agreement about how to do that would not be automatic.

Primary trait scoring thus involves a lot of hard thinking about rhetorical situations and some judgment calls about what is, in fact, *the* most important demand of the writing task. Then it involves trying out the task on a number of students to see if, in fact, they grasp the imperative and respond to it in the predicted ways. Tryouts usually require adjustments in the scoring criteria. If all goes well, you can train readers to use the criteria quite consistently. When the scoring is over, you can report not only that some students wrote better papers than others but also in what specific ways the better papers were superior, relative to the task. If the assignment was to write a job application letter, for instance, you can report that x percent wrote letters containing all the appropriate information in a manner likely to make a positive impression; y percent wrote letters that were well enough written but left out key facts; and z percent wrote letters that both made a bad impression and left out key information. You can present the task, the specific criteria for each level of quality, and sample papers along with the percentages.

What you get with primary trait scoring, then, is a lot of information about a single aspect of writing. Pure holistic scoring gives you little information, but it is about *all* aspects of writing. Analytic scoring, modified holistic scoring, and secondary and tertiary trait scoring all represent attempts to have one's cake (rank papers reliably) and eat it, too (say something about the characteristics of good and bad papers).

In the world of essay scoring, it seems we can make reliable judgments about a tacitly understood concept of quality or about a single atom of quality, but things get muddy when we try to do both. This is because we are scoring, not evaluating, and scoring is necessarily reductive. As complex human productions, each one unique, essays do not reduce well or translate into errors and then into mathematics without severe loss of important information. All mass testing involves context-stripping and major information loss. Testers try to compensate for the losses by invoking statistical estimators of their consequences, by explaining the limitations of the methodology, and by developing chains of arguments (mathematical and otherwise) that link the test to "reality." But some kinds of information loss are beyond satisfactory compensation.

Teachers need not do any of those things and can still have some productive fun with these scoring ideas in the classroom. The trick is to do something too many teachers are reluctant to do because they have the same mistrust of students that administrators have of teachers, namely, that they are "subjective" and do not really know how to score, much less evaluate, anything. The trick is to turn the whole process of essay scoring over to the students.[18] Make the students create writing assignments. Have them debate the intrinsic intentions, the *telos*, the rhetorical situation. Have them develop the criteria—extrinsic and intrinsic—that would define good, bad, and indifferent essays. Have them write the essays and judge them as if they were scorers. Have them evaluate them as if they were teachers doing engaged evaluations. Ask them to recommend and debate strategies for improving the papers. Move on to a different topic calling for a different kind of discourse and repeat the process. Do it for social studies tasks, science tasks (for example, laboratory reports), book reports, note-taking, letters to the editor, poems, or song lyrics. Above all, *implicate students in evaluation*; make them responsible for setting standards and meeting them.

As you do so, evaluation begins to fuse with learning. No longer are you the high priest or priestess who guards mysteries that students do not understand or trust. You are instead one of them, engaged with them in a quest for the particulars of excellence and the excellence that beckons in each particular act of writing.

Footnotes

1. Michael Polanyi, *The Tacit Dimension* (Chicago: University of Chicago Press, 1966); idem, *Personal Knowledge: Toward a Post-Critical Philosophy* (Chicago: University of Chicago Press, 1974).

2. Ernest House, *Evaluating with Validity* (Beverly Hills: Sage Publications, 1980).

3. Rexford Brown and National Assessment of Educational Progress Staff, *Writing Achievement, 1969-1979*, vols. 1-3 (Denver, Colo.: Education Commission of the States, 1980, 1981); Arthur Applebee, *Writing in the Secondary School* (Urbana, Ill.: National Council of Teachers of English, 1981).

4. Michael Scriven, "Objectivity and Subjectivity in Educational Research," in *Philosophical Redirection of Educational Research*, ed. Lawrence G. Thomas, Seventy-first Yearbook of the National Society for the Study of Education, Part 1 (Chicago: University of Chicago Press, 1972).

5. John I. Goodlad, *A Place Called School* (New York: McGraw-Hill, 1984).

6. For views about this point, see William Labov, *Language in the Inner City* (Philadelphia: University of Pennsylvania Press, 1972) and Basil B. Bernstein, *Class, Codes, and Control* (London: Routledge and Kegan Paul, 1977). For counterviews, see Harold Rosen, "Language and Class: A Critical Look at the Theories of Basil Bernstein," *Urban Review* 7 (April 1974) pp. 97-114, and Susan H. Houston, "A Reexamination of Some Assumptions about the Language of the Disadvantaged," *Child Development* 41 (December 1970): 947-63. For a Marxian perspective, see Samuel Bowles and Herbert Gintis, *Schooling in Capitalist America* (New York: Basic Books, 1976) and Pierre Bourdieu and Jean-Claude Passeron, *Reproduction in Education, Society, and Culture*, trans. Richard Nice (Beverly Hills, Calif.: Sage Publications, 1977). For a counterperspective, see Christopher J. Hurn, *The Limits and Possibilities of Schooling* (Boston: Allyn and Bacon, 1978).

7. Jeannie Oakes, "Tracking and Inequality within Schools" (Paper delivered at the Annual Meeting of the American Educational Research Association, Boston, 1980).

8. Goodlad, *A Place Called School*.

9. David A. Goslin, *Teachers and Testing* (New York: Russell Sage Foundation, 1967); Thomas Kellaghan, George F. Madaus, and Peter W. Airasian, *The Effects of Standardized Testing* (Boston: Kluwer-Nijhoff, 1981); Leslie Salmon-Cox, "Teachers and Standardized Achievement Tests: What's Really Happening?" *Phi Delta Kappan* 62 (May 1981): 631-34.

10. Lee Sproull and David Zubrow, "Standardized Testing from the Administrative Perspective," *Phi Delta Kappan* 62 (May 1981): 628-31.

11. For example, see Rexford Brown, *Education Advisory, 1985* (Denver: Education Commission of the States, 1984).

12. Rexford Brown, "Minimal Competency Testing in the Language Arts," *English Record* 30 (December 1978): 7-11.

13. For example, see Arthur E. Wise, "A Critique of Minimal Competency Testing" (Denver: Education Commission of the States, 1977); Thomas F. Green, "Minimal Educational Standards: A Systematic Perspective" (Denver: Education Commission of the States, 1977); Barbara Miller, *Minimum Competency Testing* (Denver: Education Commission of the States, 1978).

14. Rexford Brown, "The Examiner Is Us," *English Education* 16 (December 1984): 220-25.

15. For a thorough description, see Miles Myers, *A Procedure for Writing Assessment and Holistic Scoring* (Urbana, Ill.: National Council of Teachers of English, 1980).

16. Paul Diederich, *Measuring Growth in English* (Urbana, Ill.: National Council of Teachers of English, 1961).

17. Eric Donald Hirsch, *The Philosophy of Composition* (Chicago: University of Chicago Press, 1977).

18. K. Klaus et al., *Composing Childhood Experience* (St. Louis, Mo.: CEMREL, 1979).

Part Three
A LOOK AT THE SCHOOLS

CHAPTER VIII

Learning to Write and Writing to Learn in the Elementary School

MARY ELLEN GIACOBBE

When I first began taking writing instruction seriously I would proudly announce that I did indeed teach the "writing process." And I thought process heaven was at the South Burlington High School, in Burlington, Vermont, the site of the Vermont Writing Program (VWP). As a member of the VWP staff I learned that the work I had been doing with Donald Graves in my classroom was more widespread than I had realized. And I learned the role Donald Murray played for high school and college teachers.[1] At the Atkinson Academy, a public school in Atkinson, New Hampshire, teachers involved in the writing research conducted by Graves, had somehow thought of Graves as the "grandfather" of writing process (not that he was that old). I soon realized, however, that Murray also deserved and needed a title and what was left but "godfather." (This was somewhat problematic because it was Graves who had a religious background and training.) For three summers when I went to the VWP I was fortunate to have the opportunity to work with both grandfather and godfather, as well as Paul Eschholz, Al Rosa, and other Vermont educators. Our common goal was to teach and learn about writing as a process. While the Vermont Writing Program was in session, National Writing Project sites, first begun by James Gray, were cropping up in forty-seven states across the country. At the top of the agenda for these projects were the jobs of preparing teachers to teach writing as a process and preparing teachers to teach writing in all courses across the curriculum.

When I first heard about writing across the curriculum or writing in the content area, I thought of "report writing"—science reports, social studies reports, health reports, and so on. I can recall teachers

131

thinking there was a need for better report writing and a better use of report writing in the classroom. No longer would multiple-choice or short-answer tests serve as the only measure of what students had learned; we could find out through written reports what a child had learned about a particular topic. If a student was lucky, not only was he tested, but he learned a lesson he could carry to the reports he would have to write in the later grades—the state report, the country report, and the term paper. In this kind of report writing, however, the product is often read as though its physical appearance was more important than what a student had to say. Students turn in neat reports with transparent, plastic covers and wait for the grade. With a stack of reports, each usually at least ten pages in length (let's see now, twenty-six students, 260 pages), teachers wonder why the papers are copied, ramble on and on, and are unfocused. If we dare, we might even ask ourselves "Why are these so boring?" We grade on how well the student follows the outline we provided. If it is a report on a country, we ask students to include information on the following: location, population, agriculture, religion, industry, capital, climate, and so on. We take into consideration all the extra work they may have done. Sometimes we check the sources in their bibliography to see if they copied. (When we find out that they did, we point this out to the students and somehow feel we have taught the essence of report writing. "You can not copy another's words.")

I can remember this kind of writing and how I, as an elementary student, would fatten up my reports: a fancy cover made out of 1/8" plywood, a title page, a table of contents (with large lettering easier for the teacher's eyes but really used so it would take up two to three pages). I would make fancy first letters for each paragraph or section to take up more space. I would include lots of illustrations, graphs, charts, maps (all copied directly from the encyclopedia—what did I know about the rainfall in Argentina?). I would add lots of magazine and newspaper articles. If the report was about Argentina, I searched through newspapers and spotted all the headings of articles with the words "South America," and clipped them out to be included in the report. I never read these articles because this was the last-minute final step before I went to bed to make sure I got the "A."

As far as I was concerned, more was always better. Please note, I don't remember what I wrote, or more accurately, copied from encyclopedias. And if you asked me now about some of the topics of my reports, my mind is blank. But who would expect me to remember something that happened twenty-five years ago?

However, my memory is jarred as I recall only eight years ago my son announcing one Sunday evening at 7:30 (8:00 is bedtime) that he is writing a report and asking if I have any information about "The

Heart." I begin in my helpful-mother, best-advice-as-a-teacher role, and think about what possible resources are at home and what I might be able to find in school the next day. I remind him that his Uncle Frank had a special heart operation as a child and he might want to interview him. And there is always . . . But John interrupts with, "But mom, my report's due tomorrow." And he must do a project to go along with it and he wants to know if I just happen to have any large pieces of poster board handy. So begins my struggle as a parent with report writing:

It's his problem. He should have started sooner.

But the poor kid; it's due tomorrow and he's in a bind so I better help him.

But I wrote all my fifth-grade reports, and I said I'd never do another one.

It's 9:30 and getting late. I better help.

No, he's going to learn a lesson. He'll never let it go until the last minute again.

It's 10:30 and he'll probably fall asleep in class tomorrow and his teachers will think I'm not a good mother.

Well, it's really not his fault. The teacher should have helped him more.

But if I don't help him he'll get a poor grade and this is the year on which middle school placement is based and he won't get into honors classes and how will I feel if he's just "basic" especially since I am a teacher and live in this school district?

And the debate continues: to help or not to help? And helping by doing it for him wins because that is all we have time for.

I remember report writing for me as a child and as a parent, but what about for me as a teacher? For years, as a kindergarten and first-grade teacher I did not consider report writing. The children in my classes were writing about things they knew about (although many times their writing helped them to discover even more about their topics). They were struggling with drawings, invented spellings, spacing, directionality, handwriting, and making sure it said just what they wanted it to say.

But then one day Jessica came to school and announced to us that she was now writing reports. She said, "It's easy to do. I watched my sister Jennifer (who was doing the fifth-grade report on a country because last year she had done the fourth-grade report on a state) and this is what you do. First you copy stuff from a book. Jen was using the book and it was taking her a long time so I just thought about what I knew and wrote that. Anyway, I don't like to copy. And then you draw some pictures and maps. I'm going to do a cover for it this morning. Wanna hear it?"

Jessica stood proudly in front of her six-year old classmates as she read her report (see figure 1).

With her sister as a model, but with no formal instruction, Jessica was able to write her first report. We sigh and say "Oh, no." We laugh because of the truth we see in this parody of the research paper. If you talk to teachers of children in the upper grades, they are still receiving reports that show no real evidence that the students have learned anything. Instead, reports are frequently copied from encyclopedias and other resource materials. In this case, however, Jessica did not copy her report. She wrote it on her own, and her report serves as a clear indicator of what Jessica knows and what she does not know. I am not sure why Jessica decided to write her report in her own words and with her own ideas, but it may have something to do with the kind of writing Jessica was used to doing in her first-grade classroom.

The Writing Workshop Classroom

From the first day of school, Jessica and her twenty-three classmates were encouraged to write. Daily time was set aside not just for reading, mathematics, social studies, and science, but for writing as well. Our writing workshop began with a mini-lesson, which was an opportunity for me as their teacher to present a skill or strategy needed by this group of writers. For instance, we talked about how to choose topics and the importance of choosing something the writer knows about—if you don't know your topic, it will be difficult to write about it. We talked about what to do if you cannot spell a word. Since they were only first graders, I knew their oral language skills in almost all cases were much more developed than their written language skills. If they were to write using their rich oral language as a source for writing, they would have to be given permission to use invented spelling. They were encouraged to say words slowly and to listen for sounds and to write the letters for the sounds they heard. Occasionally a mini-lesson would be a brief explanation of a new sound and the letter or letters representing that sound. We talked about how to add information to pieces of writing. (Early on it was obvious that while children could understand that they left important information out of their writing, they could not see how to add it without messing up the page. These children needed to see the ways in which writers add—squeeze it in, write it in where there is blank space and draw arrows, staple on another piece of paper, and so forth.)

Along with learning strategies writers might use and specific writing skills, we talked about how they could help each other with their writing by being a good listener (an audience) and trying to

In Inda Thea
wor dots on Thar
heds. Tha
A LOT had
of
wors Beekos
Tha did noT like
The Pilgroms.
The indeins wor
The
wich doTS To Tall
BoLagd faMaLee Tha.
The To. how in
1979 Thar arno mor
wors.

In India they
wore dots on their
heads. They had
a lot of
wars because
they did not like
the Pilgrims.
The Indians wore
the dots to tell
which family they
belonged to. Now in
the 1979 there are
no more wars.

The Taj Mahal

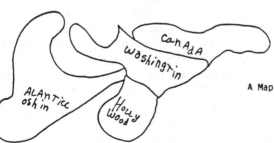

A Map

Figure 1. Jessica's Report

understand the writer's intentions. In some ways this proved to be most difficult, because the responses were often attempts to correct rather than to understand the writer's story. "You should have _____" and "Why don't you _____?" were common responses at the beginning of the year. As time passed, the quality of what they asked of each other changed. This change came about as a result of the predictable writing conferences I was having with the children after the mini-lesson. As they wrote, I circulated around the room stopping to confer with individual writers or a small group of writers. My main goal was to try to understand what the writer was trying to write and to see if the actual text written matched those intentions. I usually began by asking, "How's it going?" This was my attempt to find out what was on the writer's agenda. Throughout I was also a curious listener, trying to help the writers see that they in fact usually knew more about their topics than what was on their pages. What they wanted to write and how they were going to write it was the focus of conferences. My job as their teacher was to try to understand and not to be the evaluator who judged their writing as either right or wrong.

Toward the end of the writing workshop we came together as a group to share—a time to read and celebrate completed texts (as well as texts in progress). Jessica and her classmates saw themselves as writers—as authors of texts that were eventually published in hardcovers and cataloged to become a part of the class library. They saw themselves as children who had stories worth telling and that writing was one way for them to express those stories. They could work toward crafting a piece and eventually it would say what they wanted it to say.

Writing for my first graders had not always been like this. The change occurred when researchers Donald Graves, Lucy Calkins, and Susan Sowers began a two-year study, funded by the National Institute of Education, to observe the composing processes of six-to-nine-year olds.[2] They did not present workshops to the teachers about the best ways to teach writing. Instead, they watched what the children did as they wrote. Their interest in these children as writers served as a model, as well as an invitation for teachers to join in that research. Daily we talked about, and tried to make sense of, what children did as writers. During meetings we posed questions for ourselves, based upon our observations of our students, which forced us to think about our teaching practices.

It was not long after Jessica presented her report on India to the class that a fourth-grade teacher, Carolyn Currier, came to one such meeting, wondering how she could help her students with report writing. She had been looking at reports written during a unit on New Hampshire and realized that the outline she presented to former students did not fit in with writing process. She wondered how she could help students write reports that were as interesting as their personal writing.

As a way of answering this question, Mrs. Currier and researcher Lucy Calkins analyzed what made the students' personal writing possible. One key finding was that in personal writing students know their topics. They know what happened with their grandfather died, or when they had a flat tire on the way to the airport, or when their best friend moved away, or when they had a surprise birthday party. If students were going to write with authority and in their own words, one requirement was that students would have to know something about their topics. So Currier and Calkins proceeded to think of ways to help children learn information about topics—to help them become experts.

Report Writing: A Better Way

Mrs. Currier began by sending a letter to parents to inform them of her plan for helping their children write the fourth-grade report (in this case, on New Hampshire). To tap possible resources in the community, the children wrote to parents and friends asking for help. One way to get children beyond the encyclopedia is to help them see that there are many ways—interviewing being one—to acquire new information on topics that interest them.

Mrs. Currier ran her class as a workshop on report writing. Mini-lessons were presented on how to choose and focus topics. (For the sake of illustration, I will follow a single student, Pam, and describe how she wrote her report.) Pam's topic started as "the geography of New Hampshire," but she soon realized that was too broad. She narrowed it to the "White Mountains," and finally focused even further by choosing "The Old Man of the Mountains." She then began to list the things she wanted to know about her topic. She wrote these as questions—one question on the top of each piece of paper. As she did her research—reading, interviewing, looking at filmstrips, and so forth—she looked for answers to her questions. With her teacher's guidance she began reading in the library. Her instructions were: "Read until you are filled up. Then start writing notes without looking at the book." Pam's responses show her attempt to gather and record information and write it in her own words (see figure 2).

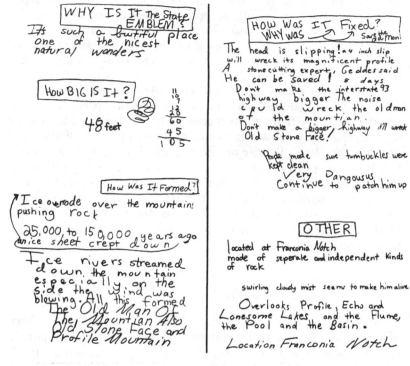

Figure 2. Pam's Notes

Students kept folders to house their research data. They had a page for a bibliography:

and a page for new words they learned as they did their research:

My Vocabulary List

As you come across words you don't
know write them down.
Look them up in the dictionary and
write the meaning.

Turnbuckles (A catch) consisting of a flat
bar that drops into a slot.

am'fa·thē'a·tor
Amphitheaters: Anything resembling this, as a
hollow surrounded by sloping hills.

Protrude: To push out or thrust forth

Leeward: In the direction toward which the
wind is blowing.

Dissect To study

Epoxy: An epoxy resin was used to fill
in cracks preventing frost pry danger.

While they were gathering data, the children were encouraged to have conferences with their classmates. Pam taught her friends about the "Old Man of the Mountains." When they asked questions, Pam did more research to answer them. She became the class expert on the "Old Man of the Mountains," and reached the point where she could talk freely and in her own language about her research.

When Mrs. Currier felt that the children had something to say about their subjects, she asked them to clear everything from their desks and try a first draft of their report. By this point in their research, the children had made their topics their own, and the drafts did not sound like replicas of encyclopedic writing. You could hear a child's voice in what they wrote. Pam's first draft shows she does indeed know something about the "Old Man of the Mountains." She begins with the dangers facing Old Stone Face and then goes on to a description of the mountain. She comments on the dangers again, and based upon what she has learned (and the fact that she is not yet driving), she has her own opinion of what should be done to save the monument. She then tells us how it was formed, its history, and why it is now in trouble. She concludes by informing the reader of the mountain's location, and she makes a sales pitch for tourists to visit it. This first draft might be considered Pam's discovery draft. As she writes, she tries to include all she knows about her topic. She addresses nine key points.

Pam's First Draft

pg. 1

Pamela Carter

Draft 1 The OLD Man OF The Mountaint Report

Whats more important a bigger and better highway or a buitiful mountian? especially one with a famous face on it, old stone face N.H. emblem. Thats a descicion trying to made. The N.H. Highway officials say Interstate 93 just isnt good enough. But what will happen if they make the highway bigger and better? The ansewer is simple. First You must know what Profile Mountain is. Its a rocky mountain with some-thing very special on top. A face Allastone face. Old Stone Face is one of his names. the others are The Old Man Of the Mountains and Profile Mountain. Its so magnificent its N.H. emblem. Now something very terrible is happening. The head is slipping! A 4 inch slip will destroy its features! Well People are trying to save him. But the

pg. 2

noise of making a highway certainly wont help! If you ask me I want the Old Man to stay The way it is. Besides I dont know and care that much about highways and I dont drive yet anyways. I suppose you wonder how a wondeful thing like this was made. I'll tell you. 25,000 to 150,000 years ago an ice sheet crept down. Ice overrode the mountians Ice rivers flowed down the mountians espesially on the side the wind was blowing. All this formed Old Stone Face. The Indians called Franconia Notch (thats where Old Stone Face is located) their temple. The early settlers discovered it in the early 1800s. But The Old Man is slipping.

B3

People are trying to fix it. Mr. Geddes was the first to go up Profile Mountian and try to fix it. It was fixed with turnbuckles a flat bar that drops into a slot. Now its becoming fixed but the desicion about the highway isnt made. Bautiful Profile Mountian is right above Echo Lake. Because of that its called The Old Mans washbowl. Also at Franconia Notch theres Profile Lake, Lonesome Lakes the Pool and Cannon Mountain. Theres a magizine called New Hampshire Profiles. Can you guess whos profile they mean. If you want to know why The Old Man was chosen for N.H.'s emblem the answers simple it one of the nicest Natural wonders of N.H. If you ever go to Franconia Notch you'll know what I mean.

As Pam experiments with how to best report her research, she tries several leads (a strategy she used in her personal writing):

Pamela
LEADS

① Mom, who carved the face?

② An ice sheet crept down over the mountain. An ice river flowed down on the side the wind was blowing. This slow moving glacier formed a face, a stone face.

③ As we were driving through Franconia Notch I looked up on the right side. Someone was spying on us.

④ It's slipping! It's slipping!

When she gets near to the end of drafting, she brainstorms a list of titles:

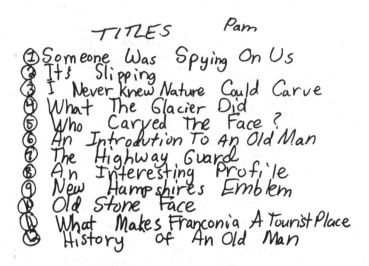

TITLES   Pam

① Someone Was Spying On Us
② It's Slipping
③ I Never knew Nature Could Carve
④ What The Glacier Did
⑤ Who Carved The Face?
⑥ An Introdution To An Old Man
⑦ The Highway Guard
⑧ An Interesting Profile
⑨ New Hampshires Emblem
⑩ Old Stone Face
⑪ What Makes Franconia A Tourist Place
⑫ History of An Old Man

Pam and her classmates were given time to practice these and other strategies they used as writers during their writing workshop time. Pam also conferred with classmates and when they asked specific questions about how the mountain was formed she did more research and rewrote her report to address what her audience wanted to know. After considering many of the leads she had written, Pam began her second draft with the story of when she first met the "Old Man." In telling her story, she presents her readers with many of the specifics about her topic—driving through Franconia Notch; the side of the mountain resembling a face, "Old Man of the Mountain"; nature being responsible; and even that it is a "48-foot stone profile." In her attempt to find the best way to present her information, she changes the organization in her second draft. As she focuses on her topic, her main goal is to show how the mountain was formed, the dangers facing it (both because of nature and man), and she concludes once again with a sales pitch.

Pam's paper took form when she decided what was important to report and what she should omit. Her classmates and teacher helped her to make these decisions by being curious listeners, trying to learn about her topic. Their questions helped her to see how her information was being interpreted. However, the decision of what she would do about it was up to her. In her second draft, she has decided what she wants her report to be about and how she can embed bits of information into her narrative. This contrasts with the usual report that begins: "My report is on the Old Man of the Mountains. It is located in Franconia Notch in New Hampshire. It is a profile that looks like a man's profile. It is 48 feet long. It is made of stone." Pam's second draft is written in a way that allows her to tell her story, while at the same time presenting information to her readers. More importantly, she has connected the information she has learned to a personal experience, which helps her extend her prior knowledge while giving her a new understanding of what she already knew.

PAM'S SECOND DRAFT

Pamela   March 5   REPORT   Page 1
Carter   2nd   History Of An Old
         draft   Man.

Someone was spying on us when we're driving
through Franconia Notch. Now don't get alarmed, it was only a stone face.
It looked just like it was spying.
     Then mom said, "look, at the
Old Man Of The Mountains, Pam."
"I dont see any old man, mom but
look at that rocky mountain up
top it looks kind of like a face
in fact it looks exactly like a face."
"That's the Old Man of the Mountains."
Mom explained. "Oh, well who carved it?"
"Nature," said mom.
Its hard to believe nature could
do such a nice job in carving.
     Ever since I found out the big
48 feet stone profile was made by
nature I wanted to know how it
was made by nature and how nature
could do such a perfect job.
I found out that it was done
by a glacier and this is what the
glacier did:
     25,000 to 150,000 years ago

Page 2

an ice sheet crept down the mountain
very, very slowly. Ice overode the mountains
pushing rock. Ice rivers flawed down the
mountain especially on the side the
wind was blowing. All this formed Old Stone
Face on Profile Mountain. I think that's
amazing. Its even complete with an Adams
Apple. (A lump at the throat.)
But something rather upsetting is happening
to the "Stone Face." Its slipping.
People are trying to fix it with
turnbuckles, a special tool. They are
also trying to fix it with a
membrane of wire coated with
a chemical called epoxy wich
would will keep out frost pry
danger. But, its also in danger
of vandalism. Its a pain
in the neck for the men
who fix it to have to do it over again.
The vandals aren't the only
ones who don't care much. The
N.H. highway officials say

page 3

the highway that goes through
Franconia Notch isn't good enough.
The noise of making a better highway
just might make the Old Man
shake a bit. I'm against the highway.
I hope the Old Man stays.
What would it New Hampshire be
without an emblem? Old Stone
Face is N.H.'s emblem.
The Old Man Of The
Mountain is very scenic.
If you ever go to
Franconia Notch you'll know
what I mean.

Throughout the report writing workshops, the students conferred regularly with Mrs. Currier and their classmates. Because these students were given time and direction as to how to go about researching and gathering data on a new topic, they did indeed become experts on their topics. I am sure Pam will remember what she learned about New Hampshire. She learned about Old Stone Face and Franconia Notch, but that is not all. She conferred daily with the other students in her class. She asked questions, read works in progress and the collection of final reports. She may have become the class expert on Stone Face, but she learned about all twenty-four topics being researched in that classroom. And, of course, she learned something about writing.

In August, during the summer after Pam's fourth-grade year, I contacted Pam and asked her if I could have some samples of her writing to share with teachers. She was most apologetic that she could not find her final draft of the "Old Man" report. As I was leaving, she asked if I might like to read a poem she wrote a couple weeks earlier. She presented me with a book of poems she had started at home when she was in first grade. "Old Stone Face" was her most recent entry:

Old Stone Face
(Old man of the mountains,
Franconia Notch, New Hampshire)

What makes Franconia Notch
    a tourist place?
A face. A stone face.
A face of boulders
And who were the molders?
Just nature.
It's a hard task for nature to do,
    but it's true.
When glaciers flowed through
    and the wind blew and blew
Thus carving Old Stone Face.

Though he's not made of gem,
It was chosen for New Hampshire's
    emblem.
I can guess why, can't you?

Pam Carter, 4th grade
Atkinson, NH

The Similarities in Writing to Learn and Learning to Write

So far, we have looked at what is commonly meant by learning to write in a particular genre (personal writing and report writing) by studying a student writing to learn about a particular topic. Although the curriculum has traditionally stressed the differences in the two (putting personal writing in one class and report writing in another), it is helpful for parents and educators to look at the similarities.

In a study for the Ford Foundation in the mid-1970s, Graves found that the problem in our schools was not that the children wrote poorly but that they seldom wrote at all. On the average, students wrote one day in ten and most of the writing was done in the context of language arts requirements. Little writing was done in other curricular areas. When they were assigned a report, students were most often assigned topics they knew little about, and it was expected that they would do it right the first time—with no time for experimenting, considering options, taking risks, and eventually being responsible for their own writing. When students finished their reports, the only audience was the teacher, and the teacher read the reports as though they were tests, looking only to see if they followed the given outline and if the words were spelled correctly.[3]

In writing to learn and learning to write, students are given the opportunity to practice their craft daily. For example, time was planned in the school day for Jessica and Pam to participate in writing workshops. Time alone does not necessarily make a difference for writers, however. What students do with the time and who is determining what they do with the time are important considerations. In learning to write and writing to learn, writers are encouraged and expected to make choices about what they do. Jessica and her classmates were responsible for choosing what they would write about. Although Pam's assignment was to write about New Hampshire, she was expected to choose something about the assigned topic that she wanted to know more about. She was guided with questions posed by the teacher and her classmates. She was also given the opportunity to pose her own questions. In such a classroom, students are encouraged to begin with what they know (both skills and information) and then to explore the unknown through writing. The writer is expected to take control of and responsibility for what she is learning. Students work toward greater understanding of the meanings of their own texts as well as subject areas.

Response is also essential for writers. Writers need the opportunity to articulate their intentions, and then to know if those intentions are indeed being understood by others. In learning to write, Jessica and Pam had opportunities to try their writing out on several audiences— their classmates, the teacher, themselves, and any other interested listener. These different audiences help the writer to know what is being understood by others; then the writer has time to consider and act on what those responses mean to her as a writer trying to produce a text and learning about a subject.

My sense is that learning to write and writing to learn are both going on at the same time in classrooms where teachers are focusing on writers who are also learners.[4] Learners need time, choice, and response. I do not think teachers need to choose between learning to write or writing to learn. A productive classroom in any subject should provide opportunities for the student to wonder, to pose questions, to pursue possible answers, to discuss with others, to come to some conclusions—all in writing and all in an attempt to come to a greater understanding of what they are trying to learn. The research done by Graves and Calkins and Sowers, and by teachers experimenting with writing workshops in their classes, indicates, as our study of Pam has, that writing can be the vehicle for learning—for learning about writing and for learning about particular topics in content areas.

FOOTNOTES

1. Donald Murray, *Write to Learn* (New York: Holt, Rinehart and Winston, 1984); idem, *A Writer Teaches Writing*, 2d ed. (Boston: Houghton Mifflin Co., 1985).

2. Lucy Calkins, *Lessons from a Child* (Exeter, N.H.: Heinemann Educational Books, 1983); Donald H. Graves, *Writing: Teachers and Children at Work* (Exeter, N.H.: Heinemann Educational Books, 1983).

3. Donald H. Graves, *Balance the Basics: Let Them Write* (New York: Ford Foundation, 1978).

4. Jane Hansen et al., editors, *Breaking Ground: Teachers Relate Reading and Writing in the Elementary School* (Exeter, N.H.: Heinemann Educational Books, 1985); Thomas Newkirk and Nancie Atwell, eds., *Understanding Writing: Ways of Observing, Learning, and Teaching* (Chelmsford, Mass.: Northeast Regional Exchange, 1982).

CHAPTER IX

The Teaching of Writing in Secondary Schools

MILES MYERS

The present reform movement in education has, among other things, outlined a new set of goals for the secondary schools by requiring skills in problem solving and interpretation, and by going beyond the traditional goal of literal comprehension with its emphasis on reading short pieces and answering machine-scored questions. In this new definition of literacy, writing refers to composing whole pieces, not just writing letters or one's name. These new goals for schools require that students know how to construct meaning in their own writing and know how to use writing and other devices as strategies for learning and discovery. As a result, most of the reform reports—from Boyer to Goodlad and to *A Nation At Risk*[1]—have called for more writing lessons taught for more minutes each day. But more of the same may not be enough.

There is ample evidence that something is awry in the content of many secondary writing courses and that simply more courses for more minutes is not an adequate public policy. Studies of the teaching of writing in secondary schools, for example, report that writing is most frequently taught in short lessons requiring students to demonstrate that they know the skills of spelling, grammar, punctuation, or some other matter of language form but not requiring them to write much beyond a phrase or sentence. On the other hand, studies of how students attain the new literacy all agree that they learn to write and think by composing pieces longer than a sentence or paragraph.[2] In this chapter, I will describe three program changes which seem necessary if secondary writing courses are to begin to provide the instruction necessary for the new standards of literacy. First, I will describe three teaching approaches that successful writing teachers use, approaches which appear to be validated by research findings and which take secondary writing instruction beyond words, phrases, and sentences, and beyond the narrow tradition of "assign it, correct it, return it." Next I will argue that the secondary writing program should be based on a different view of literacy, one in which there is an across-the-curriculum emphasis on sign systems as tools for literacy and which should be embedded, at least in some courses, in the cultural life of the surrounding community. Finally, I will comment on the relationships between curriculum content and school policies in such matters as testing, personnel evaluation, and classroom interruptions.

Three Approaches to Teaching Writing

In the best classrooms, teachers recognize that writing, like other kinds of problem solving, begins first as external social interaction and later becomes internalized mental interaction. This process of internalizing writing strategies used in collaboration with others has three zones of development: (a) actual development (what students can do alone, without the help of others); (b) potential development (what students can do with the help of others, either in collaboration with adults or more capable peers, working either in pairs or in groups); and (c) proximal development (what students can do with help now and then, that area of development between actual and potential development)[3].

In addition, in the best classrooms, the approach that is used to teach writing is the result of negotiations in which the teacher and the students jointly construct a definition of the assigned language task and the procedures to carry out that task. The evidence is clear, from both research and practice, that effective learners help construct the conditions of their own learning. In these negotiations, three approaches, often designed for students at different levels of writing ability, have been particularly useful for teachers. They are *modeling*, *processing*, and *distancing*.

MODELING

The modeling approach assumes that the learner's internal "language acquisition device" is triggered, possibly by a developmental clock; imprints on whatever models of language the learner encounters in the environment at that time; digs into the deep structure of the mind for the grammar of the language and a sense of form; and begins to develop internal models of text that young writers use for shaping their own stories and statements and for comprehending the stories and statements of others. Texts become ways to chunk experience into meaningful units, and intertextuality—the similarities and differences among texts—becomes the primary method for comparing experiences and comprehending the meaning of others. Two assumptions are essential here. The first is that students do not come to learning situations empty-headed. If nothing else, they come with some innate desire to imitate and some innate sense of basic form, either grammatical, textual, or both. The second is that school texts are not neutral, transparent views of reality. School texts are a cultural symbol system standing between the learner and the experience, shaping and mediating experience.

The modeling approach has two versions, one emphasizing whole texts and the writer at some beginning stage and the other emphasizing sentences and the writer at a more advanced stage. In the first, the teacher introduces models for writing through reading. Commenting on the teaching of college students, Ong states: "There is no way to write unless you read, and read a lot."[4] With respect to the teaching of elementary students, Smith states: "To learn to write we must read like writers. This need not interfere with comprehension; in fact, it will promote comprehension because it is based upon prediction."[5]

In this version of the modeling approach, then, student writers are surrounded by reading materials, from newspapers to literary works. Literature is presented not just as something to read but as something to imitate. This approach requires that the literature planned for a given class present forms that students can imitate—such things as parables, eye-witness accounts, argumentative essays, lyric poems, fables, letters, jokes, and so forth. In the past, many secondary English classes attempted to teach students to write essays by showing students every form of writing except the essay. The assumption was that students needed things to write about—poems, plays, and novels could provide that content—but that students did not need essay models to imitate. The modeling approach challenges that tradition.

The modeling approach has also challenged some of the most entrenched traditions of writing readiness. The assumption has been that beginning language learners, whether learning a first language or a second, should do extensive talking and reading *before* attempting to write. But Chomsky argues: "If the child writes first, the written word grows out of his own consciousness and belongs to him."[6] Smith has said: "School should be the place where children are initiated into the club of writers as soon as possible, with full rights and privileges even as apprentices. They will read like writers, and acquire full status in the club, if they are not denied admission at the threshold."[7] In secondary schools, the most successful remedial classes and classes in English as a second language do extensive modeling in their writing, modeling everything from menus to maps and stories. The teachers of these classes do not assume that reading must be brought up to grade level before writing begins.

In this first version of modeling, extensive reading must be accompanied by extensive discussion of that reading, extensive writing of whole pieces on topics negotiated by students and teachers, and finally publication and posting of student writing. Publication and posting does not refer to the reproduction and posting of just the award winner or the single piece for the PTA Newsletter. It refers instead to all students making books and magazines, having a portfolio with all their work included, and seeing their work posted in the classroom and in the hallways of the school.

A critical feature of this version of modeling is that students must see many examples of both professional and student writing. Rosch and others have shown us that it is the example or prototype that best defines our categories, not a list of features.[8] We know what a cup is by an overall model that we carry in our heads, not by a list of features such as a handle, a flat bottom, a round opening. We also define our categories of writing with prototypes, not a list of features, as holistic scoring has shown time after time. In order to internalize prototypes of good writing, students need experience doing holistic scoring in class, ranking the writing of other students and discussing the reasons for their ranking. In holistic scoring, readers rank papers on a scale from 1 to 4 or 1 to 6, using example or prototype papers to define or anchor each point on the scale. The anchor papers are selected by the readers in consensus voting. In this way, students develop an understanding of the community standards for good writing. Teachers can support students worried about their ranking by allowing them to use pen names and by giving encouragement to students with low scores.

The second version of the modeling approach gives more attention to sentence features and less emphasis to holistic impressions. Like the first version of modeling, however, it emphasizes the importance of the model or overall example, always examining features in the context of actual sentences. In lessons from this version of modeling, students imitate Christensen sentences and paragraphs,[9] using subject matter either from personal experience or from photographs assigned as a source for all students. Personal experience topics have the advantage of giving students sources that they have already partly interpreted, and photographs have the advantage of giving several students a common topic about which they can share different interpretations. Christensen structures emphasize additions as one feature of sentences: the types of additions (verbs, nouns, and adjectives) and the sequence of additions (coordinate, subordinate, and mixed). This model of the sentence provides a useful micro-model for larger units of discourse, particularly paragraphs. Gray and Benson, among others, have shown how to make the transition from sentences to paragraphs and at the same time have added a number of necessary refinements to make Christensen lessons work. These refinements include class discussion, collaboration among students, trial and error in groups, reading aloud, and the use of student models of Christensen sentences.[10]

Another approach to sentence modeling is simply the imitation of interesting sentences without any particular focus on the formalities of structure. In this approach, the sentence must make some structural demand that deviates from what students usually write. Proverbs, epigrams, and tombstone inscriptions are often very successful models, challenging the students to try new forms. The following examples show what student imitations of literary models can produce:

From Edgar Allan Poe: It was in the blue room where stood the prince, with a group of pale courtiers by his side. At first, as he spoke, there was a slight rushing movement of this group in the direction of the intruder. . .

Imitation: It was in the locker room where Al Davis stood with his coaching staff at his side. As he prepared to speak, there was a loud hushing noise which arose from the group. . .

From Joan Didion: To be married in Las Vegas, Clark County, Nevada, a bride must swear that she is eighteen or has parental permission, and a bridegroom that he is twenty-one or has parental permission. Someone must put up five dollars for the license.

Imitation: To backpack in the High Sierra, a person must obtain a wilderness permit and he or she must file a schedule of travel. Someone must contact the ranger.

The key to good lessons in sentence imitation is to read aloud both originals and imitations, thereby instructing the ear; to be prepared for failure the first time when students keep asking what to do; and finally, after students know what to do, to be prepared to make radical shifts in style from one lesson to another, thereby teaching style through contrasting imitations.

Yet another type of sentence imitation is that proposed by Strong and others.[11] In Strong's approach, the students are given the kernels of a sentence—a complicated sentence reduced to several simple sentences—and asked to combine the simple sentences into one sentence. Students work together in groups of two or three and then share their results, showing one another the variations of syntax possible with a given set of sentences. The lesson can be made more difficult by removing certain options (Do not connect any sentences with "and") and by asking students to connect several combined sentences into a paragraph, adding transitions where necessary.

Another approach to sentence modeling is that of Ponsot and Deen, in which the student is given a form for a seed sentence such as "Once I was _____; now I am _____" or "They say _____ but my experience tells me _____". The student is asked to write the sentence and then expand it into a longer piece.[12] These seed sentences are accompanied by literary readings showing these forms at work. What Ponsot and Dean accomplish is an interesting transition between the two versions of modeling, from sentence structure to the structure of whole pieces, keeping literary models at the center of the student's attention.

Beginning or basic writers have considerable success with Strong's sentences but often have great difficulty with Christensen's. The problems for these writers begin when modeling assignments begin to specify too many features. A general model can be helpful, but the assignment of several specific features can either decrease the basic student's motivation, which is often based on the student's sense of ownership of the writing, or interfere with the student's focus on overall plot and purposes, the several features of the assignment overwhelming the student's information-processing capacity. In addition to Strong's exercises, students who are still developing their fluency are also likely to have success with either the first version of the modeling approach or the *processing* approach.

PROCESSING

The processing approach makes some assumptions about how students process information and skills when they write, assuming, for example, that the limits on memory prevent students from handling more than a few unlearned and unchunked units at once; that developmental stages, partially innate and usually sequential, shape the capabilities of students, sometimes limiting students to particular strategies in the writing process; and that talk is the sea on which all other language uses and ways of knowing float.[13] This approach in the classroom focuses extensively on the structure of the writing process, particularly the importance of talk as a preliminary to writing for both professional and beginning writers and the use of learning logs and journals to monitor the generation of ideas and to get things down without having to think about correctness or even public purposes.

Because "writers can and do start anywhere—with a word, an idea, a vision, an intuition, or an argument" and because a large part of writing is the effort of trying to put into one mode (words) the images, sounds, and movement from another mode (visual, sound/ musical, kinesthetic),[14] teachers who use processing approaches introduce writing assignments in a variety of ways. They may begin with language associations connecting ideas and personal memories or with visual mapping of an idea or with a physical action and pantomime. In a physical action starter, for instance, students might be asked first to pretend to be an object (a phonograph, for example) and then to describe the object, using the details that came to mind while doing the action.

The key elements in the processing approach are the classroom journal in which the student writes, draws, or doodles regularly about writing subjects; the writing groups for discussion of drafts and papers; the learning logs, reflecting on what is being learned in class about how to write; and a sharp distinction between finished and unfinished pieces, those ready for posting and those abandoned or still evolving. The emphasis in the class is on the writing process, not on the number of finished pieces.

This emphasis presents serious problems for secondary teachers who have 150 students each day and who must be able to present a grading and evaluation record for each student. Teachers must recognize that they cannot read every piece of writing at every phase of the process. On the other hand, they must find some ways of monitoring the writing process and the student's development. Several approaches to the problem are possible, in addition to changing the school's method of evaluation. First, each student should have a portfolio in which all writing is stored, including drafts, sketches, whatever. Each finished product should have attached to it all of the relevant pre-writing, each item dated and entered on a portfolio calendar showing the work for a given day. On each draft except the first, important changes from the last draft should be circled. This information enables the teacher to make a rough estimate about the frequency and influence of pre-writing.

Second, in addition to regular journals, at the end of each week students should complete a learning log describing what has been learned during the week and identifying the evolution of pieces of writing, including interesting misunderstandings or revelations. These logs can become a major source of topics for class discussions of the writing process. In these discussions, students describe their writing processes, not their writing topics, and the sharing of these processes gives students some sense of how different writers solve processing problems. Some students seem genuinely surprised that other students not only have writer's block, for example, but have devices for dealing with it ("I just fill the page with anything"; "I read something and write about that").

Third, in order to monitor the talk in the writing groups, teachers can require that tape recorders be stationed at each group. The tapes provide a basis for evaluating writing-group processes and for training writing groups to function. Most teachers find that secondary writing groups will not work without training. Tapes of various writing groups can be played for the whole class and discussed by students in terms of effective and ineffective exchanges. In addition, teachers should conduct some writing conferences in front of the entire class. For teachers who are just beginning to develop writing groups, Macrorie's description of helping circles, Elbow's description of the believing-doubting game, and Murray's description of writing conferences are especially helpful.[15]

Three operating procedures in writing groups and teacher conferences are paramount. First, students must always bring to the writing conference or groups a piece of writing with something new in it. They cannot come empty-handed. Second, students should read their drafts aloud. While reading aloud, students will read what they intended to say, not what they have written, providing a first level of editing, and then hear what they must clarify, providing a second level of editing. Third, responders should first identify the parts they like best and then ask the writer to suggest what changes might be made, if any, or what help the writer wants.

Processing approaches help solve some of the problems of beginning writers, particularly those who feel that models impose a threatening standard or a rigid framework, but these approaches may not provide an adequate preparation for a young writer who has developed some confidence and fluency.

DISTANCING

Distancing approaches provide another alternative, one that shifts the emphasis from cognitive processing to social distancing. In distancing approaches, all language relations are organized around a communication triangle involving a speaker or writer, audience, and subject, and the essential relations are the distancing between speaker and subject and the distancing between speaker and audience. In the distancing between writer and audience, the student writer appears to follow a developmental pattern from an egocentric self to one who can take into account the points of view of others. The learner first talks to himself (journals and diaries) and to his friends (dialogues and monologues), and second to a much more anonymous school audience or the world at large. These audience relationships have parallel subject relationships moving from the concrete to the abstract, from drama and the here-and-now to narrative and the then-and-there, and from narrative to exposition and argument.

In the classroom, distancing approaches use role playing as a means of developing a student's awareness of different points of view toward audiences (readers) and subjects. In addition, writing assignments are structured with specific situations defining the audience and subject relationships. An example of a lesson that shifts audience relationships is one in which students are asked to write a letter to a friend about a particular event and then to write a newspaper report of the same event. An example of a lesson that shifts subject relationships is one in which students are asked to write the opening of a short story from the point of view of a different character.

Distancing approaches give special attention to the problem of how to make the transition from personal experience writing to exposition. One example of this transition is an assignment in which students are asked to write a description of a friend, a description of another friend who is quite different, and then a contrast of the two friends, reorganizing the two descriptions around points of difference. Another example is the "I-Search" paper in which the student is asked to select a topic for a research paper and then to write in first person about the search for information on the topic. In the next step, the student is asked to write about the topic without including any of the details about the search for information.

The best of the available approaches to writing instruction in secondary schools makes use of all three approaches—modeling, processing, and distancing. Although primarily emphasizing distancing approaches in his theoretical work, Moffett's pedagogical work with Wagner has provided an excellent integration of all three approaches.[16] The problem in secondary writing instruction at the moment is that this instruction is not embedded in some understanding of contemporary requirements for literacy; as a result, either English classes do all of the writing instruction while other disciplines ignore writing or, as is the case in some innovative programs, other disciplines provide writing instruction while English classes ignore visual and numerical sign systems. This brings me to the second theme of this paper.

The Need for Functional Literacy

There is increasing evidence that students learn best the strategies for problem solving and thinking when writing is embedded in functional situations: "[G]rowth in language power and effectiveness derives mainly from the dynamics of using language in real situations, not from studying about language."[17] Functional or "real" situations have three principal components, each an area with specialized skill and insight: (a) a stance toward objects and events, either religious or secular, poetic or transactional; (b) a set of sign systems or modes of representation—enactive (sensory-motor), iconic (visual), and symbolic (numbers and the alphabet)—each sign system with a variation of notation from concrete to abstract (from sticks to algebra in number systems, from photographs to maps in visual systems, from walking to ballet in action systems); and (c) the three basic speech events or types of discourse on which all other sign systems float. Cultural practices and functions are created by the intersection of stance, sign systems, and discourse (see figure 1).

Functional literacy in contemporary culture often refers to the extent to which students have internalized the cultural tools to manipulate stance, sign systems, and discourse. The manipulation of

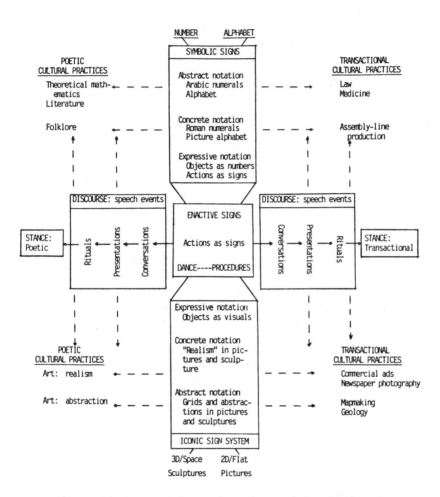

Fig. 1. Interaction of signs and discourse to produce particular cultural practices

stance refers to the ability to shift from the poetic to the transactional, from the pretend or hypothetical to the real. In the new standard of literacy, students must learn to make this shift easily, to use simulations and "what-if" scenarios to analyze and solve problems. The manipulation of sign systems refers to the ability to shift from what Bruner calls one mode of representation to another. The modes of representation are the enactive (action symbols such as gestures), the iconic (visual symbols such as pictures and maps), and the symbolic (numbers and the alphabet).[18] In the new standard of literacy, students must be able to shift easily from one sign system to another to solve problems, for example, shifting from numbers and letters to drawing and acting out to solve problems.

In addition to learning to shift from one sign system to another, students must learn something about the different kinds of notation within a sign system. Within each mode of representation or sign system, there are different kinds of notation or modes of treatment. According to Eisner, "Any form of representation can be treated in one or more of three modes: mimetic, expressive, and conventional."[19] Within a visual form of representation, for example, the expressive captures the feeling of bird's-eye view of a neighborhood, maybe brushes of color in a given direction, and the mimetic presents a picture of the neighborhood, looking down on the houses and lawns. The conventional or abstract, on the other hand, would be something like a map of the neighborhood, organized around the grid adopted by map-making institutions. Both symbolic systems (number systems, alphabet systems) and enactive systems (gestures, actions) have similar variations of notation.

Cultural activities give different priorities to different modes of representation.[20] One can know a tree through the skill of sawing it or lifting it (enactive mode, "direct" experience activity), through the skill of a drawing its overall shape (iconic, observational experience), or through the skill of listing its parts (symbolic, analytical experience). A lumber mill will give a different priority to each of these modes of representation. But the fact is that each of the ways of knowing is effective in its own right as a way of solving problems.

The ability to shift from one sign system to another and to use different modes of treatment within a sign system is part of the requirement for literacy in an age emphasizing problem solving. In fact, writing in real-life situations requires the use of numbers, drawings, and graphs to supplement words, and at many other times, words are used to supplement other media. This means that secondary schools must not only have writing-across-the-curriculum but a diversity of sign systems in English classes as well. Writing classes must give more attention to diagrams, charts, graphs, three-dimensional models, and the use of numbers to crunch data and show trends.

Finally, the new standards of literacy require that students learn to manipulate discourse. Functional literacy requires that students internalize the distinctions among different speech events, particularly conversations, presentations (lectures), and rituals (reading academic papers, presenting the oath of office, performing wedding ceremonies). These forms of discourse are used for self-regulation of behavior in all other sign systems, telling oneself in the conversational mode to do this or that, telling others in the ritual or presentational mode to do this or that. Discourse is used with enactive systems (talking one's way through changing a tire); with iconic systems (talking one's way through drawing a diagram); and with symbolic systems (talking one's way through a mathematics problem or a preliminary draft of an opening paragraph). Thus, although functional situation theory calls for attention to many different sign systems, written discourse remains the central system.

Discourse creates the style or rhetoric of engagement, determining what kinds of politics and knowledge are produced in a situation. Sometimes the style has institutional formality and logic (rituals), at other times personal formality and logic (presentations), and at other times informality and impressionistic logic (conversations). The discourse of the task shapes the student's expectation of what kinds of answers and problem-solving strategies are called for.

For example, Donaldson has shown how children in Piaget's experiments appear to be shaping their answers to fit the context suggested by the experimenter's actions and words, and when a different context is signaled, the children's answers change.[21] The children in Donaldson's report often give the wrong answer because they think the situation is social, not a test situation requiring analytical approaches. All words, both oral and written, establish their context, and this established context shapes our experience and often determines our approach to problems. According to Harste, Woodward, and Burke, even the scribble of the child is already embedded in the discourse and context of culture.[22] Can you tell in figure 2 which is Hanna's shopping list and which is her story?

In writing examinations in high school, many students who fall just below minimum competency in writing appear to misinterpret what speech event is called for. They think that a conversational event is the required underlying structure, not realizing that the presentational event is required. Sometimes teachers and researchers point to the topic as "misleading" these students, but the fact is that the students who know better are not misled. In fact, the successful students know that the conventions of the proficiency examinations

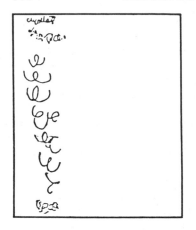 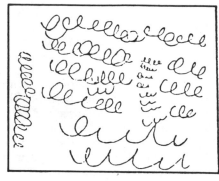

Fig. 2. Writing Samples—Shopping List and Story (Hanna, age 3)
Source: Jerome C. Harste, Virginia A. Woodward, and Carolyn L. Burke, "Examining Our Assumptions: A Transactional View of Literacy and Learning," *Research in the Teaching of English* 18 (February, 1984): 100. © 1981 by the National Council of Teachers of English. Reprinted with permission.

are signaled by more than simply the topic.[23] I suspect that these students have been able to interpret what speech event is required by attending to a number of different symbol systems and being able to translate these different systems into significant indicators for writing.

The interactions of discourse, modes of representation, and stance create the activities in which people engage. For example, the three modes or sign systems are translated into poetic and transactional forms: enactive (ballet and assembly procedures), iconic (painting and architectural plans), and symbolic (poetry and stock reports). It is the presence of these activities for fun and profit in the culture surrounding the school, activities in which students can engage as writers at some level, either in simulations or in limited contexts, that helps create the motivation for the uses of writing and other sign systems.

The creation of literacy is not simply a matter of teaching literacy in schools. Literacy must be embedded in the cultural activities surrounding the school, and teaching someone to be literate is partly a matter of involving that person in cultural activities. In this process, the student is not only learning to use new modes of representation and new mental structures but, as Luria says, is learning new motives:

[A]s the basic forms of activity change, as literacy is mastered, and a new stage of social and historical practice is reached, major shifts occur in human mental activity. These are not limited simply to an expanding of man's horizons, but involve the creation of new motives for action and radically affect the structure of cognitive processes.[24]

In summary, one form of knowledge is not equivalent to another. Each form has its own uses in problem solving and its own version of the world, and these versions of the world are embedded in cultural practices, from law to farming and industrial production. Within these practices, discourse is the sea on which all other sign systems float. Numbers, algebraic formulas, pictures, gestures, action routines—all of these signs are supplemented with and translated through discourse. Furthermore, discourse is used for self-regulation, to tell oneself to do this, do that. Through the creation of different speech events, discourse also defines the self, with presentational discourse establishing the self as an authority and with conversational discourse establishing the self as a social equal. Finally, discourse defines the apropriate logic for a given task. For example, although drawing may produce a logical answer for some questions, the testing or ritual event in language arts often eliminates drawing as an appropriate response. In the logic of some ritual speech events, drawing is equivalent to counting on your fingers—definitely a sign of illiteracy!

The new literacy requires a writing program providing opportunities for manipulating stance, sign systems, and discourse in functional situations. But how does this program differ from what now exists? First, American secondary schools too often split poetic and transactional writing into separate parts of the curriculum, with creative writing on one side and serious stuff on the other. It is clear that within writing classes there must be more opportunity for moving back and forth between the imaginary and the actual, the hypothetical and the "real."

Second, writing classes must provide more writing situations in which students manipulate other sign systems such as numbers and visuals (charts, diagrams, maps, figures). What I find odd about the present "writing-across-the-curriculum" movement among English teachers is that it appears to give English teachers a platform for telling other teachers to teach writing while the English teachers themselves ignore the sign systems of other disciplines.

Third, the notion that writing is organized around the conventions of different speech events changes much of the content of traditional writing instruction. One new assumption would be that the "rules" of composition vary from one situation or function to another. In most secondary writing courses, the clear thesis sentence, the tight conclusion, and hierarchical patterns of organization are taught as unqualified gospel for all speech events. Conversations, which serve a social function, call for close speaker-audience relations, approximations and coordinations in information, and transitory texts. On the other hand, presentations, which serve a logical function, call for distant speaker-audience relations, definite information with clear thesis sentences, hierarchical relations in information, and permanent texts.

Clear thesis sentences help produce the politics of presentational speech events in which the speaker stands as an authority. Approximations produce social equality and camaraderie among participants and turn information into social entertainment. Conversational talk is not neutral, despite the claims of those who propose teacher-student "rap groups" for all classes. In fact, there is some evidence that teacher-student conversational discussions in class contradict the values of cultures that place teachers always in the position of authority. This is a central problem for some teachers of American Indians.

Establishing a set of contrasting rules for different speech events brings to the content of writing courses in secondary schools the possibility of a critique based on varying cultural conventions. It makes the conventions of composition not so much a matter of rule as a matter of cultural interpretation. Most writing classes now teach clarity as gospel. I am advocating writing classes that debate the advantages and disadvantages of clarity from one speech event to another.

Finally, this approach to literacy suggests that secondary school students should engage in community activities in which writing is called for. One can point to a few examples: Eliot Wigginton's Foxfire work in Georgia, Fred Koury's City-as-School in New York City, and a very small effort of my own. The writing assignments in my program included the following: (a) opinion surveys designed by students, conducted in neighborhoods, with written summaries prepared by students, including charts and graphs; (b) the neighborhood profile or history for the school library, including interviews with neighborhood informants, maps, property listings, and written summary of profile; (c) preparation of an imaginary mutual fund in consultation with local broker, including a five-month report on holdings prepared for investors; and (d) a report on a jury case in the local courthouse, including observation and note taking at trial, interview of two attorneys, and diagrams of locations and events in the case. These assignments are, in part, simulations in local settings, not actual cultural tasks, but each activity required that the student go to community settings, interview people at their place of work or residence, and construct interpretations of their culture.

These individual assignments were preceded by collaborative efforts in which groups of students and even the whole class worked together on similar assignments. The opinion survey in neighborhoods, for example, was preceded by the whole class, working in pairs, conducting an opinion survey on the San Francisco-Oakland run of the mid-morning trains of the Bay Area Rapid Transit. By working in pairs, students were able to discuss and practice with each other before interviewing an informant. I will never forget that first student who, with her partner, approached a train rider who was waiting on the platform, brief case in one hand and newspaper in the other. The other students stood watching, wondering what would happen. Within a few minutes, the train rider had become an involved informant, and the two tenth graders had become opinion researchers.

Going from train to train, I observed this transformation, the students assuming an authoritative demeanor toward the adult informants and the adult informants talking among themselves about the questions and their answers. This same sense of an assignment embedded in actual cultural practices also occurred in the preparation for the courtroom assignment in which the whole class watched the first three days of a murder trial in the Superior Court of Alameda County, Oakland, California. I asked the students, based on the first day of testimony, to draw a map of the murder scene, locating all the participants and witnesses. The next morning, while waiting in the hallway for the courtroom doors to open, one of attorneys started asking the students what problems they had with the maps and which witnesses seemed most informative. Later that morning, the State presented its map of the murder scene, a map not all of the students found to be an adequate representation of the facts.

In these assignments and others like them, the students got some sense of the many uses of an authoritative position and power over language in courtroom testimony. This understanding is part of what it means to learn new motives for literacy. These students also found that in actual cultural practices sign systems are not as neatly divided as they are in school. For example, as a preliminary to the mutual fund assignment, pairs of students were given an imaginary $5,000 and asked to prepare an investment portfolio based on stock quotations from newspapers that were five and six years old. The students were given a five-year-old Standard and Poor's Index for translating abbreviations into company names, and a Wall Street guide for reading stock market returns. The whole class then went to the financial district, an invasion I had prepared for, and each pair of students met with an individual stock broker to discuss the present status of their mutual fund. In this assignment, students often had to translate from a few abbreviations to words, from a number code to visual charts, from one set of numbers to another, and from words to an actual action routine for punching in letters and getting stock quotations from computers. For these students, literacy became more than the numbers and language of school. It had to include visual signs, action routines, and special uses of numbers and words, all generated by new motives for action.

This effort to embed school writing assignments in actual cultural practices was not without its problems. One of the first problems was the bell schedule. The second problem was getting approval for students to leave the school grounds. The curriculum of the secondary school is always deeply affected by the policies that govern the organization of the school. This brings me to my third theme.

The Problem of Constraints

One major complication in curriculum change is that teachers not only introduce subject matter and help students learn; they also manage large numbers of students and implement a number of school policies not related to course content. Learning and subject matter are not the only responsibilities assigned to classroom teachers, although many teacher preparation programs and many models of teaching effectiveness seem to assume that this is the case.

One study of fourteen classrooms over one year showed that policy implementation resulted in the interruption of classes about six times each period with a combination of messages (school bulletins, student messengers from school offices, and announcements over the loud speaker in the classroom) and various other matters (attendance problems and discipline problems, for example).[25] Most of these disruptions resulted from particular school policies: discipline problems must be handled in the classroom and not sent to the office, attendance slips must be submitted every day from every class, administrators and their support personnel interrupt classes at any time to complete their work. Another set of interruptions resulted from testing policies and from the need to secure specific types of information related to special funding (surveys of school lunch needs and of speakers of English as a second language). A more general distraction is the result of policies on class size and scheduling, which give most secondary teachers in grades seven through twelve as many as 160 students each day for five days a week. Spending ten minutes per student outside class to write each student a note making suggestions for language development adds more than twenty-six hours to the already busy schedule of twenty-five hours of class time per week. In addition, teachers must complete record keeping and other administrative duties. Something must give.

To handle such problems most teachers design slot-filling and copying lessons to keep students busy and thus free the teacher for administrative duties during class time. Such lessons, which are highly structured and call for individual seatwork with no assistance from the teacher, often make little or no contribution to learning in the student's area of proximal development, but they do give the teacher some time to handle problems of discipline, tardiness, attendance, distribution of paper, and so forth. These exercises help students prepare for the battery of tests required by local and state agencies because the tests themselves require students to work without the assistance of the teacher and to fill slots so that the tests can be scored by machine. These lessons occur all too often in writing classes at all grade levels, but as long as school policies remain as they are such lessons will probably be used.

Fundamental changes in the curriculum of secondary schools cannot come about until governance policies begin to reflect what is known about teaching and learning. One policy that has a potential for distorting or harming writing instruction pertains to teacher evaluation. Let me briefly present an example of the way administrative policies can run against sound instructional practices. Many California administrators are now evaluating teachers of writing in secondary schools by using time-on-task checklists, the Stallings Observation Strategy, or some other device for measuring "direct instruction." Madeline Hunter's five-step lesson plan has become a mandated lesson form in some districts. Bloom's taxonomy of educational objectives[26] has become the recommended framework for sequences of writing assignments. These are not rare events. In fact, time-on-task and direct instruction (as concepts applied to teacher evaluation) have swept the country.

According to Rosenshine, direct instruction "refers to those activities that are directly related to making progress in reading and mathematics and to the settings that promote such activities."[27] Writing makes different demands on the classroom, however. Some of the assumptions of direct instruction seem to run contrary to the accepted procedures for writing classes, such as writing in class, reading stories to a class, and asking students questions about their personal experience in order to get early writing under way. These are valuable activities, and yet they do not immediately appear to observers as evidence of direct instruction. Rosenshine admits that "there is something grim about this picture of direct instruction: large groups, decision making by the teacher, limited choice of materials and activities by the students, orderliness, factual questions, limited exploration of ideas, drill, and high percentages of correct answers." He reports, nevertheless, that research has not shown negative side effects as a result of concentrating on direct instruction.[28] And, in fact, he has stated that "the frequency of nonacademic activities such . . . as reading stories to a group or asking questions of students about their personal experience usually is negatively related to achievement gains."[29] Similarly, in one of her studies Stallings reported that writing in class is negatively associated with gains on the Comprehensive Text of Basic Skills (CTBS).[30]

The Stallings Observation Strategy, developed by the Stallings Teaching and Learning Institute, consists of a series of instruments to be used in observing classrooms and in estimating the effectiveness of teaching. The materials are based on research findings that have associated effective classrooms with whole-class or small-group instruction, drill and practice, short quizzes and limited choices for students. Some of the features of classroom instruction that were found to be negatively associated with achievement in reading were too much time spent by students reading and writing in class, too many choices for the students, and too much time spent by the teacher working in conference with a single student.[31] These instruments have been widely used in California, in whole or in part, for evaluating teachers. In many respects, the activities recommended in the Stallings Observation Strategy are the exact opposite of those proposed by Applebee and others as the most effective forms of writing instruction.[32] It is generally accepted by composition specialists that teachers need to work individually with students on their writing, that they need to decrease the number of short-answer quizzes and increase the number of occasions for extended uses of writing, and that they need to devote much of class time to writing so that they can be available during the process to give help to students. All of these features are negatively associated with effective teaching in Stallings's research on reading instruction.

The rush to "institutionalize" an instrument like the Stallings Observation Strategy ignores a number of crucial variables. First, direct instruction may not be equally effective in all subjects. The Stallings research, for instance, used CTBS scores as the measure of effectiveness, not scores on writing samples. Second, research on direct instruction has produced what Brophy has called "'strikingly different results" for different classes.[33] And, finally, the writing class makes its own distinctive demands in classroom structure and procedures. Evertson, Anderson, and Brophy found little support for the direct instruction model in their study of seventh and eighth grade English classes, and they have suggested that the reason might be that those classes have instructional objectives more variable than those found in mathematics or basic skills classes.[34] Peterson has reported on the direct instructional model in teaching problem solving. She reports that students who receive direct instruction tend to do worse on tests of problem solving than do students who receive what she calls more "open teaching."[35] The basic problem is that instruments for evaluation of personnel and for classroom observation are often so crude that they do not allow for differences between students, between subjects, or between answering questions on a standardized test and writing an essay.

In summary, if we expect to change curriculum in writing classes, we must change those policies affecting teacher load, class schedules, and personnel and program evaluation.

Concluding Statement

Three approaches to the teaching of writing—modeling, processing, and distancing—have added to the content of secondary writing instruction a number of teaching strategies helpful for students at different levels of writing ability. But what is needed is a better understanding of contemporary definitions of functional literacy. This new definition of literacy suggests that writing is a critical instrument for learning in all subject areas, that English classes should give more attention to a diversity of sign systems, including visuals and numbers, and that students should be practicing the use of writing in community settings outside the school. Finally, there needs to be better communication between curriculum developers and policy makers and better appreciation of the impact of school policies on teaching in the classroom.

FOOTNOTES

1. Ernest Boyer, *High School* (New York: Harper and Row, 1983); John I. Goodlad, *A Place Called School* (New York: McGraw-Hill, 1984); National Commission on Excellence in Education, *A Nation At Risk: The Imperative for Educational Reform* (Washington, D.C.: U.S. Government Printing Office, 1983).

2. Arthur N. Applebee, *Writing in the Secondary School: English and the Content Areas* (Urbana, Ill.: National Council of Teachers of English, 1981); Miles Myers and Susan Thomas, *The Interaction of Teacher Roles in the Teaching of Writing in Secondary Schools* (Washington, D.C.: National Institute of Education, 1983).

3. Lev S. Vygotsky, *Mind in Society: The Development of Higher Psychological Processes* (Cambridge, Mass.: Harvard University Press, 1978), pp. 84-88.

4. Walter J. Ong, "Literacy and Orality in Our Times," in *Profession 79* (New York: Modern Language Association, 1978).

5. Frank Smith, "Reading Like a Writer," in *Composing and Comprehending*, ed. Julie M. Jensen (Urbana, Ill.: National Conference on Research in English, 1984).

6. Carol Chomsky, "Write Now, Read Later," in *Language in Early Childhood Education*, ed. Courtney B. Cazden (Washington, D.C.: National Association for the Education of Young Children, 1972), p. 125.

7. Smith, "Reading Like a Writer," p. 56.

8. Eleanor Rosch, "Cognitive Representations of Semantic Categories," *Journal of Experimental Psychology: General* 104 (September 1975): 192-233.

9. Francis Christensen, *Notes toward a New Rhetoric* (New York: Harper and Row, 1967).

10. James Gray and Robert Benson, *Sentence and Paragraph Modeling* (Berkeley, Calif.: Bay Area Writing Project, University of California, 1982).

11. William Strong, *Sentence Combining and Paragraph Building* (New York: Random House, 1981).

12. Marie Ponsot and Rosemary Deen, *Beat Not the Poor Desk* (Upper Montclair, N.J.: Boynton/Cook Publishers, 1982).

13. For research on the writing process, see Lillian Bridwell, "Revising Strategies in Twelfth Grade Students' Transactional Writing," *Research in the Teaching of English* 14 (October 1980): 197-222; Janet Emig, *The Composing Processes of Twelfth Graders*

(Urbana, Ill.: National Council of Teachers of English, 1971); Toby Fulwiler and Art Young, eds., *Language Connections: Writing and Reading across the Curriculum* (Urbana, Ill.: National Council of Teachers of English, 1982); Donald Graves, "An Examination of the Writing Processes of Seven Year Old Children," *Research in the Teaching of English* 9 (Winter 1975): 227-241; Gordon Rohman, "Prewriting: The Stage of Discovery in the Writing Process," *College Composition and Communication* 16 (May 1965): 108-10.

14. Linda Flower and John R. Hayes, "Images, Plans, and Prose: The Representation of Meaning in Writing," *Written Communication* 1 (January 1984): 156-57.

15. Ken Macrorie, *Writing to Be Read* (Rochelle Park, N.J.: Hayden, 1976); Peter Elbow, *Writing without Teachers* (New York: Oxford University Press, 1973); Donald Murray, *A Writer Teaches Writing* (Boston: Houghton Mifflin, 1968).

16. James Moffett, *Teaching the Universe of Discourse* (Boston: Houghton Mifflin, 1968); James Moffett and Betty Jane Wagner, *Student Centered Language Arts and Reading, K-13* (Boston: Houghton Mifflin, 1976).

17. Walter Loban, "The David Russell Award for Distinguished Research in the Teaching of English," *Research in the Teaching of English* 18 (February 1983): 83.

18. Jerome Bruner, "The Growth of Representational Processes in Childhood," in *Beyond the Information Given*, ed. Jeremy Anglin (New York: W. W. Norton, 1973), pp. 313-24. See especially, pp. 316-18.

19. Elliot Eisner, *Cognition and Curriculum* (New York: Longman, 1982), p. 56.

20. David Olson and Jerome Bruner, "Learning through Experience and Learning through Media," in *Media and Symbols: The Forms of Expression, Communication, and Education*, ed. David R. Olson, Seventy-third Yearbook of the National Society for the Study of Education, Part I (Chicago: University of Chicago Press), pp. 125-50.

21. Margaret Donaldson, *Children's Minds* (Glasgow: William Collins Sons, 1978).

22. Jerome C. Harste, Virginia A. Woodward, and Carolyn L. Burke, "Examining Our Assumptions: A Transactional View of Literacy and Learning," *Research in the Teaching of English* 18 (February 1984): 84-108.

23. Miles Myers, "The Speech Events Underlying Written Composition" (Doct. diss., University of California, Berkeley).

24. Alexander R. Luria, *Cognitive Development: Its Cultural and Social Foundations*, trans. Martin Lopez-Morillas and Lynn Solotaroff, ed. Michael Cole (Cambridge, Mass.: Harvard University Press, 1976), p. 161.

25. Myers and Thomas, *The Interaction of Teacher Roles in the Teaching of Writing in Secondary Schools*.

26. Benjamin S. Bloom, ed., *Taxonomy of Educational Objectives: The Classification of Educational Goals, Handbook 1: Cognitive Domain* (New York: David McKay Co., 1956).

27. Barak Rosenshine, "Content, Time, and Direct Instruction," in *Research on Teaching: Concepts, Findings, and Implications*, ed. Penelope Peterson and Herbert Walberg (Berkeley, Calif.: McCutchan Publishing Corp., 1979), p. 38.

28. Ibid., p. 47.

29. Jane Stallings, "Allocated Academic Learning Time Revisited, or Beyond Time on Task," *Educational Researcher* 9 (December 1980): 11-16.

30. Rosenshine, "Content, Time, and Direct Instruction," p. 52.

31. Materials from the Stallings Teaching and Learning Institute distributed at California State Department Workshops.

32. See Arthur N. Applebee, "Improving the Teaching of Writing," in Applebee, *Writing in the Secondary School*, pp. 99-106. See also the "Foreword" in the same volume, pp. xi-xiii, where Charles R. Cooper describes a "high school writing program certain to fail."

33. Jere Brophy, "Advances in Teacher Research," unpublished paper, nd.

34. Carolyn Evertson, Linda Anderson, and Jere Brophy, *Texas Junior High Study: Final Report of Process-Outcome Relationships*, Vol. 1 (Austin, Texas: Research and Development Center for Teacher Education, University of Texas, 1978).

35. Penelope Peterson, "Direct Instruction Reconsidered," in *Research on Teaching: Concepts, Findings, and Implications*, ed. Penelope Peterson and Herbert Walberg (Berkeley, Calif.: McCutchan Publishing Corp., 1979), p. 63.

CHAPTER X

Coming of Age in College Composition

PAUL KAMEEN

Not so long ago—as recently as 1971, when I began my graduate studies in English—college composition was little more than the dreary stepchild of what was otherwise a generally reputable family of disciplines comprising the humanities. Housed almost exclusively in departments of English, curricula in composition consisted of one or two lower-division, often required courses, the primary duties of which were to clean up the messes that students with deficits in their "skills" brought with them into the academy and/or to set the tables upon which the rest of the disciplines could serve up their more substantial portions of the academic menu.

Things have changed a great deal in the intervening fifteen years. Not everything, of course; and not, by any means, everywhere. But composition has not only acquired all of the more visible accouterment of a bona fide discipline—exclusive faculties, a wide array of advanced and elective courses, graduate areas and degrees, designated professional journals, and, in some cases, even independent departmental status; it has also accrued to itself a share of the power and prestige that inevitably accompanies the image of specialization in academic institutions. And with the more recent spread of writing-across-the-curriculum programs, composition now stands poised to insinuate itself into even the most remote appendages of the academy. This process of maturation has been fitful, uneven, often intractably complex, and it is still ongoing; like any such coming of age, it required a beneficent confluence of forces from both within and without, of both ambition and circumstance, design and coincidence. In this essay I would like to sketch some of the more prominent moments in that progress, not so much to describe the "state of the art" in composition, though that too will be part of my project, as to document the renovation of the estate in which that "art," if it can in fact be called one, is currently practiced.

Let me begin with a question I have implied in the previous sentence, a question that has contemporary application though it was formulated first toward a somewhat different purpose by Socrates, in

170

the midst of his long and testy argument with Gorgias about the purpose and status of rhetoric:

SOCRATES: Is not the position of the rhetorician and of rhetoric the same with respect to other arts also? It has no need to know the truth about things but merely to discover a technique of persuasion, so as to appear among the ignorant to have more knowledge than the expert?

GORGIAS: But is not this a great comfort, Socrates, to be able without learning any other arts but this one to prove in no way inferior to the specialists?

. . .

SOCRATES: Well, then, Gorgias, the activity as a whole, it seems to me, is not an art, but the occupation of a shrewd and enterprising spirit, and of one naturally skilled in its dealings with men, and in sum and substance I call it "flattery." Now it seems to me that there are many parts of this activity, one of which is cookery. This is considered an art, but in my judgment is no art, only a routine and a knack. And rhetoric I call another part of this general activity[1]

This highly charged critique of rhetoric, though it may seem somewhat stilted and moralistic by contemporary standards, is, I believe, more pressing, particularly in relation to the developmental structure of the discipline of composition, than it might at first seem, for it brings into focus not only the bipolar competition between value- and performance-based notions of instruction in composition (between, that is, a rhetoric whose primary injunction is, following Socrates, "know thyself" and another, whose primary injunction is, following Gorgias, "know your audience"), but it also raises the most fundamental pedagogical question: What should a rhetorician teach? Gorgias is, after all, a teacher; and Socrates is primarily concerned with what, in fact, he is teaching. This latter issue is especially apropos to composition; for composition, perhaps more than any other academic discipline, has been shaped by its long history as a teaching-intensive enterprise. Until recently, the identity of composition was constituted almost entirely by the classroom arenas in which it was "taught," and by the various competing textbooks that were the instruments of that instruction.

This helps, in part, to explain the second-class status that the academy has customarily accorded to the enterprise of teaching composition; for despite the obvious commitment to teaching as part of its mission, the university—and more recently the college and even the junior college—has defined its primary "product" not as the student it matriculates, but as the knowledge it engenders via faculty research and publication. Any discipline, therefore, whose function is primarily pedagogical will almost inevitably be relegated to a "service" role in relation to the principal business of the institution.

This is where composition resided for decades—a training ground for graduate students and part-time faculty preparing themselves for full-time positions, for junior faculty paying their dues on the way to careers as teachers (and scholars) of literature. The public discourse of the profession was almost exclusively classroom-dependent. On the most mundane level, it was a kind of "recipe-swapping" that enacted Socrates' analogy between cookery and rhetoric; on a more theoretical level, it was a chronic oscillation between value- and performance-based rationales for teaching students how to write. More recently, as composition has moved away from its service status, it has had of necessity to gear its machinery for producing knowledge not, as with literary studies, to an extant body of texts, but to the human "text" of the classroom, to students and the writing they provided. In light of this, it is easy to see how and why research in composition has been grounded until very recently not in the most immediate professional environment of traditional literary scholarship, an enterprise that can exist quite nicely (though on a much smaller scale, of course) independent of the undergraduate classroom, but in more remote, and more congenial, connections with the research apparatus of the social sciences, the primary "texts" of which are human subjects rather than historical or cultural artifacts.

One of the most significant steps along this path was the publication in 1971 of Janet Emig's *The Composing Processes of Twelfth Graders*.[2] What Emig produced was, in its own right, a notable body of controlled observations detailing, via case studies, the day-to-day business of teaching and learning writing. But more importantly, she fully appropriated a technique of inquiry from the social sciences and applied it unabridged to research in the composition classroom. The key word here is "research," a particular mode of research shaped by the methodology of the social sciences. Via this appropriation, writing teachers were enabled to produce the institutionally reputable "body of knowledge" that would be their ticket out of the servants' quarters of the academy. Thus, while the primary concerns in literary studies have always been scholarship and criticism, with the available professional roles inscribed by their mutual dependence on extant texts, composition has from the outset been constituted by its concerns with teaching and research, its available professional roles inscribed by their mutual dependence on the human subject, the student writing. This fundamental difference accounts, as I have already suggested, for much of the tension and conflict that often erupt between these two components of English studies. They have been, in fact, alien from one another in both subject and method; they have therefore had little common ground upon which intercommunication could transpire. This relationship is being renegotiated in fundamental ways these days, and I will explain more about that later; but that change did not occur before many composition programs vacated their traditional homes in departments of English and made more companionable arrangements with departments of education, psychology, speech, communications— almost anywhere that the precedents for empirical research were tenably grounded.

Emig's book was, then, instrumental in creating a disciplinary framework for research in composition, primarily by demonstrating that students' writing could be written about in recognizably "professional" ways. On a more particular level, it changed the vocabulary, and thereby the focus, of subsequent research in composition. That new vocabulary and its implications are visible in their incipient stages in her study:

Although in these linguistic studies the process of writing is sometimes purportedly under scrutiny, to this writer's knowledge none of the investigators has yet attempted to develop generalizations from their studies of specific works and authors. They have not attempted, in other words, to delineate *the*, even *a*, writing process or to ascertain whether the process has constant characteristics across writers. Rather, they have been concerned with product- rather than process-centered research.[3]

The key words here are "process" and "product," which have become so deeply entrenched in our ways of talking about the teaching of writing that they seem almost inviolable.[4] It was Emig, more than any other practitioner, who institutionalized this distinction at the center of our professional discourse. The methodological imperatives are here clearly pronounced: no longer should teachers/researchers, by way of explaining or validating their enterprise, focus on the final "products" that students generate under their tutelage (a method of inquiry that is notably and firmly grounded in the traditional practices of literary criticism) but on the manner(s) in which their writing is engendered and produced, that is, on the "composing process" (a method of inquiry that is firmly grounded in the traditional practices of "soft" scientific experimentation).

When the focus of attention shifts from *what* has been produced to *how* it has been produced, certain consequences, and certain possibilities, emerge. The teacher, for example, is suddenly dismissed (or liberated) from her customary role as the prescriptive authority on how to write, the conservator of the rules and regulations that govern the production of acceptable written discourse. And the student in the activity of composing moves to center stage, the possessor of a viable though flawed "process" which can be studied, analyzed, tinkered with—a potential experiment always in progress, available for investigation if the proper conditions can be created.

This transformation of roles led during the 1970s to a proliferation of "new" (generally performance-based) rhetorics, to a resuscitation of the concept of "invention" from classical rhetoric, to a host of heuristic procedures for facilitating composing. It also changed in fundamental ways the disciplinary understanding of the relationship between a writer and her text, situating the pedagogical locus not on the text, as was customary in the more formalistic rhetorics of the time, and not on the writer, as was customary in the many self-expressive pedagogies popular in the late 1960s and early 1970s, but on the active relationship between the two, a relationship always "in process."[5]

One can see the effects of this change of venue in even the most stalwart of composition textbooks—in, for example, James M. McCrimmon's *Writing with a Purpose*,[6] a book whose longevity has been predicated on its judicious assimilation of leading concepts in the discipline. From the fourth through the sixth editions (1967-1976) even the definition of "purpose," the governing metaphor for the textbook, underwent significant revisions, revisions that reflect the transition I have just outlined. In the fourth edition, for example, McCrimmon defines purpose as "the overall design which controls what the writer is to do in the essay."[7] The key words here are design and essay, between which the writer is sandwiched. One can see the subjugation of writerly "intent" (to use McCrimmon's word) to the more formalistic conception of "design," suggesting the degree to which his approach is rooted in classical conceptions of the patterns of exposition, those prescribed structures that govern what the writer does "in the essay," the product. For the fifth edition, purpose becomes "the controlling decisions a writer makes when he determines what he wants to do and how he wants to do it."[8] Here the writer, rather than the formal design, controls, decides, determines not merely the essay, conceived as a product (which disappears from this definition), but the "what" and the "how" of the activity of composing. In the sixth edition, purpose is even more reflexively defined as "your awareness as a writer of what you want to do, and how in general you want to do it."[9] Though this latter revision may seem a subtle one, it creates finally, through the concept of awareness, the ground upon which one can stand to study the activity, the behaviors, the habits, of composing, all toward the end of becoming conscious of and assuming a measure of control over the cognitive processes that govern the disposition of language in discourse. No longer is the design, the formal structure, of the essay predominant, as was the case in most of the traditionally formalist textbooks of the 1960s; no longer is the writer's inner self, constituted by personal experiences, the locus of invention, as was the case in the many neoromantic textbooks that were popular in the late 1960s and early 1970s. The process models, in fact, raised immediate and direct challenges to both of these systems, which had for some time constituted the poles between which renovative trends in the field had oscillated. This backdrop of conflict is briefly summarized by Gordon Brossell:

Historically, the teaching of English has vacillated between two competing traditions, each with its own view of language learning. One tradition sees language as a subject to be studied, manipulated, and mastered, and stresses rhetorical knowledge and skill as determinants of linguistic competence and power. In this view, language is a tool for achieving the specific purposes and effects of its users.

The second tradition views language as a vehicle for learning and emphasizes the language user and his attempts to discover, define, and express himself and his relation to the world. Language in this view is less a tool for achievement than an instrument for personal and social growth.[10]

One can see some similarity to the structural elements of the argument that has been ongoing since Socrates sat down with Gorgias. Of course, the vocabulary and the conditions have changed, and neither interlocutor would feel entirely comfortable with his side of this debate. But it is fair to say that prior to the "process" revolution in composition theory, instruction in writing resembled either a kind of "routine" that students were expected to master as a rite of passage into the academy or a kind of "art" that somehow endowed them with both self-understanding and civic responsibility.

The process-based approaches assumed a more functional, public stance toward the nature and purposes of discourse, refashioning not only the implicit relationship between the composer and the thing composed—the what and how of writing—but the explicit relationship between writer and reader, this latter locus, the "audience," becoming the primary determinant in shaping discourse, becoming in effect the universal "why" for writing. Among the more prominent spokesmen for this reallocation—away from writer or design and toward audience—of the motivation for composing have been Linda Flower and John R. Hayes, whose articles began appearing during the mid-1970s.

In *Problem-Solving Strategies for Writing* Flower draws the distinction this way: "If you want to be understood, it is usually not enough simply to *express* your ideas. One of the secrets of communicating your ideas is to understand the needs of your reader and to transform writer-based thought into reader-based prose.[11] The goal of writers must then be "to transform writer-based prose (which works well for them) into reader-based prose (which works for their readers as well)."[12] Writer-based prose is characterized "by one or more of these features: (a) an *egocentric focus* on the writer; (b) a *narrative organization* focused on the writer's own discovery process; (c) a *survey structure* organized, like a textbook, around the writer's information."[13] Reader-based prose, on the other hand, is organized "around a problem, a thesis, or a purpose" with "a goal or thesis as the top level of . . . a hierarchy," and it must always be "vivid and clear to the reader."[14]

Such an audience-based mode of discourse must, of course, make certain assumptions about what a "reader" is, wants, needs. Flower defines her "creative reader" and consequently her good writer, as the one who

1. Tries to fit new information into an old framework he or she already knows. *Therefore*, the writer should supply that framework by creating a context for his or her ideas.
2. Develops expectations and uses them to actively process and understand the text. *Therefore*, the writer needs to create (and then fulfill) accurate expectations that will help the reader anticipate the writer's meaning.
3. Sorts and organizes information into an unconscious hierarchical structure built around a few key concepts or chunks. *Therefore*, the writer needs to make the hierarchical structure he or she has in mind clear to the reader.[15]

Clearly, then, the role of the writer is to locate herself in service of the "knowledge," "attitudes," and "needs" of her reader.[16]

This shift in the balance of power for acts of composition is, once again, reflected in several revisions of the McCrimmon textbook. In the fourth edition, for example, the role of the reader or audience in shaping discourse is rarely mentioned and is—at least by comparison to the writer, the material or the patterns of organization—of little consequence. By the fifth edition, the reader is introduced as one of the "two relationships [that] dominate the act of writing," the other, of course, being the "one between the writer and his *subject*."[17] The reader, in fact, becomes something "a writer must think of . . . long before he begins to write." This readerly role remains fairly constant through the sixth and seventh editions (1976, 1980), though it is worth noting that in the sixth edition the subchapter "Your View of Your Subject" precedes "'Your View of Your Reader," and in the seventh edition their positions are reversed, reader preceding subject as a factor for the writer to consider. It is not until the eighth, and most recent, edition of *Writing with a Purpose* that the full impact of both audience-based approaches, and more particularly problem solving, is evident. Here even the three "stages of the writing process," which had for over fifteen years followed D. Gordon Rohman's nomenclature (prewriting, writing, and revising or rewriting)[18] have been renamed as planning, drafting, and revising, borrowing the nomenclature of the "new" process-based rhetorics. "Your View of Your Reader" becomes now "Analyzing Your Audience," a concept and a problem which are defined in terms comparable to Flower's. This edition also appropriates, almost directly, such heuristic procedures as "brainstorming" and "clustering" from the problem-solving model of composing. In effect, over a period of fifteen years, the preeminent relationship in acts of composition is transformed from the one between the writer and her subject to the one between the writer and her reader.

It is ironic I think that this very process of movement away from the dominant literary critical method of the period—a kind of neoromantic formalism—and toward the methodology of the social sciences, a movement that served generally to aggravate the tensions between these two primary factions of English studies, has also indirectly prepared a vocabulary for their ultimate reconciliation. The pivotal concept here is of course the "reader." And it is largely along an entirely different and competing line of argument that this restoration of integrity to studies in English has been lately moving.

One of the catalytic voices of this countermovement toward the recuperation of reading into composition theory has been Ann Berthoff, a longstanding complainant against the process movement in general and problem solving in particular. Though like almost all of her predecessors and colleagues she grounds her work firmly in the classroom, it is a classroom of a different sort from the one implied by the process models I have just described. In fact, she begins one of her earliest articles (1978) with a characteristic effort both to critique and to renegotiate the concept of pedagogy:

Any pedagogy is properly constituted by a method, models, and a theory. Insofar as a pedagogy is concerned with teaching reading and writing, a concern with language will be central to all three. The province of rhetoric, which is the structure and function of language, is thus coterminus with the boundaries of an English pedagogy.[19]

Embedded in this passage is much of Berthoff's theoretical lexicon. Let me begin with her concept of "method," which is central to her system and which, in itself, carried much of the weight of her explicit critique of current modes of inquiry in the discipline:

True to the spirit of the age, English pedagogues—I use the term to name all those who are concerned with methods, models, and theories—have sought to be scientific, but with very ill-formed notions of what constitutes scientific inquiry . . . . Scientific or not, we need a method that encourages critical questions about goals in conjunction with ways and means: a method that does not allow for the continual exploration of purposes and premises as well as procedures will soon become doctrinaire.[20]

Method, then, from Berthoff's point of view, is a critical stance that provides both the occasion and means for its own self-criticism. It is in short "reflexive"[21] and it is therefore radically self-conscious of the political implications and effects of its application.

It is via this conception of method, consistent with its etymological implications—"*meta + hodos, about the way*"[22]—that Berthoff dismisses not only the "skills" and "self-awareness" models of pedagogy in composition, but all models that conceive of "performance" as distinct from, and generally prior to, "criticism." By subverting the dichotomy between performance and criticism, Berthoff in effect dismantles and disallows any hierarchical conception of the production of discourse, which includes both formalistic and audience-based models for composing. What she proffers as an alternative is a dialectical system capable of managing the various bipolar constituents of the disciplinary discourse (form/content, process/product, even writer/reader) in an entirely different manner—in terms of mutual interdependencies rather than discrete levels, stages, or parts. And her claim that "without an understanding of dialectic as the heart of method, we are doomed to see one after another promising technique disappear without ever having been given a fair chance"[23] creates the ground for her subsequent redefinition of the sort of "research" that composition theorists should be engaged in. As she explains in "The Teacher as REsearcher":

REsearch, like REcognition, is a REflexive act. It means looking—and looking again. This new kind of REsearch would not mean going out after new "data," but rather REconsidering what is at hand. REsearch would come to mean looking and looking again at what happens in the English classroom. We do not need new information; we need to think about the information we have.[24]

This paragraph concludes with an exhortation on behalf of a "dialectical relationship" between "theory and practice," a recurrent motif in her work. As she explains in a subsequent essay entitled "Method: Metaphors, Models, and Maxims":

The chief purpose of a theory of composition is to provide teachers with ways to present writing so that it can indeed be learned by writing. . . . [T]heory is not the antithesis of practice and, in fact, can only serve an authentic purpose if it is continually brought into relationship with practice so that each can inform the other. . . .

Without the perspective that theory provides, there is no way of

maintaining a genuinely critical attitude towards assignments and courses. . . .
In between recipe swapping, which is the result of rejecting theory, and the
collocation and manipulation of data, which is the result of theory for theory's
sake, there is a third way. . . . This third way is best named *method*.[25]

Clearly Berthoff is seeking here to differentiate the term
"method," to "reclaim" it, from its more generic application to almost
any set of specifiable procedures, techniques, guidelines, or, to use the
current jargon, heuristics, for producing written texts. A complete
discussion of the role of "method" in contemporary theory is beyond
the scope of this essay. But it should be noted that Berthoff's
conception of method is decidedly dialectical, thereby distinguishing
it from the many hierarchical systems proffered by both classical and
contemporary rhetoric. Problem solving, for example, as some of the
above excerpts indicate, grounds not only its notions of the
production and reception of written texts, but also of human knowing
generally, in hierarchical metaphors. Dialectical systems of rhetoric
can be distinguished from such hierarchical systems by two primary
features. The first is the manner and means by which the various
constituents of the rhetorical event are ordered and arranged in
relation to one another. Hierarchical systems must, by their nature,
assign either status or temporal privileges to the various elements, or
stages, crucial to composing. Most formalistic systems presume, for
example, that thinking is prior to, and largely independent from, the
language that thinking engenders, that, in brief, thought finds form
and form finds language in a sequence of discrete stages. And most
heuristic rhetorics presume, for example, that the needs of the reader,
the audience, must take priority over those of the writer, with both of
these roles assigned always and solely to separate and discrete parties
in the rhetorical event. Dialectical systems, on the other hand, provide
for the constant interplay, even interchange, between and among the
various contraries that constitute rhetorical situations. Reader and
writer, thought and language, assume their significances not as
separable concepts and categories but by their confluences and
conflicts with one another. As Berthoff conceives it, method, the
dialectic, is not simply theory, but "the perspective that theory
provides," not simply the materials that constitute assignments and
courses, but a "critical attitude" toward those material instruments.
Which leads us to the second distinction between these two systems
for conceiving composing. Dialectical systems of rhetoric tend to be
content-dependent in their recommended modes of application;
hierarchical systems tend to be content-independent. Most formalistic
and heuristic rhetorics, for example, offer quite specific and
transferable agendas for composing, agendas (most often, as I have
noted, depicted in stages) that are designed to suffice for most if not all

sorts of rhetorical situations. They are answer-oriented. Dialectical systems are question-oriented, abjuring the security of rules or steps or recommended procedures in favor of a more problematical, exploratory mode of invention/interpretation. Thus, the actual course of both the activity of composition and the ultimate structure of the composition will be determined more by the specific issues/problems that the writer is seeking to address in their context than by a universal, preconstituted package of principles or heuristics. Briefly, in Berthoff's terms, "the *what* and the *how* depend on one another," and it is "making meaning," rather than "saying what you mean" or "let[ting] the reader see,"[26] that becomes the imperative of dialectical rhetorics.

It is largely via this shift toward such a notion of practical theory that composition has turned its renovation to a more restorative phase, reacclimating itself to its local environment in departments of English. One of the primary means by which this move has been facilitated is by the redefinition of what can legitimately function as a "text" for "reading" in the composition classroom.

Let me illustrate one version of this redefinition by asking Stanley Fish's former student's question—"Is there a text in this class?"[27]—in relation to the sort of composition class enacted in the work of W. E. Coles. Coles has published several complete assignment "sequences," each designed in terms of a particular content—what he calls the "nominal subject"—which becomes the occasion for thinking and writing and talking about writing itself. Any of these sequences could serve to make the point I want to make here. I will restrict my discussion to *Composing: Writing as a Self-Creating Process*,[28] which provides an elegant rendition, in the form of an introductory course description, of the argument on behalf of a dialectical method for imagining the intrinsic relationships that must exist among language, self, subject, and reader in the activity of composing.

Let me ask the question first in the terms that Fish designates as its apparent meaning in the first-day-of-class context: "Is there a *textbook* in this class?" From the very first sentence Coles makes clear that in his class there is not, at least not in the sense of a published text claiming auspices of authority in the classroom arena: "The assignments of this text are designed to be used for a course in writing, a course in which writing, specifically your writing, is the center."[29] What Coles is suggesting here is that, yes, there is a "text" in this class: the one that the students themselves produce and are always in the process of producing. But what exactly is the status and authority of such a text, to shift a bit in the direction of the second possible reading of Fish's student's question? Perhaps it is easier to begin by saying what it is not. It is not, for example, the single essay that each student happens just to have written, nor the one that is being talked about in

student text as center
real subject is language
KAMEEN 181

any single class session; it is neither a new text every week, the sum of all essays submitted in response to a particular assignment, nor any combination or collocation of these various discrete products. For, when student writing displaces the "textbook" at the center of a writing course, it must function at two textual levels simultaneously. On the one hand, each student will be composing her own text as the semester proceeds, which means most immediately that it can never, and should never, have the sort of immutable authority accorded to "finished" textbooks. It is fairer, I think, to say that it accrues its own authority in the process of its emergence. On the other hand, there must also be, as a means of production and revision of the first kind of textuality, the ongoing, commonly shared, dialogical "text" that is enacted in class discussion, which itself is engendered by students writing in response to the course's assignments. In that case, one might fairly ask the question in this form: "If there is no textbook located at the center of authority in this class, and if the student's texts do not yet exist, is it not the assignments that function, covertly, as the "real" text of the course?" Not so, Coles insists:

> It must be emphatically said that the assignments themselves are not an argument. They contain no doctrine, either individually or as a sequence. . . . Above all, the questions of the assignments must be understood as invariably open, as questions to be addressed rather than answered. In fact, the assignments are arranged and phrased precisely to make impossible the discovery in them of anything like a master plan. They are put together in such a way as to mean only and no more than what the various responses they are constructed to evoke can be made to mean, a meaning that will be different for different teachers and students as well as differently come by.[30]

While there is, then, an agenda that the assignments make possible, it is neither a hidden nor a prefigured one. The assignments are, like student essays, clearly textual in that they are there to be read and written, reread and rewritten; but they are not, in themselves, the "text" of the class. But is then, as the above passage can be taken to suggest, the "subject" of the assignments the course's text? Again Coles's answer is no:

> The nominal subject of the assignments is teaching and learning. This subject provides you with something relevant to your immediate experience to think and write about, and serves also to give class conversation a focus, the day-by-day movement of a course some kind of shape and direction. But the real subject of the assignments is language, and their real function is to involve you with the activity of language using, of *composing* in the largest sense of the word.[31]

The key words here are "movement," "function," "activity," and most particularly "composing," all of which suggest that there neither is nor can be anything resembling a fixed and static "text" at the center of the course. The real text of this class is, quite simply, the activity of reading and writing texts, which are themselves constituted of and by the languages through which they are enacted. It is perhaps best to say then that *because* there is *no* text in this class, *everything* in this class is a text: assignments, subjects, selves, perception, thinking, writing, reading, everything, in that all are equally "composed" of and by language. Thus, at least in part via an effort to dismiss reading—in its most formulaic, "literary" terms—from the writing classroom, the *activity* of reading has been brought into a more companionable relationship with writing, as a comparably reflexive mode of interpretation, of making meaning, of composing not any particular universe of discourse—that is, one centered in traditional forms, or in the self, or in an audience—but of apprehending these various universes *as* discourse.

Method-based conceptions of interpretation have been instrumental more recently in, to use the current metaphor, "bridging the gap" between the two primary constituents of English studies: literature and composition or, more generally, reading and writing. This reconciliation has been initiated via the just described way of talking about reading and writing as dialectically inseparable activities, as companionable contraries rather than separable opposites. And it bears repeating here, as I make this passage in my own analysis, that both Berthoff and Coles envision this merger, or perhaps more accurately presume it, when they talk, as they invariably do, about "teaching reading and writing" as if all three activities are simultaneously interrelated, sharing in common the centrality of language.

Winifred Bryan Horner summarizes this position in her introduction to *Composition and Literature: Bridging the Gap*:

In reality, literature and composition cannot be separated either in theory or in teaching practice. Composition theory and critical theory are indeed opposite sides of the same coin, and the "teaching" of writing and the "teaching" of literature are applications of theories that are closely connected, often inseparable, and always fundamental to the study of language. Not only are composition theory and critical theory philosophically connected, but research in one can enlighten and enrich knowledge of the other.[32]

Which is, of course, another way of saying what I have already said, except that Horner introduces the contributory effect of recent developments in literary "critical theory" in the movement toward reconciliation. A detailed account, if one is even possible, of the manner and degree to which critical theory has facilitated the confluence of literature and composition, the "teaching of reading and writing," is clearly beyond the scope of this essay. Even the essays that comprise the collection Horner has edited, written by some of the most prominent "names" in the profession, do not adequately unravel, decode, deconstruct, or, in general, "read" the issues fully. But it is safe to say that one of the primary effects of the multiple movement toward deconstructionist, reader-response, and hermeneutical systems of interpretation has been to redefine both the status and function of the "reader" in relation to the "text." And whether one chooses to describe the activity of reading as compositional or decompositional, the readerly role is an active one, much like, in that respect, the writer's. Reading, in short, becomes as much an act of production— rather than reproduction—as is writing; it becomes in fact a manner of writing, just as, conversely, writing becomes a manner of reading.

This integration, in both theory and practice, of the teaching of reading and writing has begun, on the one hand, to draw composition (now more broadly defined to include both reading and writing under the more general rubric of interpretation) back into its more customary habitat in departments of English. But it has not by any means relegated composition to its former subservient role in relation either to literary studies or to the curriculum in general. In part because composition acquired during the 1970s, on the terms that were then available, a well-defined and quite expansive domain of its own, along with the intrinsic authority to oversee its various provinces, the discipline is not likely to be reassimilated into the local setting of any other particular department. In many cases in fact, for the short run at least, composition programs are more likely to sustain and preserve the allies they choose, whether they be in literature programs or education programs, both of which are under considerable pressure to retrench their estates for a variety of institutional, economic, and cultural reasons.

But, paradoxically, this same integration of reading with writing has also made possible one of the more dramatic movements for general curricular revision of the last twenty years, a movement that could well lead to the gradual demise of composition as a disciplinary entity: writing across the curriculum.

An early and persistent spokesman for this movement, which originated in the mid-1970s, has been Elaine P. Maimon; and, quite appropriately, given all I have said thus far about the teaching-intensive character of composition, one of the clearest expressions of the nature and purposes of writing across the curriculum is her *Instructor's Manual to Accompany Readings in the Arts and Sciences*. As she explains, picking up a theme I have just discussed, the two companion texts in this series "are based on the following assumptions: (a) writing and reading are inseparable activities; (b) writing and reading are central to learning in all disciplines; (c) writing and reading are essential modes of discovery."[33] Though one might argue over precisely how these imperatives are to be enacted (Maimon is, for example, heavily process-oriented in her conception of writing), these are reasonable expressions of the common ground of assumptions for most writing across the curriculum programs. Maimon addresses this manual primarily to teachers of composition, preserving, it would seem, the predisciplinary character of the enterprise and the status distinction between composition and the rest of the curriculum:

> We believe that the composition course can prepare students to understand disciplinary differences without assuming that perceived disharmonies create a cacophony. We provide guidance in reading and writing about textbooks and about original scholarship in the humanities and in the social and natural sciences.[34]

But her method also represents a significant redefinition of the relationship between these two components of the curriculum, suggesting that all of the "content" areas, what I earlier called the "menu," of the academy are in fact discourse-dependent in their essence. In other words, all disciplinary "knowledge" and "research" are fundamentally rhetorical, and practitioners of these more specialized modes of inquiry need to become more conscious of, to locate themselves in a reflexive relationship with, the specific discourses that shape and constrain their activities.

These implications are evident even in Maimon's defense of the necessity of a predisciplinary composition course: "Composition courses are often criticized because they seem to be without content, to be *about* nothing. We believe that a composition course should be about writing and reading in college, that is, *about* our students' intellectual heritage."[35] Clearly, if writing is to acquire any status "across the curriculum," every discipline must begin to assume its share of the responsibility for literate participation in the "conversation" that constitutes both "education" and, in the weightier language of the above passage, "our . . . intellectual heritage." In effect, every discipline must find ways of imagining its own practices as *about* nothing, nothing that is beyond the discourse that makes its own highly specialized disciplinary "something" possible. The thrust then of almost all writing across the curriculum programs is to disperse the "teaching of reading and writing"—that is, interpretation or composing—throughout the academy. The long-range effects of this distribution of authority on the disciplinary status of composition are difficult to specify at these early stages of implementation. For the time being, "specialists" in composition are likely to serve as expert consultants in designing, implementing, and evaluating such programs. Because composition has for so long functioned as the primary "servant" of the rest of the curriculum, at least in regard to matters of verbal literacy, it is the only agent now capable of functioning as the "master" of such a curricular transition.

Ironically, it is the very contentlessness of the discipline that accords it now a privileged status in writing across the curriculum programs. While Gorgias (primarily through his mouthpiece, Polus) advances one of the possible arguments on behalf of the meta-disciplinary "power" of rhetoric, one could turn as well to Aristotle, who argues the same point, somewhat more wholesomely perhaps— that is, that rhetoric is both powerful and instructive in relation to "the rest of the arts and sciences" precisely because it has, in its own right, "no special application to any distinct class of subjects." Unlike Gorgias, Aristotle locates rhetoric firmly on the side of "truth and justice,"[36] which is, of course, what makes it "valuable as a means of instruction."[37] Thus, the very contentlessness—or, in the terms I previously employed, "textlessness"—of the discipline, which served originally to confine it to the lower-division classroom, has now become the means by which it has constituted not only itself but also, to a certain degree, the entire university curriculum.

By the same token, once this work is accomplished there is, theoretically, no longer any need for such a "discipline." For if writing across the curriculum does, in time, transform the identity of the academy; if the long-standing territorial boundaries between and among the constituent disciplines of the curriculum do in fact begin to blur, even break down; if the various disciplines do in fact create a common ground for mutual discourse about their discourses, share a common understanding that on the most fundamental level all of their "bodies of knowledge" are constituted of and by their various "rhetorics," there would be little need for exclusive programs in "composition." I doubt very much that such a transformation will take place easily, or soon, if it does at all. But just imagining it is one of the best ways I know for coming to understand the peculiar and surprising forces, from both without and within, that have shaped the maturation of the discipline over the last fifteen years.

FOOTNOTES

1. Plato, "Gorgias," trans. W. D. Woodhead, *Plato: The Collected Dialogues*, ed. Edith Hamilton and Huntington Cairns (New York: Bollingen Series, Random House, 1963), pp. 242-46.

2. Janet Emig, *The Composing Processes of Twelfth Graders* (Urbana, Ill.: National Council of Teachers of English, 1971).

3. Ibid., p. 15.

4. This distinction has become very recently a subject for discussion and critique. See, for example, Louise Wetherbee Phelps, "Dialectics of Coherence: Toward an Integrative Theory," *College English* 47 (January 1985): 12-29.

5. For a more complete discussion of these approaches, see Paul Kameen, "Rewording the Rhetoric of Composition," *Pre/Text* 1, no. 1 (1980): 73-93.

6. James M. McCrimmon, *Writing with a Purpose* (Boston: Houghton Mifflin, 1950).

7. Ibid., 4th ed., p. 12.

8. Ibid., 5th ed., p. 18.

9. Ibid., 6th ed., p. 5.

10. Gordon C. Brossell, "Developing Power and Expressiveness in the Language Learning Process," *The Teaching of English*, ed. James R. Squire, Seventy-sixth Yearbook of the National Society for the Study of Education, Part 1 (Chicago: University of Chicago Press, 1977), p. 39.

11. Linda Flower, *Problem-Solving Strategies for Writing* (New York: Harcourt Brace Jovanovich, 1981), p. 121.

12. Ibid., p. 144.

13. Ibid., p. 149.

14. Ibid., pp. 157-58.

15. Ibid., p. 134.

16. Ibid., p. 123.

17. McCrimmon, *Writing with a Purpose*, 5th ed., p. 4.

18. D. Gordon Rohman appears to be most responsible for popularizing both the concept of prewriting and this tripartite division of the writing process. See D. Gordon Rohman, "Pre-Writing: The Stage of Discovery in the Writing Process," *College Composition and Communication* 16 (May 1965): 106-112.

19. Ann Berthoff, *The Making of Meaning* (Montclair, N.J.: Boynton/Cook, 1981), pp. 48-49. All following page references are to this text of collected works. I have indicated in my argument the narrative sequence of their original publication. Sources for original publication are noted in the book, preceding each article.

20. Ibid., p. 49.

21. Ibid., p. 51.

22. Ibid.

23. Ibid.

24. Ibid., p. 31.

25. Ibid.

26. Flower, *Problem-Solving Strategies for Writing*, p. 12.

27. Stanley Fish, *Is There a Text in This Class? The Authority of Interpretive Communities* (Cambridge, Mass.: Harvard University Press, 1980), pp. 303-321.

28. William E. Coles, Jr., *Composing: Writing as a Self-Creating Process* (Rochelle Park, N.J.: Hayden Book Co., 1974).

29. Ibid., p. 1.

30. Ibid., pp. 3-4.

31. Ibid., p. 1.

32. Winifred Bryan Horner, ed., *Composition and Literature: Bridging the Gap* (Chicago: University of Chicago Press, 1983), p. 2.

33. Elaine P. Maimon, *Instructor's Manual to Accompany Readings in the Arts and Sciences* (Boston: Little, Brown, and Co., 1984), p. 4.

34. Ibid., p. 3.

35. Ibid.

36. Aristotle, *The Rhetoric*, trans. Lane Cooper (Englewood Cliffs, N.J.: Prentice-Hall, 1932), p. 8.

37. Ibid., pp. 4-5.

Part Four
POSTSCRIPT

CHAPTER XI

On the Road to Shanghai:
A Three-Year Project with the Public Schools

ANTHONY R. PETROSKY

I remember very clearly the first day I sat in Francis Rifugiato's office. There I was, fresh from a big research project on reading and writing, newly promoted to associate professor, a writer, and a writing teacher with a program for changing teachers. It was simple, I thought; first we needed thirty teachers willing to be trained as the district's teacher trainers. We would meet a few days a month on company time and two weeks during the summers for three years. Once we had the volunteers, we would begin writing district essay tests to create a need for writing instruction. After we had the tests in place, we would start conducting in-service programs on the teaching of writing to answer the needs created by the tests.

As the Director of the Division of Curriculum for the Pittsburgh Public Schools, Mr. Rifugiato bore the responsibility for all the district's in-service, testing, and curriculum work. As a twenty-year veteran teacher, principal, and now administrator, he had seen change in its strange costumes come and go—individualized instruction, mastery learning, values clarification, computer-assisted teaching, behavioral objectives. He was skeptical about me and my ideas, and he was certain, as he told me later, that I had to change my attitude and become a team player or *we* were not going to accomplish anything.

Luckily, Rifugiato and a number of other people took me under their wings. They could have left me on my own, as I wanted to be, as I had been taught to be as a researcher accustomed to producing "deliverables," and as a university professor used to measuring my productivity against others rather than with them.

That was three and a half years ago, when at the request of the Superintendent of the Pittsburgh Public Schools, I became the

188

director of a program called the Critical Thinking Project—a district-wide effort to teach and test inquiry skills in social studies through writing and classroom discussions. My staff and I were responsible for teaching thirty teachers (the steering committee) from grades three through eleven to be teacher trainers in writing and discussion, so that they could then teach other teachers. Our work included the development of district diagnostic essay tests, the design and implementation of workshops on various aspects of writing, discussion, and questioning. We were also responsible for beginning a similar project at the district's teacher center, Schenley High School, with forty high school teachers from a number of subjects—English, art, mathematics, science, social studies, and special education.

Our goals seemed straightforward and within reach, especially given our three-year timetable. We wanted to initiate a process of teachers teaching teachers to use writing, discussion, and what, for lack of better language, we called "higher-order questions" in their teaching. A number of national studies, including the Third National Assessment of Reading and Literature for which I served as a project director, pointed to youngsters' problems with these "critical thinking skills," and the district's new superintendent, Richard C. Wallace, in a bold and unusual move, took instruction, especially instruction in these areas, as one of his top priorities. The Richard King Mellon Foundation and later the Rockefeller Foundation gave us the financial backing to set the project in motion.

Now, at the end of my tenure with the project and after seeing it receiving funding for three more years, I want to take this opportunity, as I prepare to leave for the Shanghai Foreign Languages Institute in China, to discuss what we set in motion. Since I have been close to large-scale change, I have changed; and I think it is useful to discuss how my change, as a "teacher educator," enters into the picture, especially in the context of this book—filled as it is with advice from experts on how writing is, might, or ought to be taught in the public schools and universities.

I will spare you the frustrations of that first year when I spent a good deal of my time visiting principals and teachers, explaining our ideas and asking for volunteers. After six months, we had twenty-five skeptical teachers willing to serve on the steering committee. Then the difficult work began.

During those day-long meetings with our teachers, we talked about writing, about teachers writing, about students writing drafts and revising and editing, about teachers holding conferences, about the use of essay exams, about rating guides for these exams, and about teachers teaching teachers. The group listened, agreed that the program and its goals were important, but, they said, you are going to have a hard time because you are making the following mistakes: *You are asking teachers to do something they were not taught to do, you are giving teachers extra work, you are taking time from the material they are required to cover, and, with the essay tests, you are making people nervous about accountability.* Yes, I said, but we can teach them to teach writing, we can help them become writers, we can show them how to weave the extra work into their teaching, and the tests will help them decide what kinds of writing their students need help with.

Three and a half years later, even though writing in social studies has increased dramatically, even though the essay tests are administered by every social studies teacher three times a year, even though many teachers have participated in the Western Pennsylvania Writing Project (our National Writing Project site), and even though students now receive writing instruction and do more interpretive writing than they did before, it is clear that we underestimated the teachers' concerns and our abilities to help them. And it is also clear that we underestimated their abilities to help us and each other.

Before going on to discuss their concerns, it is important to say that initially we saw ourselves as outside experts. Maybe, initially, that was all that was possible for us. We learned that we would have to become coconspirators to work with the teachers, but that could only happen after we understood each other, after we had shared goals and problems, after we stopped telling each other what we knew and started talking about specific problems—like, for instance, what the sequence of in-service writing workshops might look like.

We had to learn to work with the teachers. This meant we had to teach their classes and talk with their students, so that we could know the situations they faced as they attempted to weave writing into their classes. It is important to recognize the conspiratorial nature of this work. To make large-scale changes, even though they happen with individual teachers in individual classes, you have to manipulate a system, a system that includes thousands of teachers and students, bureaucratic routines designed to maintain the status quo, and—most decisively—pressures like tests, courses of study, forty-five minute class periods, and one hundred and fifty students per teacher—pressures that pick and poke at attempts to teach writing. If you are going to change a bureaucratic system, you have to recruit coconspirators.

The first concern we grappled with, asking teachers to do something they had not been taught to do, took us in two directions. The straightest had us raising and answering questions about why writing was important in the first place, particularly in places other than the English class. Our teachers sympathized with the arguments that writing was a way of thinking and of solving problems and with those who claim students receive practice at different kinds of thinking with different kinds of writing tasks. The next step was to deal with teachers' anxiety. Most of our teachers were master teachers. They had advanced degrees, an average of ten years of teaching experience, and yet almost no experience with writing or the teaching of writing. As a result, these teachers had trouble talking about writing or imagining the problems a writer might face and the forms of instruction that might help. As we found through a district survey, few of them had taken courses in college that asked them to write, and most of the teaching models they had been exposed to were similar to those they used—lectures and recitations. Suddenly, we were asking them to write writing assignments, to speak to students about their writing, and to make suggestions for revision. We were also urging teachers to use conferences and writing workshops; we wanted them to teach their students how to talk about writing so that they, in turn, might help each other.

We were asking a lot. Our teachers hardly ever questioned the usefulness of what we asked, but they taught us how to appreciate their situations—both the personal aspects of learning how to teach and use writing and the professional aspects of trying to do it under institutional pressures and constraints. Together we worked out a system of workshops that borrowed from other in-service models. To begin with, we decided that teachers teaching teachers was the way to go. It lent credibility to the project, assured ongoing work after the university people left, and put the problems in the hands of those who faced them—the teachers.

We then decided on a series of topics for the workshops. First, following the National Writing Project model, we wanted teachers to write, to discuss their writing, and to revise. Having the teachers write became one of our goals. We also wanted to direct attention to the kinds of tasks that might be good writing assignments, so we joined forces with another project underway on questioning and designed a set of in-service workshops on "higher-order questioning"—those tasks that ask students to interpret and evaluate the ideas and events they encounter in their studies. We also felt we needed to provide teachers with information on and practice with specific aspects of writing instruction, so, after compromises on all our parts, we designed workshops on "Ideas for Writing" (prewriting and group activities), "Responding to Students' Writing" (techniques for giving students feedback on their work), and "Questioning and Discussion" (information on and practice in question writing and class discussions). At first we saw these as sequential, but scheduling problems made it impossible for us to deliver them that way, so we began cycling all the teachers through the questioning and discussion workshop first and then through the others as scheduling would permit. The problem was, of course, that everyone needed everything all at once, but early on it became clear that it would take three years to cycle all the district's social studies teachers through these workshops and through other ones we were already conducting on the use and rating of the essay tests. All in all, we had to provide about one hundred hours of in-service work to approximately six hundred teachers at all grade levels.

The in-service workshops will go into their second year during the 1985-86 school year, but already we have seen the need to move beyond them and establish procedures to support teachers in their schools, so that they can try teaching writing and receive immediate feedback on their attempts. The workshops without the school-level support systems for practice and appraisal only scratch the surface by providing teachers with knowledge and limited practice. The critical step in any writing project is, I think, the opportunity to practice and receive comments on that practice. As I leave the project, this is one of the major tasks facing the new director. He and his staff will begin addressing it by teaching the department chairs to observe and confer with their teachers as they teach writing.

As for the teachers' second concern, extra work, there can be no doubt that using and teaching writing where there had been little or no writing adds work for teachers. Composing the writing assignments, doing prewriting activities, reading the papers, writing comments on them, holding conferences with students, and conducting class discussions of the papers all add work. The solutions we came to are difficult to implement, some were beyond our abilities to handle, and others are connected to the third concern that our teachers expressed, taking time from required subject matter.

We grappled with the extra work by first arranging for the teachers to receive released time from duty work (supervision of study halls, cafeteria, and so forth) to rate the essay exams. We then began thinking about how to use class time for other tasks like talking to students about their writing. We finally arrived at another of our compromise positions by recommending that teachers spend two to three days a month using class time to give students feedback, either through individual conferences, peer conferences, small groups, or whole-group demonstrations. This may seem small, especially in light of the current calls to arms for writing as the mainstay of instruction in content area classes, but it represented a big step for us and our teachers.

The heart of the problem as we saw it was threefold: too many students in classes (the average for the district is from thirty to thirty-five students per class), too many classes (five a day), and too much subject material to cover. I will begin with the latter, because it covers two of the concerns teachers expressed.

In his chapter in this book, Applebee points to the problems of "covering the material," but the problems are more far-reaching than he claims. Teachers feel compelled to cover the material in either the textbook or the course of study, and usually "covering the material" means getting it from the book into the students' heads through lectures, recitations, and multiple-choice type worksheets. On the surface this looks like an issue of technique or strategy—using lectures rather than discussions or using workbooks rather than essay assignments—but it is a much deeper and more profound issue than a question of technique or method, for these practices represent assumptions about knowledge, and about teaching and learning. By and large, our teachers saw themselves transmitting information from their books to their students. Knowledge, in this sense (as Paulo Freire and others have pointed out), is thought of as the accumulation of information from experts. Knowledge—the kind of knowledge represented by writing and discussion—is collaborative, made by learners, and subject to change or revision.

We were not asking teachers simply to change their techniques; we were asking them to think about knowledge, teaching, and learning differently—to see their jobs not so much, or not exclusively, as the imparting of information, but also as encouraging the making, sharing, and revising of knowledge, knowledge derived from individual histories and cultures and not just from textbooks. It is not fair, though, to point exclusively at the teachers—as usual, the picture is more complicated, because the entire system, with its textbooks, workbooks, courses of study, forty-five minute periods, five classes a day of thirty to thirty-five students a class, supports these assumptions. Perhaps it is more accurate to say that the system is built on these assumptions.

Teaching writing brings us close to the problem because it offers a way out of metaphors of "accumulation" and "transmission" into social, collaborative metaphors, where knowledge is something that people make and remake in their continuing dialogues with each other. This is not to say that we do not need information, but it is to say that accumulating information and making knowledge are different and, I think, in desperate need to be balanced in education. We have a lopsided compulsion for imparting information, for facts, rather than a concern for making knowledge. Our obsessions with facts and information allow us to be caught in the trap of believing that once we have the facts and the information we know what is going on. The trouble is that we see the information differently, and knowledge comes from the critical exchange and revision of our ways of seeing.

Other than recommending smaller and fewer classes, situations we could not influence, we began thinking about writing in relation to the courses of study. By and large, they present course material with equal weight in a survey fashion, and there are few opportunities to treat material in depth. The more we argued about the courses of study, the more it became clear that they were in dire need of revision. We are beginning to reexamine the courses of study for each grade level, starting with the high school social studies courses, to determine what could be eliminated, treated in survey, and treated in depth. This project will continue in the district for at least the next three years. When the teachers started the redesign, they imagined using writing and discussion, including writing and discussion from primary sources (not just the textbook) for the sections of the courses that would be treated in depth, and lectures, recitations, and workbook-type activities for the sections that would be treated in a survey manner. The big problem, of course, is to redesign the curricula throughout the grades so that the scope and sequences complement rather than overlap and duplicate each other as they do now.

This is an enormous task, and like most of the others we encountered in the schools, it relates directly to testing and issues of teacher and student accountability. Before going on to discuss these concerns, I want to say that the workload problem is far from solved in our district. At times, I think the only way it can be solved is through smaller and fewer classes, so that teachers and students can have more time together and so that teachers can have more time to plan and practice using writing in their classes, but I also know that just having smaller and fewer classes will not change anything. If teachers are to put the additional time to any good use, they have to have training in writing and its instruction, they have to be committed to writing, and they have to assign it and talk about it in their classes under the supervision of someone knowledgeable enough to give them feedback. On the other hand, I have to say that it seems a terrible waste of professional time to have teachers overseeing study halls, hallways, and cafeterias. I cannot imagine any circumstances, except the obvious but demeaning financial ones, that make it sensible for teachers to do these things in lieu of professional work.

Finally, as I hinted earlier, our teachers' fourth concern, testing, has its nasty fingers in every pie in the schools. We began this project believing that what gets tested determines what gets taught, and continue to believe this is true. As I have already mentioned, one of the pressures that testing brings to bear on teachers has to do with the compulsion to cover material that will be tested. If the success of students, and therefore of teachers, is measured by standardized tests of information, then that information will be what teachers teach. Our district was no different from others on this account, although the emphasis on essay tests in English and social studies put pressure as well on developing essay test writing skills. I say "essay test writing skills" instead of "writing skills," because the tests did indeed bring teachers to ask for help with writing, but they were more concerned with helping their students do well on the essay tests than they were with helping their students use writing more generally as a tool for learning. Consequently it was not unusual to see teachers teaching simple formulas—the five-paragraph essay, for example—to students to ensure that they could write well under the pressure of an essay test, and this was often the only writing instruction they gave.

Still, I have a difficult time complaining about something where there was nothing or very little, and, frankly, it is difficult to know where the essay tests will finally lead. I can imagine, a few years down the road, that they will have served their purposes well—creating the need in teachers for in-service work in writing and providing them with diagnostic information on their students' writing abilities. I can also imagine, though, that they will become the be-all and end-all of writing instruction in any district not committed to in-service work. The dangers seem obvious, especially given what we know about writing being used predominately and almost exclusively for testing in many places, but the fact of the matter also seems clear: Unless essay tests are used, teachers will have a difficult time taking writing seriously; they will, instead, teach to whatever tests are being used. That fact now seems to me as natural as breathing.

From our teachers' concerns and our collaborative attempts to help them, I can draw some conclusions. First, it is important for would-be writing teachers, no matter what subject area expertise they hold, to be given the opportunity to do what they expect their students to do—that is, to write. In addition, they will need about one hundred hours of in-service work to acquire the basic experience with writing instruction that will help them cope with their anxiety about doing something they are unaccustomed to. More importantly, though, they need support systems to allow them to practice and to receive feedback on their practice. As they begin to use writing in their teaching, they will have to come to grips with the problems of workload and "covering the material." Finally, testing will play a heavy hand in what they teach and how seriously they take the teaching of writing.

Before closing, I want to mention briefly the changes I went through as I worked with these teachers. When I attended those first meetings with Mr. Rifugiato, I was truly an outsider with a prescription for change, with a list of do's and don'ts for fixing what was wrong with teachers and the system. As I worked with and became a part of a problem-solving group, the steering committee, I had to establish my credibility, and I learned there was only one way to do that—to teach in the system. After I spent time teaching classes, I understood, once again, the situations teachers live in, and they understood that, finally, they could talk to me and I would listen. I would say, now, that was my most important transition—learning to listen to teachers and administrators and teaching them to listen to me.

While I came into the schools with a prescriptive voice and manner, I am leaving believing in my usefulness as an outside agitator or catalyst, in the importance of listening, in the importance of offering advice in the form of "here's what others have tried" and then soliciting teachers' opinions on what to do next. I did not solve any of the important problems we faced, although as a group *we* solved many of them; and almost all of the solutions were ones I had not imagined. If we are concerned with the failure of such things as the process approach to the teaching of writing, as a number of the chapter authors are in this book, we need to broaden the discussion to include a critical examination of the kinds of training and support teachers receive, the ways they are given it, and the changes or lack of changes implemented in curriculum and testing to support writing instruction. Most importantly, we need to imagine change in the context of the underlying assumptions about knowledge, teaching, and learning inherent in our educational system. These assumptions work against teachers seeing the role of writing in the making of knowledge and, at the same time, work in favor of reducing everything, including writing, to forty-five minute drills.

Name Index

Abrams, Meyer Howard, 30, 33, 43, 46
Adams, Marilyn J., 91
Adams, Vernon Ardell, 93, 94
Airasian, Peter W., 129
Allen, Harold, 35, 47
Alloway, Evans, 94
Anderson, Linda, 166, 169
Anderson, Richard C., 69, 92
Anderson, Valerie, 76, 92
Anglin, Jeremy, 168
Applebee, Arthur N., 41, 47, 95, 112, 129, 166, 167, 169
Applebee, Roger, 47
Aristotle, 10, 11, 12, 20, 21, 22, 23, 29, 32, 39, 72, 77, 185, 186
Atwell, Nancie, 147

Barham, I. H., 93
Bartholomae, David, 1, 64, 70
Becker, Alton, 39, 43, 47
Benson, Robert, 151, 167
Bereiter, Carl, 73, 75, 76, 81, 86, 91, 92, 93
Berkenkotter, Carol, 58, 69
Berlin, James, 32, 33, 34, 38, 42, 43, 46, 47, 48
Bernstein, Basil B., 129
Berthoff, Ann E., 43, 48, 61, 69, 177, 178, 179, 180, 182, 186
Bissex, Glenda L., 58, 69
Bizzell, Patricia, 49, 68
Blake, William, 1, 2, 4, 5
Bloom, Benjamin S., 165, 168
Booth, Wayne C., 22, 23, 29, 39
Bourdieu, Pierre, 129
Bowles, Samuel, 129
Boyer, Ernest L., 148, 167
Braddock, Richard R., 48, 92, 96, 112
Brannon, Lil, 58, 60, 63, 69
Brewer, William F., 92
Bridwell, Lillian, 167
Britton, James N., 55, 56, 59, 62, 63, 68, 97, 112
Brophy, Jere, 166, 169
Brossell, Gordon C., 175, 186
Brown, Rexford, 4, 114, 129, 130
Bruce, Bertram C., 92
Bruffee, Kenneth A., 65, 70
Bruner, Jerome, 113, 158, 168

Burgess, T., 68
Burke, Carolyn L., 159, 160, 168
Burke, Kenneth, 40

Cairns, Huntington, 185
Calkins, Lucy M., 83, 84, 85, 93, 136, 137, 147
Carroll, Joyce, 94
Cazden, Courtney B., 167
Child, Francis J., 34
Childers, Nancye M., 69
Chomsky, Carol, 150, 167
Christensen, Francis, 31, 151, 153, 167
Cole, Michael, 168
Coles, William E., Jr., 7, 70, 180, 181, 182, 186
Connors, Robert, 29, 33, 46
Cooper, Charles R., 46, 169
Corbett, Edward P. J., 39, 41, 47, 60, 69
Crane, Richard S., 39
Crosby, Harry, 39
Currier, Carolyn, 136, 137, 139, 145

Deen, Rosemary, 152, 153, 167
Denney, Joseph Villiers, 47
Dewey, John, 42
Diederich, Paul, 130
Donaldson, Margaret, 69, 159, 168
Duhamel, Albert P., 39, 41, 47
Dyson, Anne Haas, 112

Ede, Lisa, 29
Eisner, Elliot, 158, 168
Elbow, Peter, 53, 68, 154, 168
Eliot, Charles W., 34, 47
Elley, W. B., 82, 93
Emig, Janet, 55, 56, 59, 68, 71, 91, 94, 96, 97, 112, 167, 172, 173, 185
Eschholz, Paul, 131
Evertson, Carolyn, 166, 169

Faigley, 85, 86, 88, 93, 94
Farrell, James T., 64, 70
Fine, Jonathon, 81, 93
Fish, Stanley, 180, 186
Florio, Susan, 112
Flower, Linda, 56, 57, 65, 68, 81, 93, 168, 175, 176, 177, 186

Fogarty, Daniel, 31, 32, 33, 34, 46
Freedle, R. O., 93
Freedman, Sarah W., 92
Freese, John Henry, 29
Freire, Paulo, 193
Frost, Robert, 20
Frye, Northrop, 77
Fulkerson, Richard, 30, 31, 33, 34, 37, 38, 41, 43, 46, 47, 48
Fulwiler, Toby, 63, 69, 168

Gage, John T., 8
Gartshore, Sondra, 81, 93
Gauntlett, James Frederick, 94
Geertz, Clifford, 1
Gere, Anne Ruggles, 30, 47
Giacobbe, Mary Ellen, 131
Gintis, Herbert, 129
Glaser, Robert, 91
Glenn, Christine G., 80, 84, 93
Goelman, Hillel, 69
Goodlad, John I., 121, 122, 129, 148, 167
Gorgias, 171, 175, 185
Gorrell, Robert, 39
Goslin, David A., 129
Graves, Donald H., 58, 59, 69, 85, 93, 111, 112, 113, 131, 136, 146, 147, 168
Gray, James, 131, 151, 167
Green, Thomas F., 130
Greenberg, Karen, 70
Gregg, Lee, 93
Grobe, Cary H., 92

Haley-James, Shirley, 29
Halliday, Michael K., 108, 113
Hamilton, Edith, 185
Hansen, Jane, 147
Harrington, David V., 41, 47
Harste, Jerome C., 159, 160, 168
Hartwell, Patrick, 7, 70
Hayes, John R., 56, 57, 65, 68, 81, 93, 168, 175
Heath, Shirley Brice, 58, 69, 112
Hemingway, Ernest, 72
Hill, Adam Sherman, 34, 35, 36, 47
Hillocks, George, Jr., 71, 77, 78, 92, 93, 94, 104, 105, 106, 111, 112, 113
Himley, Margaret, 70
Hirsch, Eric D., Jr., 16, 29, 31, 127, 130
Horner, Winifred Bryan, 182, 183, 186
House, Ernest, 114, 129
Houston, Susan H., 129
Hudelson, Earl, 3, 4, 6, 7
Hughes, Richard E., 39, 47

Humes, Ann, 112
Hunter, Madeline, 165
Hurn, Christopher J., 129

Irmscher, William, 25, 29, 39

Jarvella, Robert J., 113
Jensen, Julie M., 167
Johannessen, Larry R., 77, 78, 92, 94, 113

Kahn, Elizabeth A., 77, 78, 92, 94, 113
Kameen, Paul, 170, 186
Kamil, Michael L., 92
Karp, Walter, 29
Keith, Philip M., 47
Kellaghan, Thomas, 129
Keroes, Josephine, 112
King, Barbara, 94
Kitzhaber, Albert, 37, 47
Klaus, K., 130
Koury, Fred, 162
Kneupper, Charles W., 47
Knight, Melinda, 69
Knoblauch, C. H., 60, 63, 69
Kuhn, Thomas, 32

Labov, William, 45, 129
Lamb, H., 93
Lamme, Linda Leonard, 69
Langer, Judith A., 74, 75, 92, 101, 106, 107, 108, 109, 112, 113
Larson, Richard, 39
Levelt, William J. M., 113
Lloyd-Jones, Richard, 48, 92, 96, 112
Loban, Walter, 168
Lunsford, Andrea, 29
Luria, Alexander R., 160, 168

Macrorie, Ken, 154, 168
Madaus, George F., 129
Maimon, Elaine P., 63, 70, 183, 184, 186
Mandl, Heinz, 92
Marcotrigiano, Isabella, 94
Marshall, J. D., 112
Martin, Nancy, 62, 68, 69
Martlew, Margaret, 93
Matsuhashi, Ann, 81, 93
McCleary, William J., 92
McCrimmon, James M., 174, 176, 186
McKeon, Richard, 39
McLeod, A., 68
McQuade, Donald, 70
Miller, Barbara, 130
Mischel, Terry, 71, 91

Moe, Alden J., 92
Moffett, James, 97, 112, 156, 168
Montague, William E., 69, 92
Murray, Donald, 69, 131, 147, 155, 168
Myers, Miles, 130, 148, 167, 168

Neverow-Turk, Vera, 69
Newell, George E., 112
Newkirk, Thomas, 147
Nice, Richard, 129
Nold, Ellen W., 92
Nystrand, Martin, 112

O'Hare, Frank, 93
Oakes, Jeannie, 122, 129
Oberg, Antoinette A., 69
Odell, Lee, 46
Olson, David R., 58, 69, 168
Ong, Walter J., 64, 70, 150, 167
Ortony, Andrew, 92
Orwell, George, 55

Parker, Robert P., 88, 90, 94
Passeron, Jean-Claude, 129
Perl, Sondra, 58, 59, 69, 71, 91
Peterson, Penelope, 166, 168, 169
Petrosky, Anthony R., 65, 70, 188
Phelps, Louise Wetherbee, 186
Piaget, Jean, 159
Pianko, Sharon, 57, 59, 68, 71, 72, 91
Pike, Kenneth, 39, 43, 47
Plato, 9, 10, 185
Polanyi, Michael, 129
Policastro, Margaret, 80, 93
Ponsot, Marie, 152, 153, 167

Riesman, David, 77
Rifugiato, Francis, 188, 195
Rohman, D. Gordon, 41, 47, 52, 53, 68,
  168, 176, 186
Rosa, Al, 131
Rosch, Eleanor, 151, 167
Rose, Mike, 7, 64, 70
Rosen, Harold, 68, 129
Rosenshine, Barak, 165, 168
Rumelhart, David E., 92

Sager, Carol, 86, 87, 92, 94
Salmon-Cox, Leslie, 129
Salvatori, Marolina, 65, 70
Scardamalia, Marlene, 73, 75, 76, 86, 91,
  92, 93
Schoer, Lowell, 48, 92, 96, 112
Schwartz, Mimi, 58, 69

Scott, Fred Newton, 37, 38, 47
Scriven, Michael, 118, 129
Shaughnessy, Mina P., 61, 62, 63, 64, 69,
  86, 94
Silberman, Charles, 30, 46
Sinclair, Anne, 113
Smart, David, 92
Smith, Frank, 69, 150, 167
Smith, Jeffrey, 94
Smith, Shirley, 47
Socrates, 9, 10, 11, 12, 15, 16, 19, 20,
  170, 171, 172, 175
Sommers, Nancy, 58, 59, 65, 69, 70
Sowers, Susan, 136, 147
Spicer, Willa, 94
Spiro, Rand J., 69, 73, 91, 92
Sproull, Lee, 129
Squire, James R., 47, 186
Stallard, Charles K., 71, 72, 83, 91, 93
Stallings, Jane, 165, 166, 168
Stein, Nancy L., 80, 84, 92, 93
Steinberg, Erwin, 93
Stewart, Murray F., 92
Stratton, R. E., 70
Strong, William, 152, 153, 167

Thomas, Lawrence G., 129
Thomas, Owen, 39
Thomas, Susan C., 167, 168
Trabasso, Tom, 84, 92
Tripp, Janice A., 47
Troyka, Lynn Q., 92

Vopat, James, 70
Voss, James F., 74, 92
Vygotsky, Lev S., 108, 110, 113, 167

Wagner, Betty Jane, 156, 168
Walberg, Herbert J., 168, 169
Wallace, Richard C., 189
Warriner, John E., 95, 112
Weaver, Richard M., 39, 47
White, E. B., 55
Wigginton, Eliot, 162
Willing, M. H., 4, 7
Winterowd, Ross, 39
Wise, Arthur E., 130
Wlecke, Raymond, 52, 53
Woodhead, W. D., 185
Woods, William F., 31, 33, 34, 38, 41,
  42, 43, 46, 47, 48
Woodard, Virginia A., 159, 160, 168
Wyllie, M., 93

Young, Art, 69, 168
Young, Richard, 31, 32, 33, 34, 38, 39,
  40, 41, 42, 43, 44, 46, 47

Zubrow, David, 129

Subject Index

Academic expository writing: approach to, in writing across the curriculum, 64; criticism of, by writing teachers, 52-53; difficulties with, for "basic writers," 64-65

Black English, 45

Classical rhetoric: emphasis of, on process, 49-50; revival of interest in, 34, 60-61

Commission on Composition, Position Statement of, 67-68

Committee of Ten (1892), 42

Composing processes: aspects of, 49, 71; emphasis on, in classical rhetoric, 50; Flower-Hayes model of, 56-57, 81; growing interest in, 50-51; implications of research on, for curriculum, 66-68; learning of, as a socialization process, 65; recursive quality of, 57-58; research on contexts of, 59-62; Rohman-Wlecke model of, 52, 53; studies of, 55-56, 71-72; 172-73

Composition: emergence of, as a discipline, 170-73; emphasis on process, in research on, 173; three ideologies of, in antiquity, 12-13; use of social science methods in research on, 172

Composition pedagogy: beginnings of, at Harvard, 34-35; challenges to current-traditional model of, 37-43; collaborative learning in, 65-66; complexities in describing current approach to, 32-34; effects of use of model compositions in, 82-83; emphasis on usage in, 35; examples of issues facing, 44-45; journal-centered approach to, 61, 62-63; lack of coherent philosophy in, 34-35; lack of graduate courses in, 35; New Rhetoricians' approach to, 43; questions central to models of, 46; sentence combining and sentence construction in, 85-86; tagmemic approach to, 40-41; textbooks on, 35, 39, 53, 60, 174, 175, 176-77, 180-84; time and expediency as dominant factors in, 45-46; use of criteria for judging quality in,

86-87; weakening of models of, by borrowed terminology, 44. *See also,* Teaching of writing.

Conference on College Composition and Communication, 33, 45

Critical judgment, as principle aim of education, 22

Critical Thinking Project (Pittsburgh Public Schools): concerns of social studies teachers in, 190-95; emphasis on essay tests in, 194-95; examination of courses of study in, 193-94; focus of, on writing assignments, 191-92; in-service workshops in, 191-92; role of experts in, 190

Current-traditional model, of writing instruction: absence of coherent philosophy in, 34-39; challenges to, 37-43; features of, 31-32; misuse of prewriting in, 42; origins of, 34-37; prominence of grammar in, 44-45

Curriculum, implications of research on composing processes for, 66-68

Dartmouth Conference, 33, 41, 42

Definitions, research on teaching the writing of, 77-78

Direct instruction, 165-66

Distancing approaches, to teaching of writing, 155-56

English departments: focus of, on literature and style, 50; revival of interest of, in rhetoric, 39-40

English studies, changes in, 50-51

Environmental approach, to teaching of writing, 105-6, 111

Essays: analytic scoring of, 126-27; editing of, as form of evaluation, 116-18; grading of, 3-4; holistic scoring of, 125-26, 151; involvement of students in evaluation of, 128-29; use of, in evaluating writing, 124-29

Evaluation: humanists' preferences in, 114; prominence of quantitative models in, 115; use of norm-referenced tests in, 123-24

Expressivist approach, to teaching of writing, 41-42

Ford Foundation, 146

Form, declarative and procedural knowledge of, in relation to writing performance, 78-87

Functional literacy, requirements of, in contemporary culture, 157-60

Functional situations, components of, in language use, 156-57

Grammar: effects of study of, on writing performance, 79, 81, 120; prominence of, in current-traditional model, 44-45; reasons for teaching and evaluating knowledge of, 120-23

Greek philosophers, views of, on reasons for writing, 9-13

Harvard Reports, on composition instruction, 36-37, 45

Harvard University, composition instruction at, 34-37

Instruction: instructional scaffolding in relation to aspects of, 108-110; need for reconceptualizing nature of, 107-8

Inventions, forms of, in composition, 40-41

Journals, use of, in composition pedagogy, 61, 62-63, 153-54

Knowledge: types of, in relation to writing performance, 72-73, 78-79, 87-88; views of, in antiquity, 12

Method, Berthoff's concept of, in relation to composition, 177-80

Modeling approach, to teaching of writing, 149-53

Narratives, criteria for judging quality of, 86-87

National Assessment of Educational Progress, 100, 101, 105, 121

National Commission on Excellence in Education, 111

National Conference on Uniform Entrance Requirements in English, 42

National Council of Teachers of English, 33, 67, 120

National Institute of Education, 136

National Society for the Study of Education, Twenty-second Yearbook of, 2, 4

National Study of Writing in the Secondary School. 98, 100, 101, 107

National Writing Project, 97, 131, 191

Natural process approach, to teaching of writing, 88, 90

New Rhetoricians, approach of, to composition pedagogy, 43

Norm-referenced tests, use of, in evaluating writing performance, 123-24

Personal style pedagogy, in writing classes, 53-55, 59

Pittsburgh Public Schools, Critical Thinking Project in, 188-96

Prewriting, 40, 41, 42, 52, 71, 100

Process approach, to writing instruction: activities associated with, 95-96; consequences of shift to, 173-74; critique of Hillocks's conclusions regarding, 104-6; difficulties in implementation of, 102-4; emphases in, on stages of composing, 14; key elements in, 154-55; need for reconceptualization of, 107; reconceptualization of instruction in relation to, 109-111; reflection of, in composition textbooks, 174-77; research findings related to, 96; sparse utilization of, 96-101

Product-centered pedagogy, dissatisfaction with, 50-51

Progressive Education Movement, 51

Reading: integration of, with writing, 182-85; role of, in modeling approach to teaching of writing, 150-51

Reading comprehension, role of prior knowledge in, 73-74

Remedial programs, 45

Report writing, in elementary grades: common practices in, 132-33; examples of, 135, 138-45; workshops for, 134-45

Rhetoric: Aristotle's view of, 10-12, 21, 32; emphasis in, on style, 50; establishment of departments of, 38; reentry of, in English departments, 39; small impact of, on composition pedagogy, 40; Socrates' views of, 10, 171; textbooks on, 39-40

Rhetoric Society of America, 39, 40

Richard King Mellon Foundation, 189

Rockefeller Foundation, 189

Sophists: handbooks of, 10; Socrates' attacks on, 9-10, 15, 19

Speech Association of America, 38

Stallings Observation Strategy, 165-66
Substantive knowledge: effects of, on writing performance, 74-75; procedures for analysis of, in writing, 75-78

Tagmemic approach, to teaching of composition, 40-44
Teachers of writing: examples of differences among, 2-4; interest among, in composing processes, 52
Teaching of writing: analysis of current theories of, 30-34; approaches to, 30-32, 41-42, 43, 88, 90, 95, 105-6, 149-56; constraints on, in secondary schools, 164-66; critique of technical approach to, 14-22; features of classes in, that promote thinking, 26-28; importance of using functional situations in, 156, 161-63; separation of philosophy and teaching rhetoric in, 39; survey of practices in (1923), 3. *See also,* Composition pedagogy.
Third National Assessment of Reading and Literature, 189

University of Chicago, literary criticism at, 39

Vermont Writing Program, 131

Western Pennsylvania Writing Project, 190
Writing: Aristotle's defense of, 10-12, 23; criteria for good ideas for, 20-21; integration of, with reading, 182-85; reasons for, as viewed by Greek philosophers, 9-13; relationship of, to thinking and learning, 22-26; students' superstitions about, 16-18; view of, as skill versus an intellectual process, 13-15. *See also,* Composing, Composition pedagogy, Teaching of writing.
Writing across the curriculum: approach to expository writing in, 64; assumptions underlying, 183-84; different foci on, in United States and in Great Britain, 62-64
Writing classes: Coles's concept of text for, 180-82; features of, to promote thinking, 26-28; staffing of, in college, 51; student writing as text for, 53
Writing performance: knowledge of substance and form in relation to, 73-87; problems in evaluation of, 118-20; study of grammar in relation to, 79, 81; study of model compositions in relation to, 79-80, 82-83; use of norm-referenced tests in evaluation of, 123-24
Writing to learn, 8, 146-47
Writing workshops, 134-37

INFORMATION ABOUT MEMBERSHIP IN THE SOCIETY

There are two categories of membership, Regular and Comprehensive. The Regular Membership (annual dues in 1986, $20) entitles the member to receive both volumes of the yearbook. The Comprehensive Membership (annual dues in 1986, $38) entitles the member to receive the two-volume yearbook and the two current volumes in the Series on Contemporary Educational Issues. For their first year of membership, full-time graduate students pay reduced dues in 1986 as follows: Regular, $16; Comprehensive, $34.

Membership in the Society is for the calendar year. Dues are payable on or before January 1 of each year.

New members are required to pay an entrance fee of $1, in addition to annual dues for the year in which they join.

Members of the Society include professors, researchers, graduate students, and administrators in colleges and universities; teachers, supervisors, curriculum specialists, and administrators in elementary and secondary schools; and a considerable number of persons not formally connected with educational institutions.

All members participate in the nomination and election of the six-member Board of Directors, which is responsible for managing the affairs of the Society, including the authorization of volumes to appear in the yearbook series. All members who have contributed to the publications of the Society are eligible for election to the Board of Directors.

Each year the Society arranges for meetings to be held in conjunction with the annual conferences of one or more of the major national educational organizations. All members are urged to attend these sessions. Members are also encouraged to submit proposals for future yearbooks or for volumes in the series on Contemporary Educational Issues.

Further information about the Society may be secured by writing to the Secretary-Treasurer, NSSE, 5835 Kimbark Avenue, Chicago, Ill. 60637.

PUBLICATIONS OF THE NATIONAL SOCIETY FOR THE STUDY OF EDUCATION

1. The Yearbooks

NOTICE: Many of the early yearbooks of this series are now out of print. In the following list, those titles to which an asterisk is prefixed are not available for purchase.

*First Yearbook, 1902, Part I—*Some Principles in the Teaching of History.* Lucy M. Salmon.

*First Yearbook, 1902, Part II—*The Progress of Geography in the Schools.* W. M. Davis and H. M. Wilson.

*Second Yearbook, 1903, Part I—*The Course of Study in History in the Common School.* Isabel Lawrence, C. A. McMurry, Frank McMurry, E. C. Page, and E. J. Rice.

*Second Yearbook, 1903, Part II—*The Relation of Theory to Practice in Education.* M. J. Holmes, J. A. Keith, and Levi Seeley.

*Third Yearbook, 1904, Part I—*The Relation of Theory to Practice in the Education of Teachers.* John Dewey, Sarah C. Brooks, F. M. McMurry, et al.

*Third Yearbook, 1904, Part II—*Nature Study.* W. S. Jackman.

*Fourth Yearbook, 1905, Part I—*The Education and Training of Secondary Teachers.* E. C. Elliott, E. G. Dexter, M. J. Holmes, et al.

*Fourth Yearbook, 1905, Part II—*The Place of Vocational Subjects in the High-School Curriculum.* J. S. Brown, G. B. Morrison, and Ellen Richards.

*Fifth Yearbook, 1906, Part I—*On the Teaching of English in Elementary and High Schools.* G. P. Brown and Emerson Davis.

*Fifth Yearbook, 1906, Part II—*The Certification of Teachers.* E. P. Cubberley.

*Sixth Yearbook, 1907, Part I—*Vocational Studies for College Entrance.* C. A. Herrick, H. W. Holmes, T. deLaguna, V. Prettyman, and W. J. S. Bryan.

*Sixth Yearbook, 1907, Part II—*The Kindergarten and Its Relation to Elementary Education.* Ada Van Stone Harris, E. A. Kirkpatrick, Marie Kraus-Boelté, Patty S. Hill, Harriette M. Mills, and Nina Vandewalker.

*Seventh Yearbook, 1908, Part I—*The Relation of Superintendents and Principals to the Training and Professional Improvement of Their Teachers.* Charles D. Lowry.

*Seventh Yearbook, 1908, Part II—*The Co-ordination of the Kindergarten and the Elementary School.* B. C. Gregory, Jennie B. Merrill, Bertha Payne, and Margaret Giddings.

*Eighth Yearbook, 1909, Part I—*Education with Reference to Sex: Pathological, Economic, and Social Aspects.* C. R. Henderson.

*Eighth Yearbook, 1909, Part II—*Education with Reference to Sex: Agencies and Methods.* C. R. Henderson and Helen C. Putnam.

*Ninth Yearbook, 1910, Part I—*Health and Education.* T. D. Wood.

*Ninth Yearbook, 1910, Part II—*The Nurses in Education.* T. D. Wood, et al..

*Tenth Yearbook, 1911, Part I—*The City School as a Community Center.* H. C. Leipziger, Sarah E. Hyre, R. D. Warden, C. Ward Crampton, E. W. Stitt, E. J. Ward, Mrs. E. C. Grice, and C. A. Perry.

*Tenth Yearbook, 1911, Part II—*The Rural School as a Community Center.* B. H. Crocheron, Jessie Field, F. W. Howe, E. C. Bishop, A. B. Graham, O. J. Kern, M. T. Scudder, and B. M. Davis.

*Eleventh Yearbook, 1912, Part I—*Industrial Education: Typical Experiments Described and Interpreted.* J. F. Barker, M. Bloomfield, B. W. Johnson, P. Johnston, L. M. Leavitt, G. A. Mirick, M. W. Murray, C. F. Perry, A. L. Safford, and H. B. Wilson.

*Eleventh Yearbook, 1912, Part II—*Agricultural Education in Secondary Schools.* A. C. Monahan, R. W. Stimson, D. J. Crosby, W. H. French, H. F. Button, F. R. Crane, W. R. Hart, and G. F. Warren.

*Twelfth Yearbook, 1913, Part I—*The Supervision of City Schools,* Franklin Bobbitt, J. W. Hall, and J. D. Wolcott.

*Twelfth Yearbook, 1913, Part II—*The Supervision of Rural Schools.* A. C. Monahan, L. J. Hanifan, J. E. Warren, Wallace Lund, U. J. Hoffman, A. S. Cook, E. M. Rapp, Jackson Davis, J. D. Wolcott.

*Thirteenth Yearbook, 1914, Part I—*Some Aspects of High-School Instruction and Administration.* H. C. Morrison, E. R. Breslich, W. A. Jessup, and L. D. Coffman.

*Thirteenth Yearbook, 1914, Part II—*Plans for Organizing School Surveys, with a Summary of Typical School Surveys.* Charles H. Judd and Henry L. Smith.

*Fourteenth Yearbook, 1915, Part I—*Minimum Essentials in Elementary School Subjects— Standards and Current Practices.* H. B. Wilson, H. W. Holmes, F. E. Thompson, R. G. Jones, S. A. Courtis, W. S. Gray, F. N. Freeman, H. C. Pryor, J. F. Hosic, W. A. Jessup, and W. C. Bagley.

*Fourteenth Yearbook, 1915, Part II—*Methods for Measuring Teachers' Efficiency.* Arthur C. Boyce.

*Fifteenth Yearbook, 1916, Part I—*Standards and Tests for the Measurement of the Efficiency of Schools and School Systems.* G. D. Strayer, Bird T. Baldwin, B. R. Buckingham, F. W. Ballou, D. C. Bliss, H. G. Childs, S. A. Courtis, E. P. Cubberley, C. H. Judd, George Melcher, E. E. Oberholtzer, J. B. Sears, Daniel Starch, M. R. Trabue, and G. M. Whipple.

*Fifteenth Yearbook, 1916, Part II—*The Relationship between Persistence in School and Home Conditions.* Charles E. Holley.

*Fifteenth Yearbook, 1916, Part III—*The Junior High School.* Aubrey A. Douglass.

*Sixteenth Yearbook, 1917, Part I—*Second Report of the Committee on Minimum Essentials in Elementary-School Subjects.* W. C. Bagley, W. W. Charters, F. N. Freeman, W. S. Gray, Ernest Horn, J. H. Hoskinson, W. S. Monroe, C. F. Munson, H. C. Pryor, L. W. Rapeer, G. M. Wilson, and H. B. Wilson.

*Sixteenth Yearbook, 1917, Part II—*The Efficiency of College Students as Conditioned by Age at Entrance and Size of High School.* B. F. Pittenger.

*Seventeenth Yearbook, 1918, Part I—*Third Report of the Committee on Economy of Time in Education.* W. C. Bagley, B. B. Bassett, M. E. Branom, Alice Camerer, J. E. Dealey, C. A. Ellwood, E. B. Greene, A. B. Hart, J. F. Hosic, E. T. Housh, W. H. Mace, L. R. Marston, H. C. McKown, A. E. Mitchell, W. C. Reavis, D. Snedden, and H. B. Wilson.

*Seventeenth Yearbook, 1918, Part II—*The Measurement of Educational Products.* E. J. Ashbaugh, W. A. Averill, L. P. Ayers, F. W. Ballou, Edna Bryner, B. R. Buckingham, S. A. Courtis, M. E. Haggerty, C. H. Judd, George Melcher, W. S. Monroe, E. A. Nifenecker, and E. L. Thorndike.

*Eighteenth Yearbook, 1919, Part I—*The Professional Preparation of High-School Teachers.* G. N. Cade, S. S. Colvin, Charles Fordyce, H. H. Foster, T. S. Gosling, W. S. Gray, L. V. Koos, A. R. Mead, H. L. Miller, F. C. Whitcomb, and Clifford Woody.

*Eighteenth Yearbook, 1919, Part II—*Fourth Report of Committee on Economy of Time in Education.* F. C. Ayer, F. N. Freeman, W. S. Gray, Ernest Horn, W. S. Monroe, and C. E. Seashore.

*Nineteenth Yearbook, 1920, Part I—*New Materials of Instruction.* Prepared by the Society's Committee on Materials of Instruction.

*Nineteenth Yearbook, 1920, Part II—*Classroom Problems in the Education of Gifted Children.* T. S. Henry.

*Twentieth Yearbook, 1921, Part I—*New Materials of Instruction.* Second Report by Society's Committee.

*Twentieth Yearbook, 1921, Part II—*Report of the Society's Committee on Silent Reading.* M. A. Burgess, S. A. Courtis, C. E. Germane, W. S. Gray, H. A. Greene, Reginia R. Heller, J. H. Hoover, J. A. O'Brien, J. L. Packer, Daniel Starch, W. W. Theisen, G. A. Yoakum, and representatives of other school systems.

*Twenty-first Yearbook, 1922, Parts I and II—*Intelligence Tests and Their Use,* Part I—*The Nature, History, and General Principles of Intelligence Testing.* E. L. Thorndike, S. S. Colvin, Harold Rugg, G. M. Whipple, Part II—*The Administrative Use of Intelligence Tests.* H. W. Holmes, W. K. Layton, Helen Davis, Agnes L. Rogers, Rudolf Pintner, M. R. Trabue, W. S. Miller, Bessie L. Gambrill, and others. The two parts are bound together.

*Twenty-second Yearbook, 1923, Part I—*English Composition: Its Aims, Methods and Measurements.* Earl Hudelson.

*Twenty-second Yearbook, 1923, Part II—*The Social Studies in the Elementary and Secondary School.* A. S. Barr, J. J. Coss, Henry Harap, R. W. Hatch, H. C. Hill, Ernest Horn, C. H. Judd, L. C. Marshall, F. M. McMurry, Earle Rugg, H. O. Rugg, Emma Schweppe, Mabel Snedaker, and C. W. Washburne.

*Twenty-third Yearbook, 1924, Part I—*The Education of Gifted Children.* Report of the Society's Committee, Guy M. Whipple, Chairman.

*Twenty-third Yearbook, 1924, Part II—*Vocational Guidance and Vocational Education for Industries.* A. H. Edgerton and others.

*Twenty-fourth Yearbook, 1925, Part I—*Report of the National Committee on Reading.* W. S. Gray, Chairman, F. W. Ballou, Rose L. Hardy, Ernest Horn, Francis Jenkins, S. A. Leonard, Estaline Wilson, and Laura Zirbes.

*Twenty-fourth Yearbook, 1925, Part II—*Adapting the Schools to Individual Differences.* Report of the Society's Committee. Carleton W. Washburne, Chairman.

*Twenty-fifth Yearbook, 1926, Part I—*The Present Status of Safety Education.* Report of the Society's Committee. Guy M. Whipple, Chairman.

*Twenty-fifth Yearbook, 1926, Part II—*Extra-Curricular Activities.* Report of the Society's Committee. Leonard V. Koos, Chairman.

*Twenty-sixth Yearbook, 1927, Part I—*Curriculum-making: Past and Present.* Report of the Society's Committee. Harold O. Rugg, Chairman.

*Twenty-sixth Yearbook, 1927, Part II—*The Foundations of Curriculum-making.* Prepared by individual members of the Society's Committee. Harold O. Rugg, Chairman.

*Twenty-seventh Yearbook, 1928, Part I—*Nature and Nurture: Their Influence upon Intelligence.* Prepared by the Society's Committee. Lewis M. Terman, Chairman.

*Twenty-seventh Yearbook, 1928, Part II—*Nature and Nurture: Their Influence upon Achievement.* Prepared by the Society's Committee. Lewis M. Terman, Chairman.

*Twenty-eighth Yearbook, 1929, Parts I and II—*Preschool and Parental Education.* Part I—*Organization and Development.* Part II—*Research and Method.* Prepared by the Society's Committee. Lois H. Meek, Chairman. Bound in one volume. Cloth.

*Twenty-ninth Yearbook, 1930, Parts I and II—*Report of the Society's Committee on Arithmetic.* Part I—*Some Aspects of Modern Thought on Arithmetic.* Part II—*Research in Arithmetic.* Prepared by the Society's Committee. F. B. Knight, Chairman. Bound in one volume.

*Thirtieth Yearbook, 1931, Part I—*The Status of Rural Education.* First Report of the Society's Committee on Rural Education. Orville G. Brim, Chairman.

Thirtieth Yearbook, 1931, Part II—*The Textbook in American Education.* Report of the Society's Committee on the Textbook. J. B. Edmonson, Chairman. Cloth. Paper.

*Thirty-first Yearbook, 1932, Part I—*A Program for Teaching Science.* Prepared by the Society's Committee on the Teaching of Science. S. Ralph Powers, Chairman.

*Thirty-first Yearbook, 1932, Part II—*Changes and Experiments in Liberal-Arts Education.* Prepared by Kathryn McHale, with numerous collaborators.

*Thirty-second Yearbook, 1933—*The Teaching of Geography.* Prepared by the Society's Committee on the Teaching of Geography. A. E. Parkins, Chairman.

*Thirty-third Yearbook, 1934, Part I—*The Planning and Construction of School Buildings.* Prepared by the Society's Committee on School Buildings. N. L. Engelhardt, Chairman.

*Thirty-third Yearbook, 1934, Part II—*The Activity Movement.* Prepared by the Society's Committee on the Activity Movement, Lois Coffey Mossman, Chairman.

Thirty-fourth Yearbook, 1935—*Educational Diagnosis.* Prepared by the Society's Committee on Educational Diagnosis. L. J. Brueckner, Chairman. Paper.

*Thirty-fifth Yearbook, 1936, Part I—*The Grouping of Pupils.* Prepared by the Society's Committee. W. W. Coxe, Chairman.

*Thirty-fifth Yearbook, 1936, Part II—*Music Education.* Prepared by the Society's Committee. W. L. Uhl, Chairman.

*Thirty-sixth Yearbook, 1937, Part I—*The Teaching of Reading.* Prepared by the Society's Committee. W. S. Gray, Chairman.

*Thirty-sixth Yearbook, 1937, Part II—*International Understanding through the Public-School Curriculum.* Prepared by the Society's Committee. I. L. Kandel, Chairman.

*Thirty-seventh Yearbook, 1938, Part I—*Guidance in Educational Institutions.* Prepared by the Society's Committee. G. N. Kefauver, Chairman.

*Thirty-seventh Yearbook, 1938, Part II—*The Scientific Movement in Education.* Prepared by the Society's Committee. F. N. Freeman, Chairman.

*Thirty-eighth Yearbook, 1939, Part I—*Child Development and the Curriculum.* Prepared by the Society's Committee. Carleton Washburne, Chairman.

*Thirty-eighth Yearbook, 1939, Part II—*General Education in the American College.* Prepared by the Society's Committee. Alvin Eurich, Chairman. Cloth.

*Thirty-ninth Yearbook, 1940, Part I—*Intelligence: Its Nature and Nurture. Comparative and Critical Exposition.* Prepared by the Society's Committee. G. D. Stoddard, Chairman.

*Thirty-ninth Yearbook, 1940, Part II—*Intelligence: Its Nature and Nurture. Original Studies and Experiments.* Prepared by the Society's Committee. G. D. Stoddard, Chairman.

*Fortieth Yearbook, 1941—*Art in American Life and Education.* Prepared by the Society's Committee. Thomas Munro, Chairman.

Forty-first Yearbook, 1942, Part I—*Philosophies of Education.* Prepared by the Society's Committee. John S. Brubacher, Chairman. Paper.

Forty-first Yearbook, 1942, Part II—*The Psychology of Learning.* Prepared by the Society's Committee. T. R. McConnell, Chairman. Cloth.

*Forty-second Yearbook, 1943, Part I—*Vocational Education.* Prepared by the Society's Committee. F. J. Keller, Chairman.

*Forty-second Yearbook, 1943, Part II—*The Library in General Education.* Prepared by the Society's Committee. L. R. Wilson, Chairman.

Forty-third Yearbook, 1944, Part I—*Adolescence.* Prepared by the Society's Committee. Harold E. Jones, Chairman. Paper.

*Forty-third Yearbook, 1944, Part II—*Teaching Language in the Elementary School.* Prepared by the Society's Committee. M. R. Trabue, Chairman.

*Forty-fourth Yearbook, 1945, Part I—*American Education in the Postwar Period: Curriculum Reconstruction.* Prepared by the Society's Committee. Ralph W. Tyler, Chairman.

*Forty-fourth Yearbook, 1945, Part II—*American Education in the Postwar Period: Structural Reorganization.* Prepared by the Society's Committee. Bess Goodykoontz, Chairman. Paper.

*Forty-fifth Yearbook, 1946, Part I—*The Measurement of Understanding.* Prepared by the Society's Committee. William A. Brownell, Chairman.

*Forty-fifth Yearbook, 1946, Part II—*Changing Conceptions in Educational Administration.* Prepared by the Society's Committee. Alonzo G. Grace, Chairman.

*Forty-sixth Yearbook, 1947, Part I—*Science Education in American Schools.* Prepared by the Society's Committee. Victor H. Noll, Chairman.

*Forty-sixth Yearbook, 1947, Part II—*Early Childhood Education*. Prepared by the Society's Committee. N. Searle Light, Chairman. Paper.

Forty-seventh Yearbook, 1948, Part I—*Juvenile Delinquency and the Schools*. Prepared by the Society's Committee. Ruth Strang, Chairman. Cloth.

Forty-seventh Yearbook, 1948, Part II—*Reading in the High School and College*. Prepared by the Society's Committee. William S. Gray, Chairman. Cloth. Paper.

*Forty-eighth Yearbook, 1949, Part I—*Audio-visual Materials of Instruction*. Prepared by the Society's Committee. Stephen M. Corey, Chairman. Cloth.

*Forty-eighth Yearbook, 1949, Part II—*Reading in the Elementary School*. Prepared by the Society's Committee. Arthur I. Gates, Chairman.

*Forty-ninth Yearbook, 1950, Part I—*Learning and Instruction*. Prepared by the Society's Committee. G. Lester Anderson, Chairman.

*Forty-ninth Yearbook, 1950, Part II—*The Education of Exceptional Children*. Prepared by the Society's Committee. Samuel A. Kirk, Chairman.

Fiftieth Yearbook, 1951, Part I—*Graduate Study in Education*. Prepared by the Society's Board of Directors. Ralph W. Tyler, Chairman. Paper.

Fiftieth Yearbook, 1951, Part II—*The Teaching of Arithmetic*. Prepared by the Society's Committee. G. T. Buswell, Chairman. Cloth, Paper.

Fifty-first Yearbook, 1952, Part I—*General Education*. Prepared by the Society's Committee. T. R. McConnell, Chairman. Cloth, Paper.

Fifty-first Yearbook, 1952, Part II—*Education in Rural Communities*. Prepared by the Society's Committee. Ruth Strang, Chairman. Cloth, Paper.

*Fifty-second Yearbook, 1953, Part I—*Adapting the Secondary-School Program to the Needs of Youth*. Prepared by the Society's Committee: William G. Brink, Chairman.

Fifty-second Yearbook, 1953, Part II—*The Community School*. Prepared by the Society's Committee. Maurice F. Seay, Chairman. Cloth.

Fifty-third Yearbook, 1954, Part I—*Citizen Cooperation for Better Public Schools*. Prepared by the Society's Committee. Edgar L. Morphet, Chairman. Cloth, Paper.

*Fifty-third Yearbook, 1954, Part II—*Mass Media and Education*. Prepared by the Society's Committee. Edgar Dale, Chairman.

*Fifty-fourth Yearbook, 1955, Part I—*Modern Philosophies and Education*. Prepared by the Society's Committee. John S. Brubacher, Chairman.

Fifty-fourth Yearbook, 1955, Part II—*Mental Health in Modern Education*. Prepared by the Society's Committee. Paul A. Witty, Chairman. Paper.

*Fifty-fifth Yearbook, 1956, Part I—*The Public Junior College*. Prepared by the Society's Committee. B. Lamar Johnson, Chairman.

*Fifty-fifth Yearbook, 1956, Part II—*Adult Reading*. Prepared by the Society's Committee. David H. Clift, Chairman.

*Fifty-sixth Yearbook, 1957, Part I—*In-service Education of Teachers, Supervisors, and Administrators*. Prepared by the Society's Committee. Stephen M. Corey, Chairman. Cloth.

Fifty-sixth Yearbook, 1957, Part II—*Social Studies in the Elementary School*. Prepared by the Society's Committee. Ralph C. Preston, Chairman. Cloth, Paper.

*Fifty-seventh Yearbook, 1958, Part I—*Basic Concepts in Music Education*. Prepared by the Society's Committee. Thurber H. Madison, Chairman. Cloth.

*Fifty-seventh Yearbook, 1958, Part II—*Education for the Gifted*. Prepared by the Society's Committee. Robert J. Havighurst, Chairman.

*Fifty-seventh Yearbook, 1958, Part III—*The Integration of Educational Experiences*. Prepared by the Society's Committee. Paul L. Dressel, Chairman. Cloth.

Fifty-eighth Yearbook, 1959, Part I—*Community Education: Principles and Practices from World-wide Experience*. Prepared by the Society's Committee. C. O. Arndt, Chairman. Cloth, Paper.

Fifty-eighth Yearbook, 1959, Part II—*Personnel Services in Education*. Prepared by the Society's Committee. Melvene D. Hardee, Chairman. Paper.

*Fifty-ninth Yearbook, 1960, Part I—*Rethinking Science Education*. Prepared by the Society's Committee. J. Darrell Barnard, Chairman.

*Fifty-ninth Yearbook, 1960, Part II—*The Dynamics of Instructional Groups*. Prepared by the Society's Committee. Gale E. Jensen, Chairman.

Sixtieth Yearbook, 1961, Part I—*Development in and through Reading*. Prepared by the Society's Committee. Paul A. Witty, Chairman. Cloth.

Sixtieth Yearbook, 1961, Part II—*Social Forces Influencing American Education*. Prepared by the Society's Committee. Ralph W. Tyler, Chairman. Cloth, Paper.

Sixty-first Yearbook, 1962, Part I—*Individualizing Instruction*. Prepared by the Society's Committee. Fred T. Tyler, Chairman. Cloth.

Sixty-first Yearbook, 1962, Part II—*Education for the Professions*. Prepared by the Society's Committee. G. Lester Anderson, Chairman. Cloth.

Sixty-second Yearbook, 1963, Part I—*Child Psychology*. Prepared by the Society's Committee. Harold W. Stevenson, Editor. Cloth.

Sixty-second Yearbook, 1963, Part II—*The Impact and Improvement of School Testing Programs*. Prepared by the Society's Committee. Warren G. Findley, Editor. Cloth.

Sixty-third Yearbook, 1964, Part I—*Theories of Learning and Instruction.* Prepared by the Society's Committee. Ernest R. Hilgard, Editor. Paper, Cloth.

Sixty-third Yearbook, 1964, Part II—*Behavioral Science and Educational Administration.* Prepared by the Society's Committee. Daniel E. Griffiths, Editor. Paper.

Sixty-fourth Yearbook, 1965, Part I—*Vocational Education.* Prepared by the Society's Committee. Melvin L. Barlow, Editor. Cloth.

*Sixty-fourth Yearbook, 1965, Part II—*Art Education.* Prepared by the Society's Committee. W. Reid Hastie, Editor.

Sixty-fifth Yearbook, 1966, Part I—*Social Deviancy among Youth.* Prepared by the Society's Committee. William W. Wattenberg, Editor. Cloth.

Sixty-fifth Yearbook, 1966, Part II—*The Changing American School.* Prepared by the Society's Committee. John I. Goodlad, Editor. Cloth.

*Sixty-sixth Yearbook, 1967, Part I—*The Educationally Retarded and Disadvantaged.* Prepared by the Society's Committee. Paul A. Witty, Editor. Cloth.

*Sixty-sixth Yearbook, 1967, Part II—*Programed Instruction.* Prepared by the Society's Committee. Phil C. Lange, Editor. Cloth.

Sixty-seventh Yearbook, 1968, Part I—*Metropolitanism: Its Challenge to Education.* Prepared by the Society's Committee. Robert J. Havighurst, Editor. Cloth.

Sixty-seventh Yearbook, 1968, Part II—*Innovation and Change in Reading Instruction.* Prepared by the Society's Committee. Helen M. Robinson, Editor. Cloth.

Sixty-eighth Yearbook, 1969, Part I—*The United States and International Education.* Prepared by the Society's Committee. Harold G. Shane, Editor. Cloth.

Sixty-eighth Yearbook, 1969, Part II—*Educational Evaluation: New Roles, New Means.* Prepared by the Society's Committee. Ralph W. Tyler, Editor. Paper.

*Sixty-ninth Yearbook, 1970, Part I—*Mathematics Education.* Prepared by the Society's Committee. Edward G. Begle, Editor. Cloth.

Sixty-ninth Yearbook, 1970, Part II—*Linguistics in School Programs.* Prepared by the Society's Committee. Albert H. Marckwardt, Editor. Cloth.

Seventieth Yearbook, 1971, Part I—*The Curriculum: Retrospect and Prospect.* Prepared by the Society's Committee. Robert M. McClure, Editor. Paper.

Seventieth Yearbook, 1971, Part II—*Leaders in American Education.* Prepared by the Society's Committee. Robert J. Havighurst, Editor. Cloth.

Seventy-first Yearbook, 1972, Part I—*Philosophical Redirection of Educational Research.* Prepared by the Society's Committee. Lawrence G. Thomas, Editor. Cloth.

Seventy-first Yearbook, 1972, Part II—*Early Childhood Education.* Prepared by the Society's Committee. Ira J. Gordon, Editor. Paper.

*Seventy-second Yearbook, 1973, Part I—*Behavior Modification in Education.* Prepared by the Society's Committee. Carl E. Thoresen, Editor. Cloth.

Seventy-second Yearbook, 1973, Part II—*The Elementary School in the United States.* Prepared by the Society's Committee. John I. Goodlad and Harold G. Shane, Editors. Cloth.

Seventy-third Yearbook, 1974, Part I—*Media and Symbols: The Forms of Expression, Communication and Education.* Prepared by the Society's Committee. David R. Olson, Editor. Cloth.

Seventy-third Yearbook, 1974, Part II—*Uses of the Sociology of Education.* Prepared by the Society's Committee. C. Wayne Gordon, Editor. Cloth.

Seventy-fourth Yearbook, 1975, Part I—*Youth.* Prepared by the Society's Committee. Robert J. Havighurst and Phillip H. Dreyer, Editors. Cloth.

Seventy-fourth Yearbook, 1975, Part II—*Teacher Education.* Prepared by the Society's Committee. Kevin Ryan, Editor. Cloth.

*Seventy-fifth Yearbook, 1976, Part I—*Psychology of Teaching Methods.* Prepared by the Society's Committee. N. L. Gage, Editor. Paper.

*Seventy-fifth Yearbook, 1976, Part II—*Issues in Secondary Education.* Prepared by the Society's Committee. William Van Til, Editor. Cloth.

Seventy-sixth Yearbook, 1977, Part I—*The Teaching of English.* Prepared by the Society's Committee. James R. Squire, Editor. Cloth.

Seventy-sixth Yearbook, 1977, Part II—*The Politics of Education.* Prepared by the Society's Committee. Jay D. Scribner, Editor. Paper.

Seventy-seventh Yearbook, 1978, Part I—*The Courts and Education,* Clifford P. Hooker, Editor. Cloth.

*Seventy-seventh Yearbook, 1978, Part II—*Education and the Brain,* Jeanne Chall and Allan F. Mirsky, Editors. Paper.

Seventy-eighth Yearbook, 1979, Part I—*The Gifted and the Talented: Their Education and Development,* A. Harry Passow, Editor. Paper.

Seventy-eighth Yearbook, 1979, Part II—*Classroom Management,* Daniel L. Duke, Editor, Paper.

Seventy-ninth Yearbook, 1980, Part I—*Toward Adolescence: The Middle School Years.* Mauritz Johnson, Editor. Paper.

Seventy-ninth Yearbook, 1980, Part II—*Learning a Second Language,* Frank M. Grittner, Editor. Cloth.

Eightieth Yearbook, 1981, Part I—*Philosophy and Education*, Jonas F. Soltis, Editor. Cloth.
Eightieth Yearbook, 1981, Part II—*The Social Studies*, Howard D. Mehlinger and O. L. Davis, Jr., Editors. Cloth.
Eighty-first Yearbook, 1982, Part I—*Policy Making in Education*, Ann Lieberman and Milbrey W. McLaughlin, Editors. Cloth.
Eighty-first Yearbook, 1982, Part II—*Education and Work*, Harry F. Silberman, Editor. Cloth.
Eighty-second Yearbook, 1983, Part I—*Individual Differences and the Common Curriculum*, Gary D Fenstermacher and John I. Goodlad, Editors. Paper.
Eighty-second Yearbook, 1983, Part II—*Staff Development*, Gary Griffin, Editor. Paper.
Eighty-third Yearbook, 1984, Part I—*Becoming Readers in a Complex Society*, Alan C. Purves and Olive S. Niles, Editors. Cloth.
Eighty-third Yearbook, 1984, Part II—*The Humanities in Precollegiate Education*, Benjamin Ladner, Editor. Paper.
Eighty-fourth Yearbook, 1985, Part I—*Education in School and Nonschool Settings*, Mario D. Fantini and Robert L. Sinclair, Editors. Cloth.
Eighty-fourth Yearbook, 1985, Part II—*Learning and Teaching the Ways of Knowing*, Elliot Eisner, Editor. Cloth.
Eighty-fifth Yearbook, 1986, Part 1—*Microcomputers and Education*, Jack A. Culbertson and Luvern L. Cunningham, Editors. Cloth.
Eighty-fifth Yearbook, 1986, Part II—*The Teaching of Writing*, Anthony R. Petrosky and David Bartholomae, Editors. Cloth.

Yearbooks of the National Society are distributed by

UNIVERSITY OF CHICAGO PRESS, 5801 ELLIS AVE., CHICAGO, ILLINOIS 60637

Please direct inquiries regarding prices of volumes still available to the University of Chicago Press. Orders for these volumes should be sent to the University of Chicago Press, not to the offices of the National Society.

2. The Series on Contemporary Educational Issues

In addition to its Yearbooks the Society now publishes volumes in a series on Contemporary Educational Issues. These volumes are prepared under the supervision of the Society's Commission on an Expanded Publication Program.

The 1986 Titles

Academic Work and Educational Excellence: Raising Student Productivity (Tommy M. Tomlinson and Herbert J. Walberg, eds.)

Contributions of Social Science to Educational Policy and Practice (Jane Hannaway and Marlaine Lockheed, eds.)

The 1985 Titles

Adapting Instruction to Student Differences (Margaret C. Wang and Herbert J. Walberg, eds.)

Colleges of Education: Perspectives on Their Future (Charles W. Case and William A. Matthes, eds.)

The 1984 Titles

Women and Education: Equity or Equality? (Elizabeth Fennema and M. Jane Ayer, eds.)

Curriculum Development: Problems, Processes, and Programs (Glenys G. Unruh and Adolph Unruh, eds.)

The 1983 Titles

The Hidden Curriculum and Moral Education (Henry A. Giroux and David Purpel, eds.)

The Dynamics of Organizational Change in Education (J. Victor Baldridge and Terrance Deal, eds.)

The 1982 Titles

Improving Educational Standards and Productivity: The Research Basis for Policy (Herbert J. Walberg, ed.)

Schools in Conflict: The Politics of Education (Frederick M. Wirt and Michael W. Kirst)

The 1981 Titles

Psychology and Education: The State of the Union (Frank H. Farley and Neal J. Gordon, eds.)

Selected Issues in Mathematics Education (Mary M. Lindquist, ed.)

The 1980 Titles

Minimum Competency Achievement Testing: Motives, Models, Measures, and Consequences (Richard M. Jaeger and Carol K. Tittle, eds.)

Collective Bargaining in Public Education (Anthony M. Cresswell, Michael J. Murphy, with Charles T. Kerchner)

The 1979 Titles

Educational Environments and Effects: Evaluation, Policy, and Productivity (Herbert J. Walberg, ed.)

Research on Teaching: Concepts, Findings, and Implications (Penelope L. Peterson and Herbert J. Walberg, eds.)

The Principal in Metropolitan Schools (Donald A. Erickson and Theodore L. Reller, eds.)

The 1978 Titles

Aspects of Reading Education (Susanna Pflaum-Connor, ed.)

History, Education, and Public Policy: Recovering the American Educational Past (Donald R. Warren, ed.)

From Youth to Constructive Adult Life: The Role of the Public School (Ralph W. Tyler, ed.)

The 1977 Titles

Early Childhood Education: Issues and Insights (Bernard Spodek and Herbert J. Walberg, eds.)

The Future of Big City Schools: Desegregation Policies and Magnet Alternatives (Daniel U. Levine and Robert J. Havighurst, eds.)

Educational Administration: The Developing Decades (Luvern L. Cunningham, Walter G. Hack, and Raphael O. Nystrand, eds.)

The 1976 Titles

Prospects for Research and Development in Education (Ralph W. Tyler, ed.)

Public Testimony on Public Schools (Commission on Educational Governance)

Counseling Children and Adolescents (William M. Walsh, ed.)

The 1975 Titles

Schooling and the Rights of Children (Vernon Haubrich and Michael Apple, eds.)

Systems of Individualized Education (Harriet Talmage, ed.)

Educational Policy and International Assessment: Implications of the IEA Assessment of Achievement (Alan Purves and Daniel U. Levine, eds.)

The 1974 Titles

Crucial Issues in Testing (Ralph W. Tyler and Richard M. Wolf, eds.)

Conflicting Conceptions of Curriculum (Elliot Eisner and Elizabeth Vallance, eds.)

Cultural Pluralism (Edgar G. Epps, ed.)

Rethinking Educational Equality (Andrew T. Kopan and Herbert J. Walberg, eds.)

All of the preceding volumes may be ordered from

McCutchan Publishing Corporation
P.O. Box 774
Berkeley, California 94701